Empty Hand

Kenei Mabuni

In cooperation with Masahiko Yokoyama

Empty Hand

The Essence of Budō Karate

Edited by Carlos Molina

Translated from Japanese
by B. Winter

Palisander

As to the notation of the Japanese personal names: On the cover and the title sheet the name of the author has been written according to the conventions of the English-speaking countries, i.e. in the order first name, last name. In the text of the book the usual notation of Japanese names is used, i.e. the last name followed by the first name.

The publisher would like to thank Jörg Seidel, Chemnitz, for proofreading the English edition. Furthermore he thanks Patrick McCarthy, Brisbane (Australia) for putting the photograph of Itosu Ankō at his disposal.

First English Edition
1st ed. May 2009
Original title:
武道空手への招待 ("Invitation to Budō Karate")

Translation from Japanese by B. Winter

Cover design: Anja Elstner, using a drawing by Matthias Stein and the Shitō ryū emblem.
Publisher's editor: Frank Elstner
Setting: Frank Elstner
Printing and binding: druckspecht offsetdruck & service gmbh
Printed in Germany
ISBN 978-3-938305-13-3

www.palisander-verlag.de

Sōke Mabuni Kenei (2001)

Union Shitō ryū Europe
Internet: www.shitoryu-europe.org

The Author

Mabuni Kenei, holder of the 10th Dan, was born in 1918 on Okinawa, the birthplace of karatedō. As the son of Mabuni Kenwa, the founder of the Shitō ryū and one of the most important karate experts in history, from his childhood on he was in touch with karate and some of its greatest masters. At the age of 34 he became the head of Shitō ryū. Even today, in his old age, he holds seminars in different parts of the world where he teaches authentic karatedō.

The Publisher

Carlos Molina, the editor, holder of the 7th Dan, was born in 1947 in Quetzaltenango, Guatemala. He became one of the first disciples of Mabuni Kenei in Latin America. Since 1976 he has introduced the Shitō karate in the Federal Republic of Germany. Today he is the Shitō ryū representative in Germany.

Sōke Mabuni Kenei and Shihan Carlos Molina (2007)

Acknowledgement

The editor thanks his disciple Mrs Silvia Pellegrini for her extraordinary efforts to realize this project.

Illustrations

On many of the photos Mizuguchi Hirofumi – sometimes together with the author – can be seen demonstrating techniques.

Preface by the Editor

I met *sensei* Mabuni Kenei for the first time in November 1965. At that time I was 18 years old and *sensei* Mabuni came to my hometown Quetzaltenango for a karate demonstration together with a group of karateka from the capital Guatemala City. Already in ancient times Quetzaltenango was a Maya city and it is the second largest city of Guatemala today.

Sensei Mabuni had already been staying in Central America for a year, at first in Mexico following an invitation by *sensei* Murata Nobuyoshi, and then in Guatemala where at that time about one thousand karateka were practicing *Shitō ryū*.

I still had no karate experience, nevertheless I realized that there was a great difference between the way of moving demonstrated by *sensei* Mabuni and the performance of the other karateka representing various schools. I was so impressed that I decided on the spot to study karate. So, I joined the *Shitō ryū* club in my hometown. My first teachers were Jorge Sosa and Nobuyoshi Murata. I learned the basics of *Shitō ryū* and a lot about the history of the Mabuni family from *sensei* Murata.

In 1969 when I received the 1st *kyū* I got the chance to attend a lesson by *sensei* Mabuni in Guatemala City. This was a great honor for me. About 20 disciples, all of them holders of the 1st *kyū* degree participated in this lesson. We all had studied different karate techniques for several years, but Sensei Mabuni exclusively trained breathing techniques with us. After two hours of such exercises, of the 20 participants only a friend of mine and myself were ready to continue. The other ones left the training room because they could not bear the constraints caused by the breathing techniques any longer. When the two of us were alone with *sensei* Mabuni he said: "Now you can begin to study *karatedō*."

Sensei Mabuni stayed for another year in the Guatemalan capital. To attend his lessons we traveled every week the 120 miles between Quetzaltenango and Guatemala City.

In 1974 Sensei Mabuni came for the last time to Guatemala. At that time I held the 2nd *dan*. In 1976 I decided to visit my Sensei in Japan. However, on the way to Japan first I came to Europe – to Berlin. Here I met a lot of people who asked me to teach them karate. So, I stayed there.

I met Sensei Mabuni again only in 1984 – on Corsica. He was invited by *sensei* Nakahashi Hidetoshi who had been living in France for many years. Hence I became a disciple of *sensei* Nakahashi until *sensei* Mabuni accepted me as his *uchi deshi*[1]. Since then I have been trying very hard to deepen my understanding of *Shitō ryū* karate under the guidance of *sensei* Mabuni and supported by *sensei* Nakahashi and Sensei Hatano. Thanks to *sensei* Mabuni I could learn a lot about the essence of *budō* karate. He always emphasized that karate is no sport but a way of life that can be helpful in any situation.

I feel grateful and happy that *sensei* Mabuni has decided to express his ideas in this book that has become not only a source of the *Shitō ryū* but also shows the history of the origins of karate as martial art and way of life. When I look back to my first steps in *karatedō*, trying to compare my personal character of those days with the present one I realize how much I have changed. Only now I begin to understand what he ceaselessly has taught since then. Sensei Mabuni always stressed the importance of values like politeness, charity, respect and grace, and he always warned us of the dangers of mistrust, laziness, pride and envy. Although I am not always able to achieve all of this in my own life I begin to understand that these values are the basis of social and human existence. There is a motto he always uses to repeat and that is now deeply ingrained in my heart: "Try to improve, become better today than you were yesterday, and tomorrow become better than today."

I am deeply grateful that *sensei* Mabuni gave us this book. It is a treasury of wisdom!

Shihan Carlos Molina, Corsica, 1 August 2007

---

[1] *Uchi deshi*: Jpn. Internal disciple, i.e. a disciple to whom his master transmits the complete authentic teachings of his school. – Publisher's comment.

Introduction

A Martial Art for Everyone

I was born in 1918. I have been happy to spend all my life with karate. My father, Mabuni Kenwa, who founded the *Shitō* karate, always said: "Anyone can practice karate, young and old people, men and women." Karate can meet different needs of different people. It can be used to take care of the health and to maintain beauty and fitness, and of course it can be a means of self-defense or of real fighting. But that is not all. In particular *budō*[2] karate is not only a system of physical techniques, called *taijutsu*, but also rich in mental techniques, called *shinjutsu*. Once during a *kata* performance by an experienced karateka, I heard a bystander saying: "Just by feeling this spiritual energy, I understand that karate is something of great value."

Other people like karate as a means of artistic expression. For example, at the Sydney Olympic Games in 2000 the Austrian team in synchronized swimming caused considerable public discussion because they included a karate *kata* called *Heian yondan* into their performance. In August 2001 in the Nihon Budōkan the 3rd Shitō Karate World Meeting took place. I met a famous Japanese dancer there who told me: "I can see a connection between karate and dance."

To my mind karate can be compared with a huge mountain that can be climbed via many different paths, which will reveal very different sights according to the point of view or to the season. Neither the aims nor the paths of this mountain hiking adventure are fixed. Some walk slowly up the hillside to build up their physical strength, others, the ambitious mountaineers, want to climb the highest and steepest summits at any cost.

---

[2] *Budō*: Jpn. "Martial way" or "the way of war". The term is composed of *bu* (martial) and *dō* (way). Totality of the Japanese martial arts practiced as ethical way (*dō* or *michi*), as way for the perfection of the human being in his quest for himself. – Habersetzer, R. and G.: Encyclopédie des Arts Martiaux. Paris: Amphora 2004.

Karate as a Means for Physical, Martial and Spiritual Education

Education and development in karate comprise three main elements: the physical, the martial and the psycho-spiritual aspect. As a means of physical education it improves the health and provides the basis for a long and healthy life. It helps to build up fighting abilities, and as a method to strengthen mind and soul it can contribute to reach a high level of vitality and mental energy. These different elements are closely connected and support each other. Which of the aspects is prevailing depends on the practitioner's motivation and aims.

With regard to the fighting abilities there are some common misunderstandings. Many people are afraid when they hear words like "real fight karate" or "street fighting karate". "Real fight situations" can be considered as rather rare occasions in the everyday life of average people unless such situations are provoked deliberately or one searches for them. But in the past few years, more and more cases of unprovoked attacks or conflicts escalating into violence in the streets or in public transport facilities have happened to occur even in Japan, which is considered as one of the most secure and most disciplined societies of the world. Especially in times of change, family members or friends might be threatened and forced to fight. So, one should be prepared. The best way to escape such situations is to avoid the attack of an enemy or to hit him at vital points in order to gain time to flee.

Normal people are only confronted with a real fight when they have to defend themselves. For the samurai in times of feudal wars, or for the soldiers in the world wars "real fighting" meant simply to kill each other. At this point I must admit that the masters of karate, like myself, practice day by day a *bujutsu*[3] karate that surpasses the limits of self-defense. And, frankly speaking, techniques that surpass the limits of self-defense are techniques to kill people, called *satsuhō*. It sounds a little bit daring to say it, but this was the starting point of karate as *budō*, i.e. as "martial way" or

[3] *Bujutsu*: Jpn. "Combat techniques". Totality of the techniques used by the warriors of ancient Japan to conquer the enemy in the battlefield. – Habersetzer, R. and G.: Encyclopédie des Arts Martiaux. Paris: Amphora 2004.

"warrior's way". But it should be taken into consideration that by practicing *budō* karate one is doing the same as members of military units are doing who acquire techniques to kill in order to defend their homeland, the land of their ancestors.

The techniques of "minimal" self-defense that are not designed to kill people were developed from techniques that had the purpose to kill.

The Emergence of Modern Karate

The man who later was called "founder of modern karate" was Itosu Ankō (1830-1916), also named Yasutsune. He was the greatest master of the *Shuri-te*, which represents the original Okinawan hand-fighting techniques, *te*.[4] Master Itosu reorganized karate when it became part of the official curriculum of middle school education in Meiji-era Japan.

Master Itosu chose traditional techniques and modified them in such a way that they could be used for physical education. According to the ideals of modern physical education, highly dangerous techniques where replaced by techniques that were demanding and rich in substance and at the same time efficient with regard to physical education. So, the *Passai dai kata* contains a sequence from a side sweep (*yoko barai*) to a kick (*geri*), which was originally a movement from a spear hand stab in the eyes (*kaishu metsubishi*) to a kick to the genitals (*kinteki*). – Itosu Ankō created for example the group of the five *Heian kata*, which is still very popular. According to the Japanese word *Heian*, which means calm and peaceful, this *kata* does not contain attacks on the so-called "golden targets" (e.g. the genitals and other vital points) and no dangerous techniques like the "eye crusher" (*metsubishi*).

The founder of *Kōdōkan Jūdō*, Kanō Jigorō (1860-1938), proceeded in the same way when he removed all throwing techniques (*nage waza*) and blows (*atemi*) which had the potential to kill from traditional *jūjutsu*, thus developing modern *jūdō*. These were results of the modernization process

[4] On Okinawa where karate emerged it was simply called "hand" (*ti*, Jpn.: *te*, or – when adapted to the previous syllable – *de*). – Translator's comment.

the movement for cultural reform was aiming at.

But in *Shitō* karate a lot of old *kata* remained. Although they were reformed by Master Itosu, there are numerous hidden techniques that have been handed down to us as non-written secret knowledge. Amongst them were rather cruel techniques to kill. One of my most diligent students, Terada, led the karate lessons in a club of a school that his son also used to attend. Once he told me laughingly that his son had criticized him saying: "Dad, your karate is always against the rules." This touches the question whether such dangerous techniques should be part of karate practice and whether a martial education makes sense that surpasses the limits of self-defense. As stated above, attacking in order to defend oneself is part of the essence of karate. Indeed there is a certain "borderland" in the study of karate where one learns how to kill very efficiently. That means entering the world of *budō*. This problem is in fact the most important topic of this book. But first I would like to write about today's values and the general aims of karate.

Karate and Health

My father had dedicated his life to the development of karate as a means of physical education already before I was born. In the world of martial arts he was called "Mabuni the technician". Being one of the inheritors of the authentic Okinawan hand-fighting techniques (*te*), he was generally considered to be an outstanding expert with respect to techniques. He wanted to develop and spread karate as a method to improve the health situation of the general population.

In contrast to other martial arts, in karate the physical abilities can be enhanced by *kata* practice. All in all there are about 50 classical *kata*. Of course not all of them must be learned unless one wants to become a karate teacher. *Kata* are sequences of movements of attack and defense with respect to one or several imaginary opponents. In order to execute them no training devices are needed. *Kata* are easy to practice even in larger groups of people, and their practice can be a source of joy. There are some beginners who are afraid of *kata* exercises with partners called *kumite*. But in case one practices karate exclusively for one's health, *kumite* is not needed. Furthermore one needs only little space. An area of 3.5 to 4 *tatami* mats (about 75-85 sq ft) should be sufficient.

The *Shitō* karate developed by my father contains the traditional Okinawan hand-fighting techniques of the *Shuri-te* and the *Naha-te*. Apart from some small technical differences, it is a typical feature of the *Shuri-te kata* that they consist of many effective and fast attack and defense movements designed for long-distance fighting. For the *Naha-te kata*, close-distance fighting is typical, with "heavy" movements and a special breathing technique derived from Chinese Fukien *kempō*[5]. Having such a broad basis it is easy to find the appropriate *kata* for any age and any kind of physical condition. This is the great advantage of *Shitō* karate.

Long *kata* include about 70 different techniques, shorter ones about 20. A short *kata* does not take more than one minute. During *kata* practice literally every inch of the body moves, so that results can be seen very soon. Men get strong and well-balanced bodies and women also become more beautiful. No space, no special devices or clothing is needed. So there is no easier method to improve the state of health. Even very busy people should be able to afford the few minutes a day needed to keep fit by *kata* practice. Some may think that they are already too old for it. But in principle one can start practicing *kata* at any age. Most of the masters of karate from Okinawa and mainland Japan enjoyed a long life.

The Physical Effects of Karate

I myself could be regarded as living proof. I am now 83 years of age. I have never been seriously ill. Several times a year I travel overseas to supervise karate training. I never feel any jetlag and always start practicing with the young karateka the next morning after my arrival.[6]

[5] Fukien *kempō* (Chn. Fujian quanfa): Fukien (Chn. Fujian) is a province in the southeast of China. *Kempō* is the Japanese expression for quanfa, "Chinese boxing" (see also footnote 18 on p. 23). – Publisher's comment.

[6] Mabuni Kenei has composed the present book in 2001. His statements are still fully true in 2009. – Publisher's comment.

In 1938 my father published the book *Introduction into Attack and Defense Techniques in Karate Kempō*.[7] He stressed the positive effects of training, writing: "Karate helps to gain more pleasure in all other activities", "Weak persons can strengthen their body practicing at home", "Sick and overweight persons get strong muscles and become healthy", "One drinks less alcohol in the evenings and one works more efficiently at day", or "Neuralgia and mental weakness get cured".

My father actively propagated karate as an excellent means to protect and strengthen health. In cooperation with a medical university he could scientifically prove the positive physical effects by blood tests and urinalysis. In his book there are extracts from a research report on the physiological effects of karate by marine physicians. According to their report the metabolic functions and nerve reflexes, the sense of balance and the muscle power were improved. The whole physical condition was harmonized. Thus, the positive influence of karate practice on the body was sufficiently proven.[8]

When his book was published my father had already been living on mainland Japan and propagating karate for ten years. He had brought from Okinawa a rather spiritual and even religious karate. Present-day karate is unfortunately very far from the one he wanted to spread. In his

---

[7] *Kōbō Kempō karate dō nyūmon*. – Mabuni Kenwa has written this book together with Nakasone Genwa (1895-1978). – Publisher's comment.

[8] With regard to the physical training in karate, a *kata* is similar to a Buddhist sutra (a religious rule often used as a prayer). The more this is understood, the higher the value of karate as a means of physical education can be appreciated. A sutra consists of words, which although being frequently repeated, differ in their effect and emotional influence according to the age and spiritual or mental situation of the person who reads or recites it. Compared to this, a karate *kata* could be considered as non-written sutra. One cannot learn and remember "reading" it with the eyes. One must "read" it with the whole body and "perform" it with all the heart. While being read, a written sutra nourishes the spiritual energies; "performing" a *kata* as a non-written sutra increases physical strength and abilities. Some people think that it is enough to learn a *kata* by memorizing it. But this does not develop the physical energies. A *kata* has to be executed. Some people practiced only ten *kata* through all their life. But the bodily feeling and the influence of the same *kata* on the body differ every day depending on the age and the physical condition. This influence is very strong no matter to which degree it becomes conscious. Regular *kata* practice increases the activity of each part of the body, strengthens the weak points and regulates the physiological functions. So it helps to take care of health, secures a long life and provides the ability to react spontaneously to sudden dangers. – Author's comment.

opinion, practicing karate for self-defense did not only require the training of fighting techniques but also a supporting spiritual and mental education. At the end of the book he wrote: "Once you will be confronted with a situation that demands action you will be able to act."

Karate in Dangerous Situations

Several times I had the experience of spontaneous reactions towards sudden danger. When I was 16 or 17 I went with a friend to the Shirahama beach in the Wakayama prefecture. We wanted to enjoy the view of the Senjōjiki cliffs. I was wearing a swimming suit, and I just turned my back to the sea and fixed my belt when I was suddenly hit by a huge wave. My friend, facing the sea, saw the wave coming and ran away. But I could not see it and was fully stricken. In this very moment I understood that a wave had swallowed me and that my body had lost its freedom, and so I clung instinctively to the rocks the breakers had thrown me against. Had I allowed the wave to draw me into the sea I would not have survived. Many people have lost their lives this way.

Towards the end of the Greater East Asia War[9] I was stationed on the Philippine island of Cebu. When the American troops had landed there with considerable force, we had to flee together with the Japanese settlers to the central highlands. We had to march at night because in daylight American reconnaissance aircrafts were cruising over our heads. So we were marching in total darkness, one hand touching the belt or the shoulder of the man in front. Suddenly I slipped and fell down the slope. When I regained consciousness I found myself about 15 feet below the path, and I was gripping my knapsack. Astonishingly I had remained uninjured. I thought: "Maybe it's not such a good idea to stay behind." Then I climbed up the precipice as quick as I could and managed to join the others. I re-

---

[9] The Greater East Asia War (*Dai tōa sensō*) lasted from 1937 to 1945. In 1937 the Second Sino-Japanese War had begun. In December 1941 the war reached a new level because of the Japanese attack on Pearl Harbor and the subsequent entry into the war by the USA. Often, the name Pacific War is used instead of Greater East Asia War. – Publisher's comment.

member that again I thought how helpful it was to practice karate. Once more my body evidently had spontaneously reacted to the sudden danger so that I remained unharmed in spite of the deep fall.

There were many similar occasions, maybe less dramatic, in my life to make me realize that without karate I could have lost my life or at least would have been seriously injured. Some may say that my reactions were due to special training. But this is not correct because everyone can reach the same result if only the person's karate practice is serious and continuing.

Karate as a Spiritual Martial Art

Karate has changed more and more into a competition sport. This is one of the reasons why the number of women practicing karate mainly for self-defense has recently considerably decreased. But besides health care, self-defense was the original aim and is still a very important aspect of karate.

When my father taught at the *Meijō Girls College*, he invented two special self-defense *kata* for girls. One was called *Meijō kata* according to the name of the school and meaning "bright star". The other was called *Aoyagi* (green willow) referring to elegance and gentleness. These *kata* were made for real combat. They contain techniques against typical attacks towards women like embracing from the front or from behind, and punches that use the energy of the attacker. But these real-combat *kata* are very short and not appropriate for competition and therefore unfortunately not very popular in our days.

Recently, I read an article in the newspaper *Asahi Shimbun*. It was about a high school boy in Ōsaka who was at home when a burglar came in and attacked him with a knife. But the boy was clever enough to evade the attack and managed to escape. Afterwards he told a reporter, "When I saw the knife my body reacted spontaneously. If I had not practiced karate I would have been paralyzed by fear."

To use karate for self-defense, it is not enough to study a number of techniques. One has to develop a special mental energy, *ki*[10], necessary

[10] *Ki* (Chn. *Qi*): Jpn. The soul as energetically perceptible state; life energy. – Translator's comment.

to mobilize the abilities in the very moment they are needed, that is, just when one is confronted with sudden danger. No matter how often one may have practiced the techniques, without this energy one cannot make use of them. That is why the mental education is so important.

The development of *ki* is important for all kinds of martial arts, such as *jūdō*, *kendō* or *iaidō*. The mental education is needed to get rid of any inner agitation or inner tensions and to become able to focus the whole mental energy on one point. Since karate is aiming at the ability to defend the own body with empty hands flexible mental energy is extremely important. For this reason one can consider karate as martial art of the soul (*ki no budō*).

Of course the physical condition affects the general development of a person. It could be said that people who are lacking physical self-confidence are apt to mental and psychological weakness. Because karate practice develops the whole body, even people who begin in a rather weak condition can gain strong physical confidence after a short time, building the basis for mental and psychological strength.

The Breathing Techniques in Karate

However timid and weak a person might have been, by regularly and seriously practicing karate – even if the practice is not very intense – one can experience how the body gradually fills with energy, how self-confidence grows from the ground of the abdomen and calmness installs in a quite natural way in the whole body. This is a particularity of karate.

Especially the breathing techniques (*kisoku hō*) of the *Naha-te* are a good example to explain how karate strengthens the spiritual and mental unity.[11] It goes without saying that breathing is important for all kinds of martial arts but its deliberate and systematic training is a special aspect of karate. Breathing, and in particular inhaling (*iki o suru*), is closely connected with life. The Japanese verb meaning "to live" (*iki ru*) is said to be derived form the expression "to take breath". People can live without food for about a

[11] See p. 209 et seq.

month. But as is well known, it is hard to survive without breathing.

If one gets nervous in a situation of violence one will lose. Such nervousness comes from disturbances of pulse and blood pressure, which again are caused by breathing disturbances. For this reason some people get also nervous in front of a crowd. When things go wrong somehow and life is full of trouble one often feels depressed. Unconsciously breathing becomes short, flat and throat-centered. In the worst case, one breathes only with the tip of the nose, so to speak. If someone gets used to such kind of breathing he cannot expect to be blessed with a long life.

In order to harmonize the soul one must harmonize breathing. Breathing deeply into the abdomen arranges the energies in the lower abdomen. If in this area everything is "well settled", one has good reason to hope for a long life. The effects of correct breathing will be greater the better the breathing rules are understood and followed consciously. I studied several breathing techniques like those of yoga or qigong. According to them, holding the breath (*taisoku*) is harmful. But in karate it is regarded to be very reasonable. It strengthens the heart and improves the flexibility of breathing. I am now more than 80 years of age but I do not have any problems climbing a staircase and never grasp for air.

The State of Total Inner Calmness

Karate practice develops body, spirit and fighting abilities. Since these three aspects of education are closely connected in the *kata*, *kata* training allows progress in all of them. This kind of learning is a real pleasure and can be a never-ending one.

In the Edo period (17th to 19th century) the samurai of the Nabeshima fief on Kyūshū Island (now Saga prefecture) were educated on the basis of the famous warrior code *Hagakure*[12]. The first rule a samurai had to follow was about his attitude towards aging. This rule demanded that learning and practicing should never end. No matter which level of abilities a samurai

[12] Yamamoto, T.: Hagakure. The Book of the Samurai. Mechanicsburg: Stackpole Books 2002.

may have reached, how high in the hierarchy he might be, there is no reason for conceit, no reason to stop learning and improving oneself.[13]

Those who learn only in order to win over others, to be better and stronger than others, are people who in fact learn for others. This is not the right way. A real master follows his way by continuously trying day by day, all his life, to improve himself. If one does not practice karate with joy so that nothing can stop oneself whatever people might say, this cannot be called true karate. Only if one enjoys practicing karate for oneself, not for others, if one cannot stop even if one would like to, one will experience karate as an endless path and reach a state of total concentration and inner silence.

About such a state of deep concentration called *zanmai*[14] my father once wrote the following words: "I enjoy my mind getting empty while rowing to the island of *bu*."[15]

---

[13] There is a rule with regard to the life cycle of learning. The beginner has the feeling not to progress although trying hard. He judges his abilities to be poor, and so do the others. He considers his efforts to be rather useless. In the middle stages of learning, the results still seem to be unsatisfying but the student has become able to understand his own weak points and can evaluate those of the others. When higher levels of development are reached, certain results do appear. The student feels proud and happy, likes it to be admired by others and tends to utter criticism about their failings. At this stage the student has come to real achievements. He cannot imagine any further development and is considered by others to be a strong and able person. Most people can reach this stage. One step more and it looks as if they have reached the end of their path. But if this point is passed, one will realize that things are not as they were thought of. Going beyond this point, one can understand that there are weak points left and can try to advance further, but from now on without any feelings of superiority or inferiority. As Master Yagyū said one must learn "how to win a victory over oneself not only over others". So, every day one should improve a little bit, all life long, without stopping. – Author's note.

[14] *Zanmai* (pronounced: *zammai*): Jpn. Expression for the Sanskrit term *Samadhi*: State of composure brought about by the pacification of the spirit; this state is an essential precondition for real meditation (*Dhyana*). It is a sub-step of the mystical process that should lead to wisdom (*Pjrajna*). – Habersetzer, R. and G.: Encyclopédie des Arts Martiaux. Paris: Amphora 2004.

[15] *Nanigoto mo uchi wasuretari hitasura ni bu no shima kogu ga tanoshiki.* – The character (*kanji*) used for *bu* (武) signifies "martial ability". It is for example part of the well-known word for Samurai, "*bu*-shi". But the phoneme *bu* is also represented by another character signifying "emptiness" or "nothingness" which is of essential meaning in Buddhism. – Translator's comment.

There is a Japanese term called *gunshū* meaning "learning by absorbing the smell". It is based on the idea that the odor of an object is transmitted to the person steadily handling it. If one works with wood one will gradually acquire a wooden smell. What one does and thinks day by day finally becomes part of oneself, shapes the character and gives a certain "smell". When my father was a policeman on Okinawa, visiting the karate masters at hidden places, teaching karate at the fishery school or attending karate performances, he always took me along and let me sit on his lap. That is maybe how I acquired his "smell".

I always remember my father stripped to the waist practicing with his comrades in the light of a naked bulb, encouraging each other and forgetting the world around them. After he had moved to Ōsaka, he never knew what the day would bring. Nevertheless he went on with his life devoted to the study of karate, spending time with his comrades with whom he often shared his food and shelter. He also took care of the *tatami* mats that were always worn fast by the practice of the karateka. When one of his students came home from the battlefields of the Pacific War unharmed, he was as happy as he was when I returned. All this is the "smell" of my father my body has absorbed and I shall never lose. I also shall go the way of my father, the way of karate, which has no end. I shall practice karate as long as my body can move, step-by-step, stage-by-stage. I cannot predict how far I will come. But I know that I shall move on as long as I can. Progressing and improving oneself, that is what really makes sense, provides pleasure and joy. This is special about *budō karate*, that kind of karate I would like to propagate and that is the subject of this book.

I

Budō Karate

1 The Development of Karate

1.1 Karate as Fighting Technique

Unarmed Fighting in Ancient Times

Methods of fighting without arms are mentioned in the ancient records of all peoples and therefore can be considered to be part of the common heritage of mankind. In the oldest Japanese chronicle *Kojiki*[16], a fight between the gods Takemigazuchi no kami and Takeminakata no kami is mentioned which took place on the Inasa beach in the Izumo region. The *Nihonshoki* annals report about a fight between Nomi no Sukune and Taima no Kehaya. This fight is considered to be the moment when *sumō* was born.[17] But in contrast to present-day *sumō* it must have been a life-and-death struggle. Although carried out without weapons it was nevertheless a fight without rules, since Sukune broke Kehaya's hips and then kicked him to death.

Such techniques of fighting without weapons have existed everywhere in the world since ancient times. It is even reported that in ancient India Buddha has fought against his younger brother for the right to marry a beautiful girl. I saw fights in India that were very similar to *sumō*. In ancient China there were fist-fighting techniques called *kempō* in Japanese. In the Spring and Autumn Annals[18] they were called "brave fist" (*kenyū*) or "martial art" (*bugei*), during the Warring States Period (475-221 BC) "punching technique" (*gigeki*) and in the Han period (202 BC to AD 220) simply "technique" (*gikō*) or "circular punching" (*shubaku*).

---

[16] *Kojiki*: Jpn. "Records of Ancient Matters". Annals of the early history of Japan in three volumes. Together with the *Nihonshoki* it is the first written source of ancient tales and legends, and it also comprises the description of the first deities and rulers of the country. Ōno Yasumarō edited the document in 711/712, by request of the empress Gemmei. It is a collection of mythological stories told to the author by the Master of Tradition of the court Hieda no Are, and of accounts on ancient traditions from various sources. – Habersetzer, R. and G.: Encyclopédie des Arts Martiaux. Paris: Amphora 2004.

[17] According to tradition this fight took place on the 7th day of the 7th month of the year 23 BC by command of emperor Suinin. – Publisher's comment.

[18] The official chronicle of the State of Lu covering the period from 722 to 481 BC. – Publisher's comment.

Shaolin Kempō – the Fighting Techniques of the Warrior Monks

The *Shaolin kempō* was created in the Chinese Shaolin monastery that was built in 495 (late Wei period) by order of the emperor Xiào Wén (471-499) for the Zen Buddhist priest Ba Tuo, who had come from India. The monastery is placed in the Honan province south of the Yellow River at the foot of the Songshan mountains. That is why it was also named Songshan Shaolin. It became famous because Bodhidharma[19] (Japanese: *Daruma*), who became the founder of Zen Buddhism in China, stayed there and introduced *zazen* [20]. This might be the reason why he was – probably by mistake – considered to be the founder of the temple and the father of *kempō*, too.

Fighting techniques were developed particularly in the monasteries because they owned rich treasures of art and other property that the monks had to defend in this country that was ceaselessly stricken by unrest and war. The term *Shaolin kempō* includes all techniques that were invented in the monastery itself or came from the surrounding region. Some of them got lost in the course of time, such as the "smashing fist" (*tsūhai ken*), the "animated fist" (*shin i ken*) or the "cosmic fist" (*rikugō ken*).

In the Shaolin monasteries the monks were divided into prayer monks who where specialized in religious studies and warrior monks who mainly practiced fighting techniques. Those to become warrior monks had their hair shaved and wore monks' habit immediately after entering the monastery. They spent their monastic life mostly with martial exercise rather than with Buddhist studies. The present-day Japanese style of *Shaolin kempō* (called *Shōrinji kempō*) practiced as a religious exercise is a historically new phenomenon that appeared after World War II. It was founded by Master Sō Dōshin (1911-1980).

Incidentally, since the Ming period the Shaolin monks were famous rather because of their staff fighting, *kompō*[21] or *bōjutsu*, than because of their fist-fighting techniques. The Fukien *kempō* was developed in the

---

[19] According to tradition, Bodhidharma lived from 460 to 534. – Publisher's comment.
[20] *Zazen*: Jpn. Seated Zen meditation, mostly done in upright lotus position, but sometimes in other seated positions, too. – Publisher's comment.
[21] The spelling "*konpō*" is also in use. – Translator's comment.

Fukien and Kanton provinces in southern China. This martial art, too, is said to originate from a Shaolin monastery – not the Songshan Shaolin but another one built later in the Fukien province.

The Fukien Shaolin temple does not exist anymore. Possible remains were found at different places. That is why its location could not be determined until today. Because the Songshan Shaolin monastery was located north to the Yangtze River and the Fukien Shaolin monastery south to it, their respective martial arts were also referred to as northern and southern Shaolin or northern and southern *kempō*.

As in other countries, there were times when certain religions were supported and times when they were suppressed by the rulers. So the Shaolin temple, too, experienced times of promotion and prosperity and times of suppression and destruction. There might have been monks who practiced in both temples or others who had to flee the Shaolin monasteries and found shelter in other temples were they shared their knowledge and fighting experience with their hosts. It can be supposed that their knowledge and abilities were spread even among the common people. Chinese distinguished between the "monastery or house" *kempō* of the monks and the "outsiders" *kempō* of the commoners. The *taijiquan* is an example of the latter.

That is how present-day Chinese *kempō* developed in a long historical process out of different schools and styles of fighting without weapons which influenced each other. But there is no doubt that Chinese heroism in general was inspired by the monks of the two Shaolin monasteries. Like the monks of the Japanese Hieizan monastery at the end of the medieval times they took up arms and intervened in the secular world.

So did Minamoto no Yoshitsune and Musashi Bō Benkei at the end of the Heian period (794-1185) in Japan. Yoshitsune, who as a child was called Ushiwaka-maru, lived in the Kurama monastery north of the capital Kyōto. He studied esoteric Buddhist teachings (*mikkyō*)[22] and started

[22] *Mikkyō*: Jpn. "Secret teachings". The term designates a complex of esoteric teachings from India (Tantra) and from Chinese Buddhism (Mizon) aimed at acquiring occult abilities. The roots go back to the Tendai Buddhism that was founded in the 9th century by the bonze Kukai. *Mikkyō* was adopted by ascetic mountain monks (Yamabushi), and through them they became also part of the secret teachings of the Ninja. – Habersetzer, R. and G.: Encyclopédie des Arts Martiaux. Paris: Amphora 2004. See also footnote 172 on p. 190.

to practice fighting techniques. He was said to have been taught martial arts by the long-nosed mountain spirit of Kurama called Dai Tengu[23]. To strengthen his body he walked every day from the Kurama mountains to the center of the capital. Once he encountered the fearsome warrior monk Benkei on the *Gojō* bridge of Kyōto. In a great fight he achieved a victory over him.[24] This episode is widely known in Japan because it is part of a famous *kabuki*[25] theater play.

The Influence of the Chinese Kempō on the Japanese and Okinawan Martial Arts

According to old chronicles, *kempō* was first brought to Japan by a Chinese called Chin Gempin[26] in the Edo period. He was said to have learned *kempō* at the Songshan Shaolin temple and was praised to be a true genius. He was profoundly knowledgeable not only about Confucianism, Buddhism and Taoism but also about arts like calligraphy, brush painting and poetry, or crafts like pottery, making of sweets and preparation of medicinal herbs, and also about acupuncture or moxibustion[27]. After his arrival in Nagasaki he traveled on the main island Honshū up to the region of present Nagoya. He is reported to have been received three times by the *shōgun* Tokugawa Iemitsu and to have met many other lords to speak about his knowledge and show his abilities. Fukuno Masakatsu Shichirouemon and

---

[23] See footnote 173 on p. 191 et seq.

[24] After this encounter Benkei became the most faithful follower of Yoshitsune. This story is part of the book: Habersetzer, R.: Die Krieger des alten Japan. Chemnitz: Palisander Verlag 2008. – Publisher's note.

[25] *Kabuki*: Jpn. Epic theatre style that emerged in the 17th century. In the *kabuki* plays tales about the actions of the historical heroes of Japan are performed in colorful and realistic representations. – Habersetzer, R. and G.: Encyclopédie des Arts Martiaux. Paris: Amphora 2004.

[26] Chin Gempin (1587-1670). His Chinese name was Chen Yuan-ping. Since 1659 he taught Chinese martial arts in Japan. – Habersetzer, R. and G.: Encyclopédie des Arts Martiaux. Paris: Amphora 2004.

[27] Moxibustion: Stimulation of acupuncture points by means of heat. This is realized by burning small amounts of herbs on or above acupuncture points. – Publisher's comment.

Ibaragi Sensai developed the *Kitō* style of Japanese *jūjutsu* after having been instructed by Chin Gempin.

There are other styles of *jūjutsu* whose roots can be found in China such as the famous *Yōshin ryū* that was created in Nagasaki by the physician Akiyama Shirōzaemon in the beginning of the Edo period after he had studied *kempō* during a journey in China. The *Yōshin* style became the basis for the *Tenshin Shinyō* style, which together with the *Kitō* style was the material Kanō Jigorō used to create modern *jūdō*.

But this should not lead to the conclusion that the original *jūjutsu* styles were directly derived from Chinese *kempō*. Techniques of unarmed fighting had existed in Japan since ancient times. The *Takenouchi* style, which is considered to be the oldest in Japanese *jūjutsu* originated from shortsword techniques. These techniques were taught by Takenouchi Hisamori. According to a myth, he had learned them from a hermit with long white hair who appeared while he was praying to the god of Atago to make him a master of martial arts. This happened in the beginning of the feudal wars in the 16th century, 100 years before Chin Gempin came to Japan.

Of course Chinese *kempō* had a strong influence on the Japanese *jūjutsu*. Although it was not its origin, it nourished and inspired its development. However, in *jūjutsu* highly dangerous blows (*atemi*) are not used and thus almost not practiced in order to avoid fatal injuries. But throwing and joint-locking techniques are very important. In particular, *jūjutsu* was aimed for supporting the fight with weapons. Since the beginning of the age of the samurai in the 12th century sword techniques had become crucial, and the fighting techniques with bare hands only played a secondary role.

It is also often said that the origin of karate was the Chinese *kempō*. Because of similarities with regard to techniques and terms this might be plausible, but there are no written records supporting this assumption, and consequently it cannot be considered as proven. Since ancient times there has been a kind of *kempō* on the island of Okinawa which was simply called "hand" (*ti*; Jpn. *te* or *de*), whereas Chinese *kempō* was called "Chinese hand", *tōde*.

Since the middle of the 14th century, the Ryūkyū kingdom was tributary to the Chinese Ming dynasty. The relations with China became closer than those with Japan. People from the Ryūkyūs who had traveled to China to study or as members of diplomatic missions were not only influenced by Chinese culture but also learned martial arts. Of course, many Chinese came to Okinawa, too, and imparted their knowledge to the islanders. The bodyguards and other escorts who accompanied the Chinese envoys seem to have played a special role in transferring fighting skills to the Okinawans. They were highly trained and experienced elite soldiers because they had to defend the missions against the almost omnipresent pirates during the sea passages. In the history of the Ryūkyū islands, 23 of such Chinese missions were reported. Altogether about 500 Chinese came to Okinawa in this way. When the Chinese diplomatic missions arrived on Okinawa, welcome ceremonies were held and the bodyguards performed Chinese *kempō kata*, so-called *tao*. There are some *kata* in the *Shuri-te*, like the *Wanshū* and *Kōsōkun kata*, which are said to have been named after the bodyguards who taught them to the islanders.

There is also the opinion that the term "hand" (*te*) for all Ryūkyū techniques corresponds to the general term for fighting techniques used in Japan, the "18 arts of fighting" (*bugei jū happan*)[28] because similar to the samurai on mainland Japan, the Ryūkyū *bushi*[29] also practiced different special fighting techniques.

The original Okinawan karate developed in particular during two periods of prohibition of weapon use. After Lord Oho (Shō) Hashi (1372-1439) had unified the country, King Oho (Shō) Shin (1465-1526) had the local gentry disarmed and he forced them to settle in the castle town

[28] These 18 martial arts are the following: 1. *Kyū jutsu* – archery, 2. *Ba jutsu* – riding, 3. *Yari jutsu* – lance techniques, 4. *Ken jutsu* – sword-fighting techniques, 5. *Suiei jutsu* – the art of swimming (combat swimming), 6. *Battō jutsu* – the art of drawing the sword, 7. *Tantō jutsu* – short sword techniques, 8. *Jitte jutsu*, also *jutte jutsu* – techniques with iron forked stick (similar to the *sai*, but with only a simple fork) for defending against sword attacks, or used as baton, 9. *Shuriken jutsu* – throwing stars techniques, 10. *Ganshin jutsu* – needle techniques, 11. *Naginata jutsu* – techniques for lances with curved blades (Japanese halberd), 12. *Hō jutsu* – fire arms, 13. *Torite jutsu* – grappling techniques, 14. *Jū jutsu* – weaponless falling, throwing, choking, joint locking and striking techniques, 15. *Bō jutsu* – staff techniques, 16. *Kusarikama jutsu* – techniques for sickle with chain, 17. *Mojiri jutsu* – hook knife techniques, 18. *Shinobi jutsu* – camouflage and concealment. – Translator's comment.

[29] *Bushi*: Jpn. Warrior. – Publisher's comment.

of Shuri. Furthermore he created a central government and introduced a legal system.

In 1609, almost one and a half centuries after the first prohibition of weapons the Shimazu clan conquered the Ryūkyū islands. These samurai came from southern Kyūshū, from the province of Satsuma. Again the possession of any weapons was forbidden on pain of death for the islanders. Under these circumstances, the development of fighting techniques had to focus on unarmed fighting. So, under the influence of Chinese *kempō* the Ryūkyū *kempō* was developed, the archetype of present-day karate.

If the possession of weapons had also been forbidden on mainland Japan, methods of unarmed fighting similar to karate would probably have been developed there, too. If on the other hand the possession of weapons had been allowed to the people of the Ryūkyūs, techniques assisting sword fighting similar to the Japanese *jūjutsu* might have been developed. So a unique and pure method of unarmed fighting emerged on Okinawa about which in 1934 my father wrote the following sentences in the prologue to his book *Introduction into Attack and Defense Techniques in Karate Kempō*[30]:

> *In the southwest of Japan there is a chain of islands stretching in the open sea (Jpn. oki) like a rope (Jpn. nawa). So the name of the islands of Okinawa means "rope in the open sea". Since ancient times these islands have been famous as a strongly armed country without weapons. Because its only weapons are the karate fighting techniques.*

Karate – the Fundament of Martial Arts

My father used to say: "Karate is the legitimate heir of the *bujutsu* martial arts."[31] I think that karate is in fact the basis of all *budō* fighting techniques. There are two reasons for this statement. First, fighting with nothing but the empty hands is the most elementary way of fighting. Furthermore it is justified to say that any weapons, from staff, sword, bow and arrow or gun up to present-day missiles, could be regarded as extensions of the hand.

[30] *Kōbō jizai goshinjutsu karate Kempō.*

[31] *Karate wa bujutsu no chakuryū nari.*

If one does not have any weapons one has no choice but to fight with empty hands. If a samurai was called to fight against an unarmed opponent, he would lay down his weapons without any hesitation. The tournaments in the Heian and Kamakura periods always started with archery and were followed by spear and sword fighting. When the fights became too violent the opponents got the order: "Attention! Depart!" They had to lay down their weapons and to continue fighting with empty hands.

If forced to fight with empty hands, everything within reach can be used as an assisting fighting tool. That is the logical and historical starting point for the development of the various techniques of armed fighting. *Jūjutsu* is a technical system to support fighting with a sword or other weapons, whereas karate integrates weapons to support fighting with empty hands. On the Ryūkyū Islands, for centuries several agricultural and other tools have been used to support karate fighting such as staffs (*bō*), tridents (*sai*), sticks with a side-handle (*tonfa*) or segmented staffs (*nunchaku*).[32]

There is a second reason for considering karate as the fundament of all *budō* fighting techniques: There are no forbidden techniques because the aim is to injure the opponent deadly and this aim must be reached unarmed, with empty hands. That is why the whole body is extremely well prepared for fighting. During the prohibition of arms under the Satsuma rule, the old knowledge about how to fight for life and death without weapons was transferred from generation to generation quite exactly, although not in a written form. Karate practice consisted mainly of *kata* practice which was done alone so that nobody could be hurt and therefore no kicks or thrusts or punches had to be forbidden. So karate became a worldwide unique art of fighting.

In 1938 my father wrote in this context the following:

> *If there are people who think that under the pretext of physical education kata and kumite should be changed into sports and separated from their* bujutsu *or martial arts essence just to fit into the modern times, they should be told that*

---

[32] In general, the weapon techniques of the Okinawan karate are called (Okinawan) *kobudō*. – Publisher's comment.

they are obviously not realizing that by doing so they are making the first step to commit a very serious mistake, that is they are contributing to the destruction of the original values of karate as bujutsu. *Of course in the practice of* kata *and* kumite *the movements of the arms and the legs must be evaluated in detail. But this must be done from a martial arts point of view. Rational-physiologically based preparing and supporting exercises to improve the function of the limbs and the inner organs can be integrated in the practice of karate. But no one should think that the martial content of* kata *and* kumite *practice could be improved by changing both into sports or enjoyment.*

In a certain way my father thus predicted the present form of karate and warned us of this development. The transformation of karate into competitive sports is one of the main topics of this book, too. But before coming to this point, I would like to say something more about the history of karate.

1.2 The Emergence of Karate on Okinawa

The Old Okinawa-te

On Okinawa, three different styles of karate developed in three localities – Shuri, Naha and Tomari.[33] The term karate was introduced in the years 1911-1912 when the "Okinawa Boxing" or the "Okinawa Hand" became a compulsory subject at Japanese middle schools.

At first karate was written combining the character for "Tang China" with that for "hand". The people of Okinawa called their native martial art only "hand" (*te*), and the Chinese *kempō* was called *tō-de*, i.e. "Tang Chinese hand". The three local styles were called Shuri style, Naha style and Tomari style, or *Shuri-te*, *Naha-te* and *Tomari-te*, respectively. The oldest one was the *Shuri-te*. This is an original Okinawan system of hand-fighting techniques which took an independent development nourished by Chinese *kempō*. There was a saying among the Okinawa karate mas-

[33] These three localities were situated in the area of the present capital of Okinawa, Naha. – Translator's comment.

Photo 1: Itosu Ankō (1831-1915), second from left in the second row (with white moustache). This photo was discovered only in 2006 in the archives of Kinjo Hiroshi (born in 1919, 9th *dan*, president of the International Ryūkyū Karatejutsu Research Society). It is the first known photograph showing Master Itosu. It was taken in 1909 or 1910 when Itosu Ankō had started to teach at the middle school of the Okinawan prefecture in Shuri. The picture also shows the director of the school, some teachers and *kendō* and *jūdō* students.

ters: "The only true hand (*te*) is the *Shuri-te*."[34] The youngest style is the *Naha-te* in which the Chinese *kempō* is preserved most obviously. The *Tomari-te* is somewhere in between, geographically as well as technically.

Thanks to the recommendation of an acquaintance of the family my father was allowed to join the *dōjō* of the great master of the *Shuri-te* Itosu Ankō when he was 13 years old. Many of the famous karate personalities who contributed to the creation of modern karate came from the school of Master Itosu. He was said to have hit the *makiwara* (rice straw that is bound together in bundles and attached to a wooden post or board) every day several hundred times according to a schedule he had fixed in the morning in order to harden his fists which in the end looked like black stones. A lot of stories were told about the very muscular body of Master

[34] *Hontō no te wa Shuri-te dake da.*

Itosu. His upper arm, when being hit with a thick wooden pole did not even quiver when the pole bounced. He could smash a big bamboo cane in his hand or move hand over hand along a ceiling beam across the room without any effort.

Photo 2: Mabuni Kenwa (1889-1952).

In those days karate was not as popular as today and the rooms for practice (*dōjō*) were rather simple. Quite often the own garden was used as a *dōjō* and practice was done in open air. As a child I often watched my father exercising in the garden in the light of a bare bulb hitting the *makiwara* and hardening his muscles with stone weights.

Master Itosu's *dōjō* was not open for everybody. Only very selected persons were taught by him. When my father became 19, Master Itosu allowed him to get lessons from Higaonna Kanryō (1853-1916), who was a famous master of the *Naha-te*. As a young man Higaonna had traveled to the Chinese province of Fukien and studied there the local *kempō*. After his return to Okinawa he created the *Naha-te* based on his studies in China. My father was introduced to Higaonna by Miyagi Chōjun (1888-1953), who later founded the *Gōjū ryū*. Both became favorite students of Master Higaonna and were called "Dragon and Tiger", and a lifelong friendship developed between them.

Besides the *Shuri* and *Naha* styles, my father also studied the *Tomari-te* and traditional techniques of the *Ryūkyū kobudō*. He learned *bō* techniques from Master Aragaki Seichō (1840-1920), knife techniques from Tawada Shinkatsu (1851-1920) and special *bō* techniques from Master Soeishi Yoshiyuki.

Photo 3

Photo 4

Photo 3: Higaonna (Higashionna) Kanryō (1853-1916). He was the most important representative of the *Naha-te*.

Photo 4: Miyagi Chōjun (1888-1953), Higaonna's disciple and successor, founder of the *Gōjū ryū*.

The Kata of the Shuri-te

Karate is a system of self-defense techniques which have been developed on Okinawa since the 17th century at the beginning of the Tokugawa era and passed on secretly to the following generations. It was used to fight with empty hands against opponents armed with swords and other weapons in times when the lords of Satsuma ruled over the Ryūkyū Islands and did not allow the natives to possess weapons and suppressed any resistance. That is why in *Ryūkyū kobudō* only agricultural tools were used as weapons.

Furthermore, and unlike to the sword techniques or *jūjutsu*, which were supported by the Tokugawa government in Edo and by the *daimyōs* in their fiefs, no written records existed about karate. The masters of karate had to transform the technical experience and ideas they had acquired in many dangerous situations into *kata*, i.e. certain sequences of movements that were rather different of those practiced in other martial arts. They looked similar to traditional Okinawa "boxing dances" called *genkotsu odori*. Punches, kicks and blocking techniques are carried out as a sequence of attack and defense movements against an imaginary opponent. This way of practicing might also have been helpful to camouflage the true character of the exercises. So the *kata* became the legacy of the Okinawan karate. The karate student acquires the techniques and the spirit of karate by exercising *kata*. In the old days, learning the *te* always meant practicing *kata*. The masters arranged the *kata* according to their own experience and understanding. The *Ishimine no Passai*, for example, is suitable for fighting against small opponents. So it can be supposed that master Ishimine was not a small person. There are five different variations of the *Passai kata* named after Itosu, Matsumura, Matsumora, Tomari and Ishimine.

Except for the great masters Itosu and Higaonna, it was quite normal for a karate master to teach only one *kata*. Many of the *kata* used in our days in the *Itosu* style are named after masters or places they came from like the *Chatan Yara no Kōsōkun, Tomari no Passai, Matsumura no Passai, and Ishimine no Passai*. Tomari is the name of a place.[35] Matsumura and Ishimine were martial arts teachers. *Chatan Yara no Kōsōkun* means the *Kōsōkun kata* created by master Yara from the village Chatan. This *kata*, which recently has become rather popular in competitive karate, is the most representative one for the *Shuri-te*. However, in the form transmitted by Yara it contains a circle block technique (*mawashi uke*) which is very typical for the *Naha-te*. It was modified considerably to be used as a competition *kata*. Anyway, the legitimate *kata* of *Shuri-te* are the ones taught by master Itosu.

The Jigen Sword Technique and the Shuri-te

According to certain recent research, the *tao* of Chinese *kempō* are said to be the archetype of karate *kata*. But although certain similarities may be found in the *tao*, karate is – technically and spiritually – totally different from Chinese *kempō*. This will be explained on the following pages.

As mentioned above, all Okinawan hand-fighting techniques are based on the two main styles *Shuri-te* and *Naha-te*. The *Shuri-te* was taught as se-

[35] Tomari is the port of Naha. – Translator's comment.

cret knowledge among the Shuri nobility. It was perfected by Matsumura Sōkon (1800-1896), the incomparable master of the fist. His teacher was Sakugawa Shungo (1733-1815), who was known in Shuri as an outstanding martial arts expert. He had studied the Chinese *kempō* (*tō-de*) in China and passed his knowledge on to the Shuri nobility. That is how he earned the name Tōde Sakugawa. He had learned the northern Peking style which some people think to be the archetype of the *Shuri-te*. At the age of 20 Matsumura was sent by the Ryūkyū court to the Satsuma province in southern Kyūshū. There he learned the *Jigen* sword technique and reached the highest level of perfection called *unyō* (flame cloud). At the age of 27 he returned to the Ryūkyū islands and soon had the opportunity to travel on board of a tribute ship to China. So he could study Chinese *kempō* in Peking.

In the *Jigen ryū* there are no upper, middle and lower positions of the sword but only one position called *hassō*. The sword is raised as if to thrust into the sky. Then, with a bloodcurdling *kiai*[36], one makes a step forward or lowers the stance, crashing the *tachi* sword down.

The philosophy of the *Jigen* sword technique demands full control of the oncoming situation and the readiness to win with the first strike. Kondō Isamu, member of the *Shinsen gumi*[37], remembered that there was nothing they were more afraid of than this first strike by the Satsuma men using the *Jigen* sword technique and that they were repeatedly instructed to evade it. During the war to overthrow the Tokugawa government in 1868 as well as during the samurai rebellion against the new Meiji government in 1877, the Satsuma samurai were feared because of their first strike technique that intimidated their enemies whose corpses were often found cut open by a "sash strike" from the shoulder to the navel. Some even had the guard of

---

[36] *Kiai*: Jpn. In *budō*, a *kiai* is a battle cry expressing the unity of will and action. To let out a *kiai* means to direct one's energy, *ki*, against the opponent. In fact, a *kiai* can also be soundless (*kensei*). But usually it is a sound coming from the belly (*hara*). The *kiai* is as well an attitude of mind (*shin*) as a technique (*waza*, *gi*) of the voice. It is the art of determinedly focusing the totality of one's physical and mental energy on an object. – Habersetzer, R. and G.: Encyclopédie des Arts Martiaux. Paris: Amphora 2004.

[37] Special protective squad of the Tokugawa government, formed in 1863. – Translator's comment.

their own sword stuck between the eyebrows. They had tried to stop the Satsuma sword by raising their own sword above their heads. But they had underestimated the speed of attack by far so that the defending sword was smashed into the defender's skull.

The *Jigen* sword technique was aiming at the highest speed of impact. The highest level of perfection was called flame cloud. This is described in the *Manual of Jigen Style Military Techniques* as follows: "One eighth of a minute is a *byō*. A tenth of a *byō* is called *shi*. A tenth of a *shi* is a *kotsu*. A tenth of a *kotsu* is a *kō*. A tenth of a *kō* is called *rin*. When one has reached *rin* this level is called 'Cloud of Flames' (*unyō*)."

The masters of the *Jigen* style were said to be able to cut raindrops falling from the roof three times before they hit the ground. To train the mental concentration necessary to carry out such ultra high-speed strikes, a special training method was used called "hitting a standing tree" (*tachi ki uchi*). Partner exercises were not part of the training. Instead, a branch of a *Yusu* tree was cut and used as a wooden sword to hit a wooden block diagonally from left to right with a loud *kiai*. "Hitting a standing tree" became the incentive for master Matsumura to invent the training method "hitting the punching board" (*makiwara zuki*), which is still widely used in traditional karate. As mentioned above, master Itosu, who had been taught by master Matsumura, practiced this on a regular basis.[38]

Master Nakayama Hiromichi (1869-1958), who was called the "Musashi of the Shōwa period" or the "Last of the Sword Saints", wrote the following words: "Karate turns the empty hand into a sword. This is not a mere metaphor. The karate fist is definitely a sword."

In historical plays or movies one can often see the opponents hitting each other fiercely and endlessly. Japanese call this *chanbara*.[39] In reality this is only possible if the opponents are wearing head and body protectors like in *kendō*, hitting each other several times while always keeping the right distance. In case of a real fight, the moment when the sword is drawn

---

[38] However, a theory exists saying that the *makiwara* already existed on Okinawa long before Matsumura and that the training device is possibly of Chinese origin. – Habersetzer, R. and G.: Encyclopédie des Arts Martiaux. Paris: Amphora 2004.

[39] *Chanbara* is an abbreviation of *chanchan barabara*, literally meaning bang-bang-click-click. – Translator's comment.

is decisive for victory or defeat. The first strike will decide whether one will die or live on. There is no second chance. Even if the first strike does not contain the energy of a *Jigen* strike, it will be deadly.

The fact that master Matsumura perfectly mastered the *Jigen* sword technique, the favorite style of the Satsuma samurai, has decisively marked the development of the *Shuri-te*. These samurai who occupied Okinawa since 1609 were the enemies each native Okinawan had in mind while practicing the hand fighting techniques. There is no doubt that it was master Matsumura who shaped karate according to the basic principle to kill the enemy with the first punch or kick.

The masters of *Shuri-te* took up the idea of a "deadly first strike". But there is no such idea in Chinese *kempō* where the ruling principle is called "searching for the hands and legs" (*tanshu tantai*), that is first testing the technical abilities of the opponent and studying each other. The opponents begin from higher positions (*kamae*), reduce the distance step by step and finally adopt lower *kamae*. After each clash the opponents retreat. Then they approach and fight again so that in this way a rather spectacular and dramatic action develops. But this is only possible because in Chinese *kempō* the empty hand is not a sword.

On the opposite, karate is a martial art developed to defend oneself against an enemy who could be assumed of being educated in the *Jigen* style and able to carry out the first strike on the "cloud-of-flames" level. It was a question of survival to correctly evaluate the first strike of the swordsman and at the same time to instantly perform the deadly strike. So it can be said that master Matsumura and master Itosu perfected the *Shuri-te* under the influence of the Japanese sword techniques, in particular that of the *Jigen* style.

Drawing a Circle With a Straight Line

In Chinese *kempō*, the basic movement is the circle. In boxing and kickboxing, too, all kicks and punches are carried out as circular movements. Under the influence of these techniques in the post-war era, the karate movements have become circular, too.

Some time ago a student showed me a book titled *The Secrets of Okinawan Karate: Essence and Techniques* written by Arakaki Kiyoshi. This author also had edited writings left by my father in the monthly journal *Karate Dō* as a series titled *Karate Sankoku Shi*. His book was very interesting to me. He wrote: "The essence of Japanese *budō* can be described as drawing a circle with a straight line." I was very impressed by this sentence because it expresses with words what I feel with my whole body. In *iaidō*[40] it can be well observed that the arms are drawing a straight line forward while the sword is carrying out a circle. That means that a straight line describes a circle. It is also true that the *Jigen ryū* "flame cloud" speed that is reached when the sword hits the target cannot be obtained with a circular movement alone. According to master Arakaki, the maximum energy generated by the circular motion is transferred to the target via a straight line that is the shortest possible distance. This technique of the Japanese *budō* represents the highest level of body perfection.

It is not the hardening of the hands and their transformation into weapons what makes the difference to Chinese *kempō*. It is the kind and perfection of body control in the moment of thrusting and kicking which mobilizes the whole body. When we observe the thrust movement of the fist, we can see that unlike the curved line in boxing, the thrust is carried out in an absolutely straight line by bringing the fist forward out of its back position (*hikite*) (see photos 5 to 7 on the following page). Kicking too, is not carried out in wide curved lines or circles as in Chinese *kempō* or in kickboxing. The karate kick goes straight into the target. Therefore the energy is generated from a circular movement by bending the leg inwards and swinging it up. Then the circle is drawn with a straight line (see photos 8 to 10 on page 41).

It may be surprising, but in the traditional karate *kata* there is no roundhouse kick (*mawashi geri*) and no kick in the upper level (*jōdan geri*). However, there are jumped kicks (*tobi geri*), but they are only used as final falling or sacrifice techniques (*sutemi*). Kicking in wide, curved lines causes

---

[40] *Iaidō* is the "way of drawing the sword". This martial art has evolved from the combat techniques of the *iaijutsu*. It particularly emphasizes the spiritual component of the classical *budō* arts. – Habersetzer, R. and G.: Encyclopédie des Arts Martiaux. Paris: Amphora 2004.

Photo 5

Photo 6

Photo 7

Photos 5 to 7: The execution of a punch. The fist is in the back position close to the hip (*hikite*) (5). It comes from the *hikite* position (6), and a thrust is carried out in an absolutely straight line (7).

instability because it opens the own weak points to the enemy. It is too slow when fighting against a swordsman or other armed opponents and does not provide deadly first strike ability. Besides this, kicking may easily become ineffective if the opponent is physically stronger.

There is a special Japanese *budō* exercise called "falling tree" (*tōboku hō*) or "falling down" (*tōchi hō*). In the book cited above *The Secrets of Okinawan Karate* by master Arakaki there is a photo showing me doing this exercise. The photo has been taken from the book my father published in 1938, *Introduction into Attack and Defense Techniques in Karate Kempō*. It shows how my father is supporting or catching me, respectively. This exercise gives the experience of a tree falling down to earth using the energy of the free fall. The body does not try to resist gravity. Arakaki considers this exercise, which is peculiar to the Japanese *budō*, to be the top level of human body control. My understanding of this practice is not that much scientific and I like to use the name used in the Itosu style: "borrowing power from the earth".

The beginners in the *Itosu ryū* always start their studies with the *kata* of the *Shuri-te*. "Borrowing power from the earth" is one of the exercises of the traditional Okinawa-te, which is the kernel of the *Shuri-te*. All *Shuri-te kata* include the principle of the "falling tree". Whether this principle is

Photo 8 Photo 9 Photo 10

Photos 8 to 10: Execution of a kick. Taking the basic position or ready stance (*kamae*) (8). The leg is bent and then swung upwards (9). The kick is carried out in a straight line (10).

integrated into present-day karate is a point I would like to write about later in the context of the development of karate into a kind of competitive sport.

Photo 11: Mabuni Kenwa and his son Kenei practicing the exercise "falling tree" (*tōboku hō*).

The Emergence of the Naha-te

The *Naha-te* is said to originate from a village called Kume[41]. It was founded by Chinese who came to the Ryūkyū islands from the Fukien province in 1393. This was the time of the Ming empire. Many of their offspring were active in the China trade. From their home province they had brought along *kempō* knowledge that they obviously passed on to the Kume nobility. What they taught was probably not pure Chinese *kempō* but a style rather influenced by the *Shuri-te* and adapted to the conditions of the Ryūkyū islands.

Aragaki Seishō (1840-1920) from Kume – he was later given the name "Aragaki the Cat" – is said to have been one of the greatest martial arts masters. My father, Funakoshi Gichin and Miyagi Chōjun were among his disciples. He not only practiced karate but also *bō* techniques.

Higaonna Kanryō (1853-1916), too, learned karate from master Aragaki. Higaonna came from a Naha-based family of firewood traders. He learned *kempō*, which was normally taught only to the Kume nobility, from Aragaki. Higaonna seemed to have been blessed with a special fighting talent. At the age of 15 he traveled to the Fukien province, studied the local *kempō* and after his return created the *Naha-te*. That is why the *Naha-te* is younger than the *Shuri-te* and the Chinese influence is stronger. My father said about master Higaonna and his karate: "Master Higaonna had been to China and had studied the Fukien *kempō*. His lessons were different from the ones we are used to today."

Typical for the *Shuri-te* is distance fighting presupposing an opponent armed with a sword. *Naha-te*, however, is infighting, based on southern Chinese *kempō*. There are no thrusts and kicks which are typical elements of distance fighting. Of course *Naha-te*, too, is not pure *kempō*. It is influenced by the *Shuri-te* and adapted to the Okinawan conditions. However, techniques that are called in Chinese *kempō* "explosive energy" (*hakkei*) or "power of the moment" (*sunkei*) are particular for this style. In the *Naha-te*, these techniques were at first practiced by exercising the "three phases

[41] Kume, also called Kumemura. A village in the surroundings of the city of Naha. Here, the Chinese legation resided. – Translator's comment.

Photo 12

Photo 13

Photos 12 and 13: The hanging or laying hand (*kake-te*). Photo 12 shows the technique *kake-te* as practiced in the *Shuri-te*, and photo 13 represents the same technique as practiced in the *Naha-te*. See next pages.

kata" (*Sanchin*) and "turning-the-palms *kata*" (*Tenshō*).

A particularity of the *Naha-te* is also a breathing technique used to contract all muscles of the body. There is no such exercise in the *Shuri-te*. In the beginning it is practiced by inhaling and exhaling slowly, and at the same time slowly pulling the fist back to the hip (*hikite*) and thrusting it forward. Of course in a normal situation blocking and thrusting are carried out much faster.

The above-mentioned expression of the "power of the moment" (*sunkei*), i.e. "explosive power", describes the harmony of breathing and action in order to accumulate the inner energies and to contract the whole muscular system of the body and then releasing it "explosively". Normally this is called *kime*.

In present-day *kata* the differences between *Shuri-te* and *Naha-te* are hardly recognizable. However, the original styles differ significantly from each other. But there are not only differences with regard to the principles

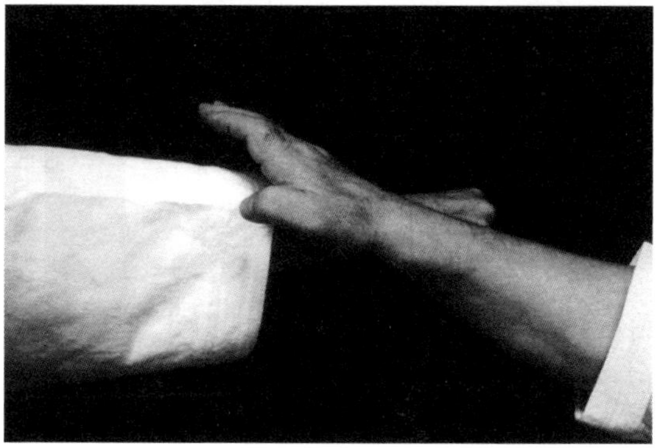

Photo 14: Analysis of the *kake-te* in the *Shuri-te*: The hand blocks and grabs.

Photo 14

of kicking and thrusting but also to single techniques. The blocking technique "laying or hanging hand" (*kake te*) may serve as an example (photos 12 to 15). This technique is used in *Shuri-te* as well as in *Naha-te*. But it is used in different ways. Because *Shuri-te* is distance fighting, the thrusting arm of the opponent is caught in a distance. The laying or hanging of the hand is carried out with a grabbing and pulling movement (photos 12 and 14). In the infight-focused *Naha-te*, the distance is reduced and the laying of the hand is carried out with the palm being raised deviating the attack with the back of the hand (photos 13 and 15)

The Origins of the Tomari-te

There are no written records about the early *Tomari-te* but it is said to have been brought to the Ryūkyū Islands by a monk from the Chinese Shandong province called Anan[42]. Nothing else is known about it. The modern *Tomari-te* was founded by Matsumora Kōsaku (1829-1898). He is said to have learned it from Teruya Kise (1804-1868) and Uku Karyū (1800-

[42] According to some sources Anan is said to be identical with master Shionja who came from the city of Fuzhou in the Chinese province of Fujian (Fukien). Shionja is also considered Matsumora's direct teacher. – Habersetzer, R. and G.: Encyclopédie des Arts Martiaux. Paris: Amphora 2004.

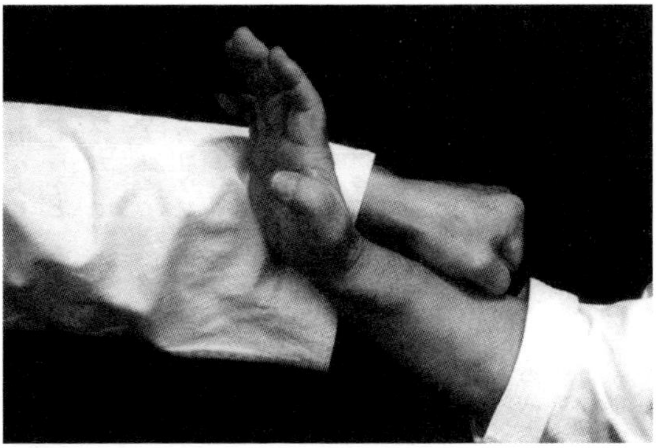

Photo 15

Photo 15: Analysis of the *kake-te* in the *Naha-te*: The hand blocks and deviates the attack.

1850), who both were students of Anan. There are a lot of *kata* in the Itosu style which were named after master Matsumora. Most of them are close to the *Shuri-te*, some of them similar to the *Naha-te*.

The Shitō Style as Heritage of the Okinawa-te

Modern karate on the Japanese main islands comprises four major currents: *Shōtōkan ryū*, *Gōjū ryū*, *Wadō ryū* and *Shitō ryū*. The *Shōtōkan* style contains parts of the *Shuri-te*. The *Gōjū* style teaches only *Naha-te*. The *Wadō* style partly includes *Shuri-te* but rearranged as *jūjutsu*. The only school to represent all of the Okinawa-te is the *Shitō* karate.

On Okinawa today there are three major currents: The *Shōrin ryū* originating from *Shuri-te*, the Okinawan *Gōjū ryū*, created on the basis of the *Naha-te*, and the *Uechi ryū*, a style derived from southern Chinese *kempō*. The *Uechi* style is even closer to the original patterns of Chinese *kempō* than the *Naha-te*. Uechi Kanbun (1877-1948) developed the *Uechi* style after his studies in the Fukien province.

In the early 1920s master Uechi went to mainland Japan and opened a karate club in the Wakayama prefecture where his style was practiced. After my father had come to mainland Japan, he from time to time needed the help of his fellow countrymen in Wakayama and there was a rather intense exchange between my father and master Uechi Kanbun. That is

Photo 16: Uechi Kanbun (1877-1948).

why some of the *kata* typical for the *Uechi* style were integrated into the *Shitō* karate. One is called *Shimpā*. Because the second half of this *kata* was missing, I completed it after my father had died.

Uechi Kanei (1911-1991), the son and successor of master Kanbun, lived in Ōsaka close to the Nishinari district where the Okinawa countrymen fellow association had some rooms. I remember that after my arrival in Ōsaka I often visited them in Nishinari; the rooms of the association were also used for regular karate training.

2 Shitō Karate – the Teachings of Mabuni Kenwa

2.1 "Captured" in the World of Budō

Striving for a Healthy Body

Some time ago I went to India as a supervising coach. There, a student came to me and told me full of joy that his son, who had practiced karate already since he was a child of six, had reached the black belt. I myself was also quite happy about this and we enjoyed a little chat. He asked me when I had started karate. I answered slightly amused that I had probably started kicking in my mother's womb. And this was not mere joking. Because wherever my mother was indoors with me, my father was somewhere nearby, fiercely practicing karate. So I was educated in karate since my birth. I was born into a world of karate and I grew up in this world. After my father had died in 1952 at the age of only 53 I practiced every day for four hours without any break, and even today all I can think of and think about is karate.

My father was born in 1889 in Shuri, which is a town in the Okinawa prefecture. Among his ancestors was a lord of the old Ryūkyū kingdom called Ōshiro Kenyū who was famous for his courage and called "demon Ōshiro". He belonged to a clan called *Ka* (*Ka uji*). The names of the Okinawan natives include a character indicating to which family the person belongs. The names of the members of the *Ka* clan contain a character with the meaning "clever" and the reading *ken*. The Mabuni family is the main family of the clan to which I belong in the 18th generation. I am the head of the family. But because I am living in Ōsaka, the families of the *Ka* clan founded an association to take care of the clan's shrine.

My father was a very frail child. His family was really worried about him. Whenever possible, he was told stories about his brave forefather, and my father seems to have been deeply impressed. It is reported that when he was a small child he was already determined to gain a strong and healthy body.

A Life Without Selfishness and Greed

After my father had graduated from middle school he served in the army and later became a policeman. But more than anything else he was interested in his beloved karate practice. He often told me that karate had been of great help to arrest criminals or in other difficult situations of his work.

In those days one needed influential warrantors to become a karate student and be accepted by a karate master. Then the decision of the student was examined several times. Finally he had to place some incense sticks in front of the Buddhist altar, sit there for a long time and do an oath. At that time one could not chose a teacher freely and enter a karate club easily. The karate itself, so to say, chose the people by whom it wanted to be studied.

As a policeman, my father got around a great deal and often he had the chance to come into contact with other kinds of *budō*. Here and there in the villages he could meet people with expert abilities not only in the *Shuri-te* or *Naha-te* but also with regard to other local forms of karate and old *kata*.

My father was a man of high character. He was generous, very sociable and popular among people. He was without selfishness and greed. Often he helped others and from time to time this brought him into trouble. After the feudal domains had been abolished and a new administrative structure based on prefectures had been introduced, the nobility rank of the Mabuni family was confirmed. This happened in the beginning of the Meiji period in the 1870s. My grandfather got a financial compensation which he used to build a sweets shop. But this shop went bankrupt after a short time. A joke was told that my grandfather had spread the sweets among his friends too generously.

My father had no special talents by nature. He did not like to play *Go* or Japanese chess and was not interested in betting or gambling. When he had reached a middle age he stopped drinking alcohol. But he liked cigarettes. "Golden Bat"[43] was his favorite brand. Since shortly after the war all

[43] The cigarette brand Golden Bat was brought onto the market on 1 September 1906, immediately after the foundation of the Japanese tobacco monopoly, and it still exists today. It was made of broken tobacco leaves from many small domestic producers and was considered a very cheap brand. – Translator's comment.

goods were rationed, tobacco was rare and of course cigarettes were very hard to get. But from time to time my father managed to get some and he used to share them with his students. He passed the packet around although often in the end not a single cigarette was left over for him. In fact he was not interested in material things at all.

Photo 17: Kanō Jigorō (1860-1938).

The only thing he felt a strong greed for was *budō*. Maybe he was also driven by the unconscious fear that the Okinawa-te could disappear in the waves of modernization like many an old tradition. So he tried hard to study all kinds of traditional Okinawa techniques. Meanwhile many people realize and highly valuate his contribution to the preservation of traditional Okinawan culture. By now 70 percent of the *kata* my father had studied are lost even on Okinawa.

Praised by Kanō Jigorō

My father's passion for karate did not become weaker. Not for one day. In 1918, the year I was born, he founded the "Society for Karate Studies" in his flat. He was then 29. All day people who had something to do with karate were coming and going. Already when I was a small child I was always at my father's side watching him teaching karate. I still can remember that his visitors and students were making fun with me and giving me sweets and that I was trying to copy their *kata* movements. When my father went to his karate lessons at schools or to *budō* performances he always took me along. Like the "novice in front of the temple gate" could read the holy books without having studied them, I was able to do karate without having learned it.

In 1924 my father quit his police career to become a karate-teacher at the Okinawan Fishery School, at the Teaching Staff Seminar and at the local Police Academy. The following year he founded the Society for Okinawan Karate Studies, opened the first *dōjō* on Okinawa and began to teach karate in his own school. The *dōjō* was right behind the house and perfectly equipped with all training devices typical for the Okinawan karate practice. Besides my father other *budō* masters were teaching here like Miyagi Chōjun, Kyoda Jūhatsu, Motobu Chōyū, Hanashiro Chōmo, Ōshiro Chōjo, Chibana Chōshin and Go Kenki, who was teaching Chinese *kempō*. The whole elite of modern karate had gathered here.

In 1921 the Princes Kuninomiya and Kachōnomiya visited Okinawa, and in 1925 a visit of Prince Chichibunomiya followed. They honored my father and his colleagues by watching their karate performances. One day, when my father and some other teachers were just discussing the daily training program, Kanō Jigorō (1860-1938), the founder of *jūdō* came into the *dōjō* to invite them to the opening ceremony of the Association of Okinawan Jūdō Masters. This was probably in 1927. Miyagi Chōjun and my father Mabuni Kenwa took the chance to give a karate performance and some explanations which deeply impressed master Kanō and made him say: "This kind of *budō* including attack and defense is ideal and should be spread all over the country."

Funakoshi Gichin Learned Kata From My Father

Already five years before, in 1922, Kanō had watched a karate performance at the *1st Exhibition on the Education in Traditional Budō* organized by the Japanese Ministry of Cultural Affairs in Tōkyō and voiced his strong interest in karate. This performance had been given by master Funakoshi Gichin (1869-1957) who later was called the "father of modern karate". At that time he was regarded in mainland Japan to be representative for the Okinawa karate. He stayed in Tōkyō and was the first to make efforts to spread karate in an environment characterized by aloofness, and under poor living conditions. What had kept him stay in Tōkyō was master Kanō. This extraordinary *budōka* was farsighted and clearly recognized the potential of karate to develop from a local to a universal art of fighting.

Master Kanō was even more impressed when he saw the performance carried out by master Miyagi and my father in the center of the karate culture coming in touch with its mainstream. This is comprehensible because at the time he had presented karate for the first time in Tōkyō master Funakoshi knew only a few of the *Shuri-te kata*. In order to expand his knowledge he decided to send his son Gigō[44] to study *kata* in my father's *dōjō* on Okinawa. Master Funakoshi Gigō was a karate teacher at the Takushoku and Waseda Universities. My father already had a good reputation in the world of karate but he was 20 years younger than master Funakoshi Gichin. This might have been the reason why my father was grateful and felt honored that master Funakoshi – represented by his son – had accepted lessons from him. Later he always was very rigid in his criticism against students who made depreciatory remarks about the *kata* of the *Shōtōkan* style master Funakoshi had founded. My father did not tell me anything about master Gigō's visit but my mother revealed it to me in her late years.

Photo 18: Funakoshi (Yoshitaka) Gigō (1906-1945) hitting the *makiwara*.

Urged by master Kanō my father quit his work as a teacher on Okinawa and went to mainland Japan without his family. This happened in 1929 when he was 41 years of age. At first he lived together with fellow countrymen in the Wakayama prefecture and then moved to Ōsaka where he settled in the south-western ward called Nishinari.

The reason my father chose Ōsaka but not Tōkyō was surely his respect and consideration towards his fellow countryman and elder colleague mas-

[44] Funakoshi Gigō (1906-1945), also called Funakoshi Yoshitaka, played an essential role in the development of modern *Shōtōkan* karate. – Publisher's comment.

Photo 19: Sitting in the center: Mabuni Kenwa. Standing from left to right: Funakoshi Gichin (1869-1957), Nakasone Genwa (1895-1978), unknown, Konishi Yasuhiro (1893-1983), Mabuni Kenei. Photograph from 1930.

ter Funakoshi who was trying hard to make karate popular in the Tōkyō area. At that time karate was absolutely unknown to the people in the Ōsaka area. When they saw karate performances they thought this to be a kind of "fighting dance". But when the karate activists started to smash tiles and break wooden boards they began to understand the power of the karate fist. One of the performances especially popular at that time was the smashing of beer bottles. This could of course not be left to the assistants but using the right technique it was a rather easy exercise. The bottle should not be fixed too tightly. It was half filled with water. When the edge of the hand chopped off the bottle-neck it jumped away with a plopping sound.

There was a lot of public criticism on karate because it was feared to be misused by ruffians as a means for street-fighting and for injuring people. Others warned not to teach karate to policemen because they could be provoked to use inappropriate force for example when arresting criminals. It was not easy to make karate popular in such an atmosphere. This time could be considered to be a preparatory period of the development of karate, although it was a rather long time.

In the summer holidays – I had just finished the 6th grade at primary school – we got my father's call from Ōsaka we had been longing for: "Come over here!" Later when I faced military service the family decided to be registered at the new residence. This was important because as long as I was registered on Okinawa I would have been called for service on the far away island of Kyūshū.

In Ōsaka I started practicing karate and it was my independent and conscious decision to do so. I was 13 – the same age my father was when he had started karate under master Itosu. I must stress that my father had never tried to force me to practice karate, not in the least.

The Creation of the Shitō Ryū

After my father had fixed a plate over the entrance with the inscription *Yōshūkan*[45] and his *dōjō* opened, nobody came in for a certain while, and so times were rather hard. The first student came from the *jūdō* club of the Kansai University. His name was Sawayama Masaru (1907-1977). Later he became the founder of Japanese *kempō* (*Nihon kempō*).

---

[45] *Yōshūkan*: Jpn. "House of rising above oneself". – Publisher's comment.

In the small space of a six *tatami*[46] room they practiced day and night. Soon the *tatami* were spoiled and for this reason covered with reed mats. Although my father quickly provided a nice floor replacing the worn out *tatami* by wooden boards the *dōjō* remained rather unknown and only two or three young men, half students and half spongers, came regularly. But finally some high school students and some students from the Kansai University dropped in, then a lawyer and the owner of the rice shop close by, who always brought along some rice. – So, somehow we managed to survive.

At that time training methods were quite different from today's training. They practiced always the same *kata* day by day until the master said, "It's alright now!" (*yoshi*). The *kata* were not explained in detail as today. When a student asked for help to understand a certain technique the master said, "Come on, try to attack me!" and made him kick and thrust freely and answered by blocking or evading the attacks and finally asking, "Well, did you get it now?!" Techniques which lasted only parts of a second were practiced not only one or two times but almost endlessly until the physical experience was deeply ingrained in the body.

After my father had moved to mainland Japan he kept contact and regular exchange with the top ranking masters of martial arts of the time like Konishi Yasuhiro (1893-1983, founder of *Shindō Shizen ryū*), Ōtsuka Hironori (1892-1982, founder of *Wadō* karate) or Fujita Seiko (1899-1966, 14th generation of *Kōga ninjutsu*). They helped each other to develop their own styles, not hesitating to offer their internal knowledge on *kata* for their studies.

After I had finished middle school my father sent me to Tōkyō for one year to the *jūdō* master Konishi. I assisted his coaching and under his guidance I learned *jūdō* joint manipulation techniques[47]. This ability was important because it could help me to make a living. My father was always afraid that I could not build up my own life only based on karate.

In the early years karate still was regarded in mainland Japan to be minor and barbarian compared to *kendō* or *jūdō*. At that time the "shrine" of *budō* was the *Dai Nihon Butoku Kai* (Great Japan Martial Arts Association). It was in particular thanks to the efforts of the masters Kanō and Konishi

---

[46] Almost 10 m^2 (about 110 sq ft). – Translator's comment.

[47] This corresponds to a chiropractor training. – Translator's comment.

that karate could finally gain an independent position in this organization. Step by step master Konishi took the lead in making karate popular and officially recognized. The first karate performance in the *Butoku Kai* was given in 1938. In 1939 the *Shitō* style my father had created was officially registered in the *Butoku Kai* headquarters. The same year the *Dai Nippon Butoku Kai* (Great Japan Martial Arts Association) awarded my father the rank of a "grandmaster of karate" (*Karate jutsu renshi*). Under the official name *Shitō Ryū Kempō Karate Dō* the *Shitō* karate had become an official and independent school of karate. At the same time the *Dai Nihon Karate Kai* (Great Japan Karate Association) was founded. From now on karate could move forward on the right tracks.

Following My Father's Footsteps

After I had spent half of my life with karate at my father's side I was called for duty in January 1940 to the 8th Ōsaka Regiment. In the beginning I served in the regiment staff in Ōsaka. Then I was sent to Taiwan and finally to the Philippine island of Cebu where I awaited the end of the war. For a certain time I was held there in a POW camp and luckily returned home in December 1945.

At that time my father was leading the karate training at the Kansai, Kansai-Gakuin and Tōyō universities. The young fellows he was sweating with in karate practice helped very much to build up and develop the Japanese Karate Association in the post war years. My father had teaching assignments at nearly all universities in the region. I helped him as an assisting karate teacher and I also gave lessons at some other universities like the state-owned Ōsaka University, the municipal, technical and economical universities in Ōsaka, and also at the Kōbe University and the Kōbe University for Foreign Languages.

From the end of the war until the death of my father in 1952 I practiced karate very close to my father. He taught me a lot of techniques but also a lot of psychological aspects I truly understood only in later years. This does not mean that I learned only by copying. Some things just need time to be understood.

From time to time I am asked how the essence of the karate the masters of the former generations had taught could be defined. Once my father was asked by some students whether there is an essence or kernel in karate. He answered that there is nothing like this. And he added, "Somehow everything can become its essence." He also said: "There is no limit to the techniques."[48] This might be the kernel of his teachings.

After I had become the head of the *Shitō* karate, I studied a lot and even changed some of the techniques. Therefore some people considered the result to be "quite different compared to the former or traditional techniques". But this is not right. My father's karate also changed according to the several stages of his life from the pre-war times, through the post-war times until his late years. Meanwhile the *Shitō* karate has split up into different sub styles. The reason might be that the masters who created the sub styles met my father in different periods of his life. People change according to their age. And the same applies to karate.

My Father's Goals

In the beginning I have tried to explain that originally there was no karate on the Okinawan islands but several fighting techniques which were called "hand" (*ti*, Jpn. *te*). Furthermore, because of the strict rule over the islands by the lords of Satsuma, no written records about techniques and psychological methods of the defense against sword attacks could be made and passed on to the following generations. The term karate was used to collect the several local hand-fighting techniques, *te*, and to shape all the physical and psychological techniques included into one system and constructed a comprehensive ideal system comparable to that of *kendō* and *jūdō*. Sadly master Funakoshi and also my father were still on the way to their great goal when they had to leave us and left the question what karate actually is, unanswered.

To determine the word "karate", master Funakoshi had taken the character meaning "sky, heaven or emptiness" and the reading *kara* from a sentence of a famous Buddhist prayer called *Hannya* Sutra: "The color is

---

[48] *Waza wa mugen.*

emptiness and emptiness is the color".[49] But until today it is not fully clear what concrete meaning he had in mind in doing so.

My father had composed the name *Shitō* of parts of the names of his main teachers Itosu and Higaonna. In doing so he had at the same time provided a clear definition of his style because both teachers represented the two main sources of karate, the *Shuri-te* and the *Naha-te*, which my father had studied with equal intensity. This made him unique and for this reason he was honored by the martial arts experts of his time with the name "Mabuni the technician" to confirm his position as the major expert in the field of *kata*.

As mentioned above, master Funakoshi, too, had learned many *kata* from my father through his son Gigō. Master Funakoshi always said: "If you have questions about *kata*, ask Mabuni." Also master Ōtsuka, who founded the *Wadō ryū*, and master Konishi, who founded the *Shindō Shizen* (also *Jinen*) *ryū*, had much of their knowledge about *kata* from my father. As an afterword to the above-mentioned book[50] by my father master Funakoshi clearly showed his respect for my father's achievements.

Memories About the Days Ten Years Ago. By Funakoshi Gichin.

Mabuni Kenwa and I are very close friends. Mabuni is a true researcher on karate rarely to be found in modern history and is the outstanding specialist in our days. When we were living on Okinawa we were trying to gather like-minded people – Mabuni in Shuri and me in Naha. We founded many practice groups and promoted our students and were so busy about it that we even forgot to eat and sleep.

Our reputation spread throughout the island, and more and more people wanted to join us. Day and night people came to our houses to ask us questions and talk about things.

Mabuni was a comrade with a warm heart and a strong character. He did not care about former conflicts between the different styles of martial arts. Age hierarchy, too, was not important to him. When there was something we did not know he even asked younger fellows for help. And when he had learned something new he did not keep it to himself. At the next occasion he would show it to others and share it as part of the joint research.

---

[49] See also p. 197 et seq.

[50] *Attack and Defense Techniques for Self-Defense in Karate Kempō.*

He prefers open discussion and has absolutely left behind the mystery mongering so typical for this sphere of life. For a very long time he has been collecting material. Now he is absolutely familiar with all kinds of hand fighting. There is nobody equal to him in this regard. I am not exaggerating to say that he is the greatest in this respect.

He initiated meetings between the Shuri-te and Naha-te fighters, was always open for criticism, improved whatever was found to be weak and struggled for joint learning and joint development. That is what he was admired and respected for by all sides. There was nobody to criticize him.

As I have learned recently he has moved to Ōsaka and built up good relations, for example with the Kansai University, and is guiding many young people, showing his devotion to our common cause, to our country and our society. I am glad to say that recently his efforts in the Kansai region have been recognized properly. Now he is well known and respected. So, we should deepen our relations and coordinate our activities in the Kantō and Kansai regions and I would like him to take over a responsible role for our common cause.

I wrote down these memories because master Mabuni has asked me to add some final remarks to his book.

When my father created the *Shitō* style, it was surely not his aim to see it splitting into several schools and drifting apart. As master Funakoshi confirmed, my father wanted to create a karate as *Nihon budō* (Japanese Way of Fighting) and in this regard had the same aim as master Funakoshi in Tōkyō.

Shitō Karate is Authentic Budō Karate

My father tried to show that the technical content and the ideas of the *Shitō* style are passed on within the Mabuni family. That is why he used the family crest of the Mabunis as the symbol for the *Shitō* style. According to my father's explanation, the circle symbolizes harmony (*wa*) while the two parallel vertical lines to the left and to the right inside the circle and their corresponding short horizontal ones symbolize the *Shuri-te* of master Itosu and the *Naha-te* of master Higaonna – the whole image stressing the harmony of the two schools.

Of course *Shuri-te* and *Naha-te* were used metaphorically representing all Okinawan hand-fighting techniques, because from the beginning my father was searching for a karate to unify all of them. Giving the family crest a new

Photo 20: The Mabuni family crest.

meaning he created a symbol of the karate he wanted to achieve. This was not just a superficial mixture of both main schools but a true and deep fusion.

When traveling abroad I am often asked about the spiritual meaning of the *Shitō* style symbol. That is because in Europe family and heraldic symbols always seem to have a spiritual message often expressed by the images of swords or lions.[51] But my father did not leave a psychological or spiritual message. He created the *Shitō* style as an unified technical system but he did not have the time to systemize its psychological and spiritual aspects. When talking to foreign students, the *Shitō* style symbol always seemed to be an interesting matter. The lines left and right inside the circle could also be understood as two human beings and the circle as the earth. So the symbol could be explained as two human beings holding the earth and maintaining its balance.

One day, when asked again at the occasion of a karate seminar abroad, I spontaneously answered without any hesitation that the crest symbol-

[51] For example, the lion as one of the most frequent heraldic animals was to symbolize power, courage and martial virtues in his capacity of king of the animals. – Publisher's note.

izes the "harmony between the human beings (*wa*)", thus being a symbol of peace. And I think that this interpretation is a good one. So, I finally added a spiritual explanation to the merely physical one. I guess my father would have appreciated this interpretation of our family crest, since in his book from 1934 he had written: "The essence of the martial art is balance (*hei*). Its final aim is harmony (*wa*)." Both characters combined build the Japanese word *heiwa* meaning peace.

At the 3rd World Convention of Shitō Karate in 2000 my explanation of the Mabuni family symbol was published in Japanese and English. That is how the message of the *Shitō* karate symbol carrying the ideas of "reforming karate" and "world peace" became internationally known.

Finally, to all those who practice karate I would like to stress again which kind of karate my father was aiming at and what is characteristic about the *Shitō* style. *Shitō* karate is *budō* karate, it is a martial way. This corresponds exactly to the meaning of the above-cited sentence. Karate was created as martial way, *budō*, not as sports and not for competition.

2.2 The Pleasure of Learning and Teaching Karate

How to Teach Karate

To my father it was extremely important to respect and to develop the individuality of each student when teaching karate. The essence of karate training is practicing *kata*. Long kata contain about 70 and short ones about 20 attack and defense techniques. Each of these individual movements has to be executed with precision. According to the aims of the student there are different ways of acquiring *kata*. They can be used to improve one's health. Studied analytically by applying analysis (*bunkai*)[52] they can become an

[52] *Bunkai*: Jpn. Interpretation of a fighting technique and the attempt of its practical use. Since time immemorial, the transmission of the techniques of the fight with bare hands was realized by means of codified forms, fighting sequences that are practiced alone, i.e. without partner. These forms are called *kata* (in Chinese quanfa, they are called *tao*). Each movement, each shift, each turn, each rhythm within a *kata* has a meaning. Sometimes this meaning is evident, sometimes it is hidden, and in some cases it is even misleading (e.g. a

abundant armory to get equipped for real fighting. Whatever karate is practiced for, the *kata* contain all the necessary techniques and ideas. My father used to say: "Karate begins with *kata* and ends with *kata*."

Meanwhile several sub-styles of the *Shitō* karate exist. One might wonder whether those who founded the different sub styles had learned the *kata* from the same master. But *kata* are something individual. This probably depends on the fact that those masters learned *kata* from my father in different stages of his life, and another reason is that his education was focused on the individuality of his students.

In the past, by watching a *kata* performance one could say at first glance which master had guided the practice. In the last few years books and video tapes are increasingly used for karate teaching. That is why *kata* have become uniform even in detail, and lost individuality. Also at the big *kata* contests *kata* performances prove excellent training results but nearly no individuality; the *kata* always look the same.

Two or three years ago a young man joined my *dōjō*. He had already practiced *Shitō* karate for a certain time with another master. But when he came to me he wore a white belt to show his readiness for a new beginning. After some months he said: "Master, you corrected my exercises in each lesson only once. Nevertheless I feel like having progressed in those few hours more than I have in the last 10 years." Well, maybe he was right. In any case it is true to say that I think a lot about the best ways to teach karate.

---

technique can be similar to a known technique, but in the actual context of this sequence it does not seem to make sense). The interpretation of the visible form depends on the previous and on the subsequent technique, but also on the – rather mental than physical – level of the practitioner. Often a *kata* is a kind of rebus – certain keys are required to understand it. With regard to *bunkai*, very different levels exist – from the most elementary to the most developed. Time and patience are needed to discover them gradually "behind" the obvious. Sometimes, a *kata* may contain real traps impeding true understanding; without such an understanding the techniques cannot be really effective, neither for fighting nor for therapeutic purposes (the sequence of a *kata* is also a technical process for the development and the arrangement of the internal energy *ki*, directly influencing the health). For this reason one can say that numerous techniques appearing in a *kata* have a *bunkai* that changes in dependence of the execution of the *kata*, i.e. the experience of the practitioner counts. – Habersetzer, R. and G.: Encyclopédie des Arts Martiaux. Paris: Amphora 2004.

Karate for Children and Youngsters

I have enjoyed the great luck to be able to practice karate all my life, as a small child, as a school child, as a youngster, as a middle aged and aged person and as an old man. My teaching is based on my own long and deep experience acquired through all stages of life. Primary school pupils do not need complicated explanations. One should rather try to become their friend and play with them, sit down and talk with them on eye-level. And the heart, too, should be open to the emotions of the children. If one can truly come together and play with them, children will open their hearts.

In the same way one should adapt oneself to middle school or university students. This means one should not try to make the others adapt to one's own level, but the opposite is right. One should try to adapt oneself to the others' level. One must try to be flexible and flow like water which cannot choose in which direction to run. Water adapts to any environment. When approaching students in this way, differences in age or language do not matter at all. It is important to meet each other at eye level and interact with joy.

I taught in many countries. There are only few I did not travel to. Only if one tries to meet people on eye-level, no matter which race, ethnical background, culture or religion they belong to, there is real chance of spiritual exchange and emotional understanding.

The Wealth of the Traditional Kata

The word *kata* is written with a character meaning form or shape but not with homophone meaning model or type. *Kata* means movement in a certain form of appearance which can differ according to the psychological situation or the level of abilities of the person to carry it out. A *kata* is not a static mould the person performing it is pressed into. A *kata* is a living form or "figure". A *kata* can be adapted to the own individuality or to breathing by slowing down the movements to a convenient speed even if it may look jerky, and it can be repeated as often as necessary until the meaning of the *kata* as a set of fighting techniques is fully understood.

Of course such *kata* are not apt to win in a *kata* contest. This may be a dilemma. But it should be understood that there are two versions of a *kata* – one for public contests and a *budō* one with respect to the fighting techniques and the martial mental attitude. Both are basically different. *Kata* for contest are destined for a broader public. They should include nice and spectacular techniques which in a situation of real fight would in fact mean total surrender. If the aspect of fighting technique is stressed on the other hand, only a few insiders can judge and enjoy it. But in any case, one should feel that the *kata* has something like a soul, that it is filled with *ki*[53].

In his book *Introduction into Attack and Defense Techniques in Karate Kempō* my father wrote:

> *The karate kata are living creatures. It is easy for the observer to see without any special explanation to which degree the person performing it has practiced and understood it. If the person performing the kata does not understand it, the performance will look ugly. If the person performing the kata has not practiced enough, it will look weak and wobbly. But if the kata is deeply understood and thoroughly practiced, its spirit will enter the person and appear as a living creature expressed by this person. Often one can see how a kata is enjoying life. So a kata is a living thing. It is a spirit turned into a living creature. The more one practices and understands a kata the greater the benefits for body and soul will be.*

In 1999, at the 1st World Convention on Okinawa,[54] *kata* performances were given by the four great old masters Tomoyose Ryūkō (*Uechi ryū*), Miyahira Katsuya and Nakazato Shūgorō (*Shōrin ryū*) and Yagi Meitoku (1912-2003, *Gōjū ryū*). Master Yagi is even older than me and I have known him since he met my father for the first time. He was wearing a karate suit he had been given from his *sensei* Miyagi Chōjun and in memory of him was performing the *Tenshō kata* his teacher had created. A younger student who had watched this said: "I don't think that a world champion in competition *kata* could perform in such a way." I do not know to which

[53] See footnote 10 on p. 16.

[54] 1st World Convention of Traditional Okinawan Karate and Other Martial Arts. – Translator's comment.

degree this student understood the technical subtleties of this performance but at least he could perceive the high level of spirituality.

Karate in Europe

After the Japanese Karate Association had been formed, competition karate emerged to be supported by the Japanese Association for Physical Education and soon began to develop internationally. Nevertheless *budō* remained the basis of competition karate.

When I travel abroad I always try to explain that karate is *budō* and not merely a competition sport and that the most important about it is something spiritual. But it should not be supposed that in foreign countries karate is treated halfheartedly. Particularly in Europe and first of all in France people seem to be more attracted by the spirituality of karate than in Japan itself.

My first trip to a foreign country was in 1962, ten years after my father's death. My destination was Mexico. Murata Nobuyoshi, who was one of my students at the Osaka University for Foreign Languages, was employed by the pharmaceutical enterprise Takeda and worked in the Mexico-City branch office. He loved karate and when his daily work was finished he led a karate training group. Because of his job he knew a lot of people, among them physicians, lawyers and politicians. Many asked him for karate lessons. Soon there were so many students that he could open his own *dōjō*. That is how he came to ask me to visit him in Mexico. At that time the exchange rate for 1 Dollar was 360 Yen and normal people could not afford to travel abroad. One had to wait four months to get a passport. Under such circumstances I worked as a supervising instructor in Mexico. Among Murata's students there were later ministers and even prime ministers. This may be one reason why karate is deeply rooted and well developed in present-day Mexico. Since this time I have been traveling to Middle and Southern America every second year. I have been to Guatemala, Honduras, El Salvador, Nicaragua, Costa Rica, Panama, to the Dominican Republic and to Cuba and have seen a lot of places in South America. I also went to the United States – to Los Angeles and San Diego.

I went to other Asian countries for the first time in 1973. The reason for this trip was the foundation of the Asian Association for Shitō Karate. The main destination was Singapore. But on this occasion I also went to Malaysia, Indonesia, Nepal, India, Hong Kong, Macao, and finally I traveled to Australia and New Caledonia. In Australia there is a great number of competing karate schools. Among them the *Shitō* karate has acquired a rather strong position. The person in the center of the Australian karate is my former student Con Kassis, who is also the head of the Shitō Karate World Federation. He is leading 26 *dōjō* in Australia; the center of his activities is in Melbourne. Thanks to his help, my teaching materials could be published in English in Australia.

Photo 21: Mabuni Kenei teaching at a seminar in Berlin.

The first time I went to Europe was in 1979 when I came to Spain. Later I traveled to Portugal, Italy, Switzerland, Germany, Belgium, Monaco and France. I travel to France every year in August to open the European Seminars in the town of Bastia on the Island of Corsica. The Japanese Nakahashi Hidetoshi who is married to a French woman is technical consultant of the French Karate Federation. Thanks to his support my teaching material could be translated into French, too. About 300 students attend the annual seminar in Bastia. They come from many European countries, not only from France but also from Spain, Italy, Switzerland and Germany. A number of them come from smaller European countries. Maybe it is related to the summer season, but often they bring family members along. A father comes with his son, a mother with her daughter. It is remarkable for the seminars in foreign countries that several family members come together from rather far places to enjoy karate. In Japan, this is quite different.

Photo 22: Summer seminar in 2007 on Corsica. Left: the publisher of the English edition of this book, Carlos Molina. Beside him is Nakahashi Hidetoshi. Right: Mabuni Kenei.

Besides this, the training conditions are also different to Japan with regard to the training times. Training facilities are normally open from 8 in the morning to 9 or 10 pm. They are used not only for karate practice but also for other kinds of *budō* or general sports. And there are a lot of small clubs. This is why often the karate teaching is done on a professional basis. In Japan training hours are normally in the evenings or at the weekends and training is not run by full time teachers.

Furthermore the membership numbers are much higher in foreign countries than in Japan. Some foreign clubs have more than 1,000 members and use several training facilities.

Because of the time restrictions public facilities like school gyms cannot be used easily and there is not enough time to go into the details. Japanese karate is very much focused on competition. There are championships on all levels. That is why karate practice in Japan today is always a preparation for some kind of competition. As a result there are many repetitions of always the same techniques. No time is left to study joint-locking, throwing and vital point techniques, or techniques with the traditional Okinawan weapons such as *bō* or *sai*. That means that there are less and less chances to get to know these techniques at all.

A Lack of True Leaders in Karate

Of course there is competition karate in Europe, too, but it is not as dominant as in Japan. The attitude towards karate is totally different in Europe and Japan with regard to tradition. Europeans do not consider karate to be nothing but a kind of sports and distinguish exactly between *budō* and competition. The reason may be that there is more state support. In Japan karate seems to be regarded only to be a sport and as far as karate is concerned the government is doing nothing to protect tradition and culture.

On the other side there is a very strong interest in the old *Ryūkyū budō* in Europe inclusive of its weapon techniques (*kobudō*). This interest becomes evident by the fact that in Europe replica of Okinawan weapons are produced. For this reason I always hold a seminar with *bō* techniques when I am in Europe. All in all, much more people than in Japan are acquainted with traditional *budō*.

Talking about karate in Japan everybody will think of thrusts and kicks. Throwing techniques are thought to belong to *jūdō*, or joint-locking techniques to belong to *aikidō*, and everything that has something to do with swords belongs only to *kendō*. But karate as *budō* is complex, and throwing and joint-locking techniques or the use of weapons are originally part of it. And this is exactly what I want to teach. Karate is the basis of any kind of *budō* and particularly the *Shitō* style is proving this. I want to continue to lead the *Shitō* karate based upon this conviction.

But there is one urgent and severe problem left: There are no real leading personalities in *Shitō* karate in Japan. There are a lot of leaders as far as competition karate is concerned, but there are, frankly spoken, absolutely not enough leaders who really understand the essence of the traditional *Shitō* karate. If there are such personalities they can be found abroad where more time and official support is provided than in Japan. Not that I like this idea very much but I might be forced to invite to Japan future karate leaders from abroad.

3 How to Overcome the Own Limits

3.1 Karate – More than Kicks and Punches

Yagyū Sekishūsai and the Art of Mutō Dori

As described above, on the Okinawan islands unique hand-fighting techniques were developed called "hand" (*te*). To defend oneself against the Satsuma samurai, who ruled over the islands and enforced a policy of total disarmament of the natives, the Ryūkyū islanders had to develop unarmed self-defense techniques to the extreme. And this is what karate is actually about.

The decisive stimulus for the birth of the techniques and ideas of karate was the anticipated enemy, first of all the *Jigen* sword technique mastered by the Satsuma samurai, the so-called "cloud of flames" (*unyō*) first strike. The mission of karate was to defend oneself, one's family and the people of the Ryūkyū Islands with empty hands against the "flame-like sword" of the Satsuma samurai.

But not only karate brought about the art of withstanding an armed enemy with bare hands. The great sword master Yagyū Sekishūsai (1527-1606) developed the *mutō dori*[55] technique, which is the peak of Japanese sword technique and the essence of the *Yagyū* style. In order to get across the *mutō dori* technique, I would like to explain how Yagyū Sekishūsai arrived at it. At first he studied sword techniques like the *Shintō* style under the guidance of Iizasa Moritsuna and the *Toda* style of *tōjutsu*[56] under Toda Seigen. In the Kōfuku-ji temple in Nara he practiced the *Hōzōin* style of *yari* spear fighting under Kakuzenbō Inei. In the middle of his 30s he had the reputation of being the greatest expert in fighting techniques in the Kinai region. But there is always a better one. In his case it was the founder of the *Shinkage* style Kamiizumi Nobutsuna (1508-1578)[57]. Nobutsuna

---

[55] *Mutō dori*: Jpn. *Mutō* (without sword), *dori* (grabbing, seizing); i.e. "seizing without sword". – Publisher's comment.

[56] *Tōjutsu*: Jpn. An ancient name for sword fighting, *kenjutsu*. – Habersetzer, R. and G.: Encyclopédie des Arts Martiaux. Paris: Amphora 2004.

[57] Also: Kōizumi Isenokami. – Translator's comment.

had been taught the secrets of the *Kage* style by Aisu Ikōsai. Later, adding a lot of own ideas, he reformed it into the new *kage* or *Shinkage* style. Even Takeda Shingen[58] invited him to become his follower offering most favorable conditions. But he strictly denied the invitation and preferred to travel around the country with some of his disciples. When the travelers reached Ise, Nobutsuna heard the rumor about the extraordinary abilities of Sekishūsai who very soon challenged Nobutsuna for a test fight. But for Sekishūsai this ended with a total defeat. Not only was he beaten by the master himself. Even Nobutsuna's master student Suzuki Ihaku thrashed him three times as if he were a schoolboy. Getting this lesson, Sekishūsai immediately asked Nobutsuna to accept him as his student. Nobutsuna was pleased to agree and in the following three days explained to him the essence of his *Shinkage* style. Furthermore Nobutsuna and his disciples accompanied Sekishūsai to his home, stayed there for half a year and practiced the *Shinkage* style together with Sekishūsai's students.

Nobutsuna was said to be very impressed by the strong will and the ingenious fighting abilities of Sekishūsai. Before he left him he asked him to think about the following *kōan*[59]: "How to control a sword without a sword?" or "How can a sword be deprived of its power?"[60], respectively. This was the ideal of the *Shinkage* style which even Nobutsuna had not reached yet although he had tried so many times. He wanted Sekishūsai to help him to solve the problem of *mutō* and find the answer of how to win being unarmed against a bare sword.

When Nobutsuna visited Yagyū Sekishūsai a few years later Sekishūsai revealed to him the result of his restless studies. Again Nobutsuna's assistant Suzuki Ihaku was chosen to be his opponent, who a few years ago had managed to defeat him in a second. The fight lasted for only a moment. A fan jumped out of Sekishūsai's hand and Ihaku hit the air. In this very moment Sekishūsai moved into the opponent, grabbed his wrist from below and wrestled the sword out of his hand. Nobutsuna saw this

[58] Takeda Shingen (1521-1573): Territorial lord (*daimyō*) and warlord during the Japanese Feudal wars in the 16th century. – Publisher's comment.

[59] Riddles or meditation sayings in Zen Buddhism. – Translator's comment.

[60] *Mutōno tachi ika ni.*

and said: "Your heart is as free as water changing its shape when filling a vessel. There is nothing I could teach you anymore." He gave Sekishūsai the master license and four picture rolls containing the secret records of his fighting techniques. This was the hour of birth of the *Yagyū ryū*.

The episode reported above may lead to the conclusion *mutō dori* were only the technique to distract the attention of the opponent and evade his striking sword using a fan. But in fact it is not merely a technique, it is a certain state of mind which Sekishūsai described with the words: "Because everything comes out of emptiness, having no weapons is the essence of fighting."[61] It is a mental and spiritual tendency which appears in the positions of body and sword, the atmosphere of the place, the distance, the movements and other aspects of fighting. It works without a fan, too. Even without having a sword one must keep calm facing the opponent using everything the situation offers and adopt a mental state of total calmness. In such a crucial moment between life and death there is no room for superficialities. One is giving up all considerations about how one looks or the judgment of others and approaches the opponent in a completely natural way. This attitude truly expresses the spirit of the way of karate, too. For karate one does not need weapons. *Mutō* means not to cling to the sword. Because the characters of karate could also be read *kū te*. *kū* means "empty" or "emptiness", and *te* means "hand". Everything can emerge from emptiness. That means that any object or any part of the body, such as hand, foot or elbow, can be used for defense in *karate*.

In the event described above Sekishūsai had pulled out his fan. In our days perhaps he would choose a ballpen. Aiming it at the head of the enemy could be an efficient means to defend oneself. Karate turns everything into a "hand". A woman for example could fight the enemy efficiently by biting with her teeth. This too could be called excellent karate, according to the ideal of *mutō dori*. It is evident that the mental attitude of the *mutō dori* is the same as that from which karate or the Okinawa-te, respectively, emerged. The further development of karate took place in close contact with other martial arts, in particular with the Chinese *kempō*. As already mentioned the Chinese ambassadors used to travel to the Ryūkyū islands

---

[61] *Manbutsu wa mu ni tai suru zo heihō mo mutō no kokoro okugi narikeri.*

accompanied by guards who were *kempō* experts. The native *bushi* (warriors) who were well educated in the traditional Ryūkyū fighting techniques (*te*), used any opportunity to secretly study the *kempō* techniques from the Chinese guards and military personnel. Others had gone to China with the tribute vessels, studied the true *kempō* in its place of origin and returned with new knowledge. By integrating the Chinese *kempō*, the Okinawa-te became a worldwide and historically unique hand-fighting technique.

Karate Turns the Whole Body into a Weapon

In the old Okinawan *kobudō* agricultural tools like the *sai*, the *kama*, the *nunchaku* or the *tonfa* were turned into weapons. Another *kobudō* weapon, the *eku*, was originally a paddle. The staff (*bō*) is called *kon* by the natives of Okinawa. They also used the *shakujō*, a staff originally used by Chinese warrior monks, which had a tinned tip and was armored with metal rings. Even throwing stars (*shuriken*) were integrated from *Kōga ninjutsu*. I myself learned how to produce and throw *shuriken* under the 14th generation *Kōga ninjutsu* master Fujita Seiko. But these weapons should not be used like mere tools. They must be mastered as if they were part of one's own body. This requires long training.

Photo 23: Fujita Seiko (1899-1966).

After my father had moved to the main island Honshū he started to study staff techniques more intensely, for example with the *jō*[62]. In the *Passai Shō kata* of the *Shuri-te* there is a set of movements anticipating an opponent who uses a staff.

[62] While the *bō* has a length of about 1.80 m (ca. 5.90 ft), the length of the *jō* is about 1.30 m (4.30 ft). – Habersetzer, R. and G.: Encyclopédie des Arts Martiaux. Paris: Amphora 2004.

As demonstrated above, the *mutō dori* of the *Yagyū* style corresponds to the point of origin of karate. This also means that karate only begins at this point and goes well beyond the *mutō dori*. Beginning with the *mutō dori*, the own body must be transformed into a weapon. Karate practically turns every part of the body into weapons. This is clearly shown by the karate *kata*.

Photo 24

Photo 25

Photo 26

Photo 27

Photos 24 to 27: A technique of the *kata Passai shō* and its application. Photo 24 shows a position of the *kata*. With a turn of the body one avoids the staff's thrust, and the staff is grasped (25). The hand of the opponent is taken by scooping it up (26). The opponent's *bō* is positioned as a joint-locking support against his own elbow joint (27).

Photo 28

Photo 29

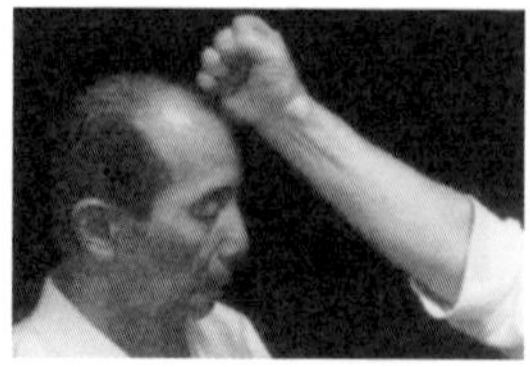

Photo 30

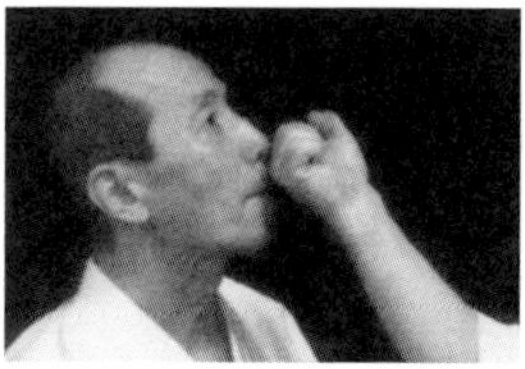

Photo 31

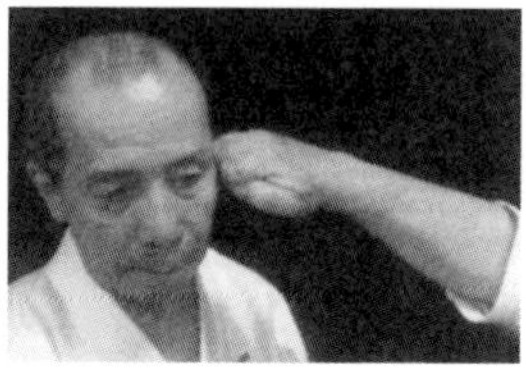

Photo 32

Photo 33

Photos 28 to 40: The hand as weapon.

Photo 28: The fist concentrated to the ankles of the middle finger and index finger called "great fist" or "great straight punch" (*daikentō*).

Photo 29: The fist concentrated to the second knuckle, "small fist" (*shōkentō*).

Photo 30: The bottom side of the fist in the hammer fist (*kentsui*).

Photo 31: The back of the fist or the ankles of the middle hand, respectively (*uraken*).

Photo 32: The bottom side of the flat fist with the fingers bent in the middle joints and with the thumb above them (*hiraken*).

Photo 33: The finger tips of the open hand called spear hand (*nukite*).

Some time ago I visited a *dōjō* in the Mie prefecture. When I asked which parts of the hand could be used for karate, even the *dan* graded students did not know exactly how to answer. Indeed there are many to think that the only useful parts are the fist and the edge of the hand. But as one can see in the following photos all parts of the hand can be used as weapon or transform the hand into a weapon, respectively.

As parts of the arm the forearm and the elbow can be used, and as parts of the foot the ball, the instep, the heel and the edge (photos on page 76). Of course, even the head and the buttocks can be used as weapons. Head thrusts can be carried out using the forehead or the back of the head or the sides.

It is often assumed that there were only punches, thrusts and kicks in

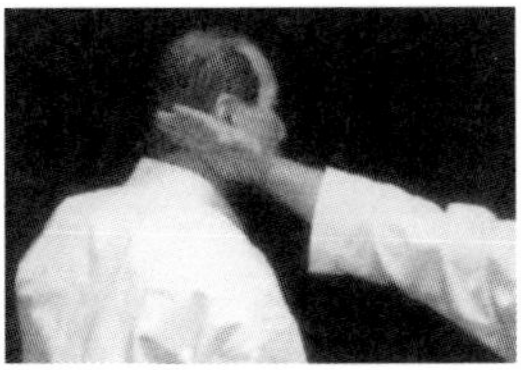
Photo 34

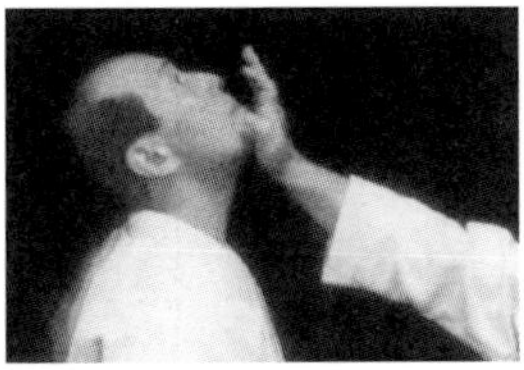
Photo 35

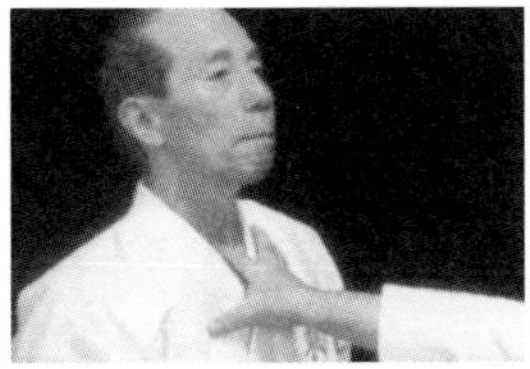
Photo 36

Photo 37

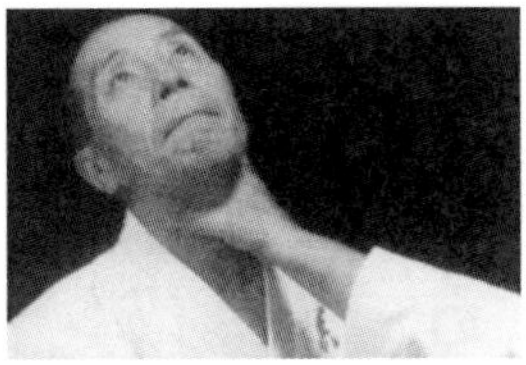
Photo 38

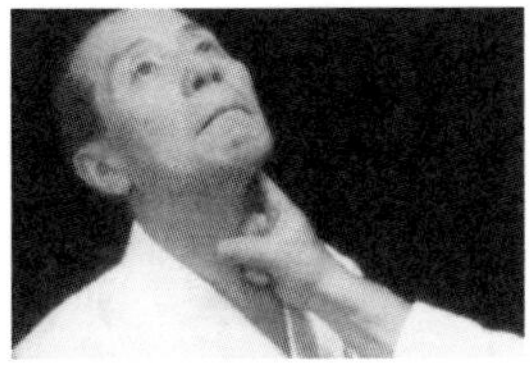
Photo 39

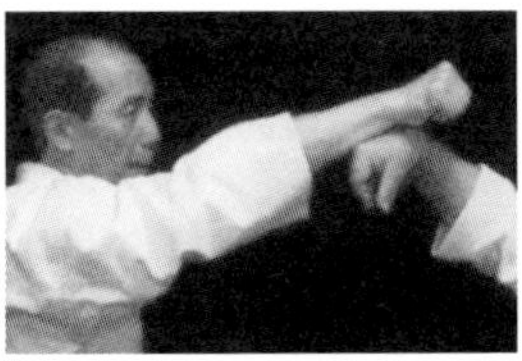
Photo 40

Photo 34: The edge of the hand or sword hand (*shutō*).

Photo 35: The heel of the hand (*shōtei*).

Photo 36: Stabbing with the index finger (*hitosashi ippon nukite*).

Photo 37: Fist with protruding middle finger, bent in the middle joint, "iron fist" (*nakadaka ippon ken*).

Photo 38: "Finger scissors" – thumb and index finger form a claw, the other fingers are bent (*yubi basami* or *yubi hasami*).

Photo 39: Scissors formed by the splayed thumb and the other fingers that are together and slightly bent – "throat scissors" or "tiger mouth" (*hira basami*).

Photo 40: The back of the bent wrist (*koken*).

karate. In reality, the techniques are not at all restricted to thrusts, punches and kicks. Joint-locking and throwing techniques are also used. The idea that karate only contains punches and kicks is a misunderstanding born in the times when in Japan karate was only studied to acquire the life-threatening *atemi* techniques which were not practiced in *jūdō*. After the World War II the Japanese Association for Physical Education had attributed the sword techniques to *kendō*, the throwing techniques to *jūdō* and the punching and thrusting techniques to karate. Besides this, the more karate developed towards competition sports, the more techniques got prohibited. This con-

Photo 41

Photo 42

Photos 41 and 42: Arm techniques (*ude*).

Photo 41: Forearm technique (*kote*). The forearm diverts a punch.

Photo 42: Elbow technique (*hiji*).

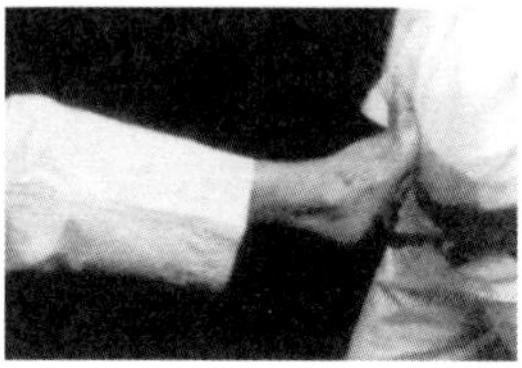

Photo 43

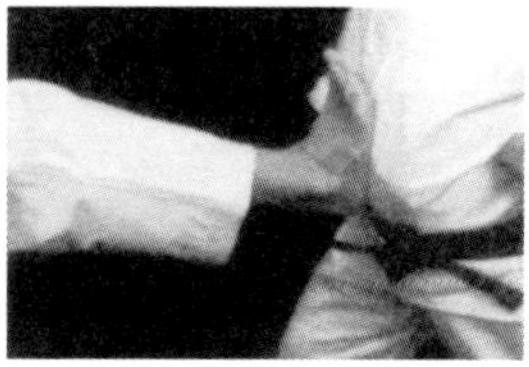

Photo 44

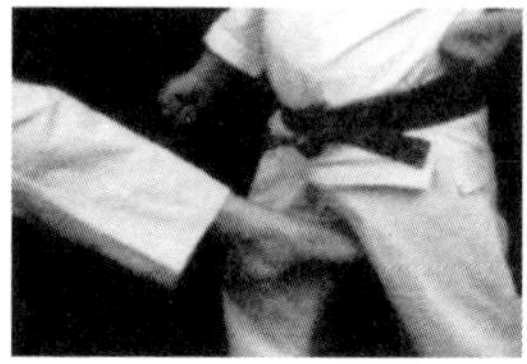

Photo 45

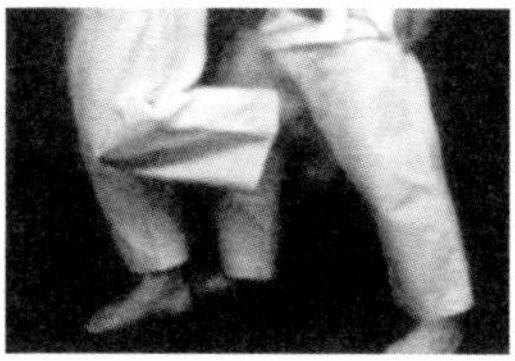

Photo 46

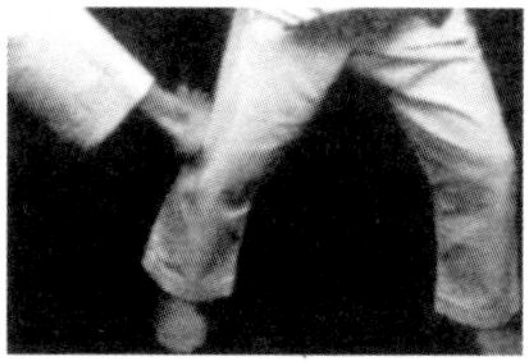

Photo 47

Photos 43 to 47 : Foot techniques (*ashi*).

Photo 43: Ball of the foot (*jōsokutei*).

Photo 44: Heel (*kasokutei* or *kakato*).

Photo 45: Instep (*kō*). Upwards kick with the instep.

Photo 46: Kick with the heel with back turned towards the opponent (*kōshō*).

Photo 47: Edge of the foot (*sokushu sokutō*). Kick or thrust with the edge of the foot against the knee joint or the ankle.

cerned in particular all joint-locking and throwing techniques. That is why the image of karate as a system of thrusting and kicking techniques became fixed. Even many of these were banned like the spear hand (*nukite*), the foot edge thrust (*ashi katana*) or the kick to the genitals (*kinteki geri*). In competition sports the only aim is to win. It is not necessary to master the techniques of original karate. It is even more efficient not to know them at all. One does not need to harden the fist or the sword hand for competition.

But if karate is used as a means for self-defense, the starting point of which is similar to that of the *mutō dori*, it is a fighting technique (*bujutsu*). In this case all the things around will become part of the "hand" and the own body will completely turn into a weapon.

This does not mean that I disapprove of competition sports. It is only that I would like to see karate studied again much more as original *budō*.

Photo 48: Two-finger sword hand in the *kata Chintei*.

How to Harden the Body

For progress in karate the *kata* must be studied thoroughly and a lot of analysis is needed. This comprises the work with the *bunkai*. In this way the karateka becomes able to understand how to use a technique in each particular case. For example the sword hand (*nukite*) is used differently according to the target. To carry out a thrust against the eyes a two finger sword hand is efficient. The *Chinte kata* includes such an attack against the eyes (see photos 49 to 53). But there is a great risk to miss the target and even to hurt one's own fingers. This is why the two-finger sword hand should be developed out of the thumb ball thrust against the chin of the opponent.

Thinking about how to effectively use the various parts of the body one should also think about hardening it. In the past there were no special devices as used in our days. Everything offered by the surroundings was used to harden the body e.g. straw bales attached to poles or trees called *makiwara*. To harden the sword hand push-ups were carried out only supported by the finger tips (*udedate fuse*). One starts with five fingers, and then step by step one reduces the number of the fingers the body is resting on. Other methods are useful, too, like thrusting the fingers into a bundle of young bamboo or into a box filled with sand.

To harden the grip traditionally big sake jars (*kame*) were used. Each hand holds a jar from above. The thumb is bent and the jar held between

Photo 49

Photos 49 to 53: The *kata Chintei*. Basic position (*kamae*) (photo 49). The opponent's thrust is directed downward and simultaneously the counterattack is carried out with the ball of the other hand against the opponent's chin (photos 50 and 51). The attack is continued with a two-finger thrust (*nihon nukite*) against the eyes (*metsubishi*) (photos 52 and 53).

Photo 50

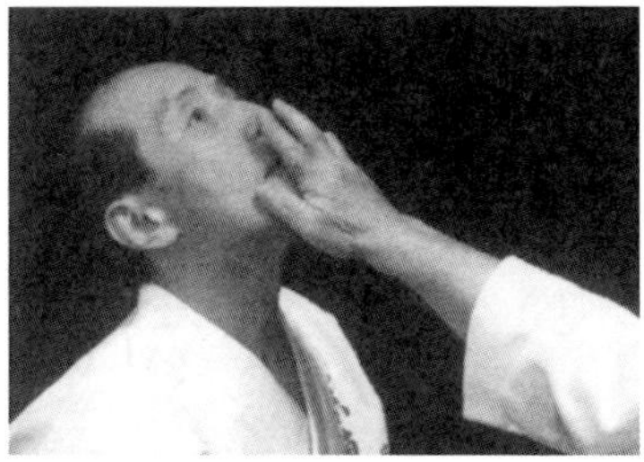

Photo 51

Photo 52

Photo 53

the inner edge of the thumb and the other four fingers. The stance for this exercise is the *sanchin dachi,* one of the basic stances of the *Naha-te.*

Initially the jars are kept empty. After one masters the grip, the jars should be filled with a certain amount of sand. After some exercise one gets used to the weight, and some more sand is poured in now. The exercise goes on until one can handle the full jars easily. Then other heavier materials like lead can be put in the vessels. Without experiencing this kind of traditional practice, karate cannot be understood in its original function as fighting and self-defense technique and one actually begins with the end.

Thrusts with Muchimi

There is one more very important point. The old Okinawan masters used to stress that a punch or a thrust should be carried out with *muchimi*. This is Okinawan dialect meaning tough or elastic. The whole body should act like a whip or a bamboo cane. Bamboo is as well hard as flexible. Without *muchimi* a really strong punch cannot be made, no matter how much one may have tried to turn one's body into a weapon. The state of *muchimi* cannot be explained. It must be experienced by one's own body.

There is no other kind of *budō* which, based on the spirit of the *Yagyū* style *mutō dori*, enables not only single parts like hands or legs but the whole body to transform and focus the energies of the environment like karate can do. The potential to do so is incorporated in the *kata*. Karate is a complex system of fighting techniques not only including a set of punches and kicks like *kempō* but also comprising *jūdō*, *kendō*, the old *Ryūkyū kobudō* and even the use of *shuriken*. The fighting positions (*kamae*) in karate, the ways to stand or to move, suit to any kind of *budō* and to the use of all kinds of weapons. All this supports my assumption that karate is the foundation of all *budō* because it is the legitimate heir of the traditional Japanese fighting techniques, and furthermore also integrates all kinds of fighting techniques invented by mankind.

Karate as Support for Every Budōka

There are many examples proving that understanding karate helps to progress in other kinds of *budō*. This is particularly obvious with regard to *kendō* and *iaidō*. This is easy to understand because karate has developed out of the climax of Japanese sword techniques. But practicing karate can become a great advantage for the practice of other kinds of *budō*, too. Because the whole body is involved and besides punching and kicking, joint-locking and throwing techniques are included, it is much easier for an experienced karate student to master *jūdō* or *jūjutsu*.

In the December 2000 edition of the monthly journal *Gekkan Karate Dō* there was an article titled *The Three Great Personalities in Karate*. The author reminded us of the words Kanō Jigorō uttered when for the first time he had seen a karate performance by my father: "You did show abilities worth to be awarded *jūdō* 4th *dan* on the spot."

I had a similar experience in 1947. I wanted to establish a bone-healer practice and therefore needed a license as *jūdō* chiropractor. At that time in order to get a healer license for dislocations, bone fractures and the like, a *jūdō* examination had to be passed. Of course I could have done this because I knew some *jūdō*. But I was the first to get the right to undergo a karate examination instead. I wanted to perform the *Seienchin kata*. One of the members of the commission was willing to act as my partner so I could also present the *bunkai* of the *kata*. In those days karate was still not very popular and most of the examining staff had not seen karate yet. Nevertheless they all seemed very impressed. Since that time many students have got the permission to undergo a karate examination to get the chiropractic license.

3.2 Blocking is Attacking – Without Beat

Starting With a Block

All karate *kata* begin and end with blocking. "There is no first attack in karate."[63] This philosophy or concept is learned not by words but by practicing *kata*. It can be explained as well in psychological terms as in technical and physical ones. I will discuss the psychological aspects in the second part of the book. Here I would like to have a closer look at the physical or merely technical side of the problem.

The first action of a *kata* is always blocking. That is why there are many who regard karate as a rather passive kind of *budō*. But this is actually not true. In the ancient Chinese book *The Art of War* by Sun Tsu[64], the following statement can be found: "If you know the enemy and yourself you will

---

[63] *Karate ni sente nashi.* Doctrine by Funakoshi Gichin, adapted to karate according to an ancient rule of the Japanese *bushidō*. – Publisher's comment.

[64] Sun Tsu, also Sūn Zǐ or Sun Wu, was a Chinese general and military strategist who lived from about 534 BC to about 453 BC, "The Art of War" consists of 13 chapters and is considered as the first book on strategy, and as one of the best. – Publisher's comment.

win hundreds of battles. If you know only yourself but not the enemy you may win or lose. If you do not know neither the enemy nor yourself, fighting will become dangerous." This offers an explanation why *kata* always begin with a block. It is necessary for studying the opponent. Except for an attack that hits the opponent absolutely by surprise, the first attack can easily be defended and integrated into the opponent's tactics.

Mentally weak people are often short-tempered, tending to get angry easily and to attack quickly. This is what happened to Sasaki Kojirō, an outstanding master of the long sword, in a famous fight that took place in 1612 on the island of Ganryū-jima[65]. His power was at least equal to his opponent's, Miyamoto Musashi. The fight was to begin at 8 am. But Musashi deliberately came three hours later. He had used the time to carve a wooden sword (*bokutō*) from a paddle during his passage. So Musashi had already humiliated Kojirō before the beginning of the fight. He had, so to speak, attacked him psychologically. When he saw his opponent coming towards him with his blank sword, Musashi yelled: "Kojirō, I will destroy you!" So he made him even angrier provoking his attack. But he had one of his younger followers secretly measure the length of Kojirō's sword in advance and had made a *bokutō* that was 33 cm (a *shaku*) longer than Kojirō's sword. So he finally won due to a length difference of one *shaku*. Kojirō on the opposite had already lost in the beginning when he attacked Musashi first because Musashi was offered the opportunity to counterattack. At first the opponent must be studied. As long as the opponent's potential is unknown one must not attack. This is the real meaning of the fact that *kata* always begin with a block.

Blocking the Opponent's Attack With a More Powerful Counterattack

There are many *kata* like the *Passai dai kata* starting with supported blocking that is used if the situation demands special precaution (see photo 54 on p. 82). When practicing *kumite* (practice with a partner) one adopts a ready stance (*kamae*) while making a step backward. This corresponds to the

[65] Uninhabited island in the Shimonoseki straits. – Translator's comment.

Photo 54: Supported blocking. The first action (*dai itte*) in the *Passai dai kata*. The blocking or receiving hand is supported by the other hand.

same logic of precaution. However, this does not mean that karate is a defensive martial art. In *Shitō* karate there is a rule: "The blocking hand is the attacking hand." As explained above karate literally means fighting without a weapon, with empty hands. Considering karate to be passive because it always starts with blocking, arises from mixing it up with other kinds of fighting techniques. But one must not forget that it is fighting with bare hands and empty fists which are turned into weapons.

Fighting techniques which use weapons demand a blocking action first. The counterattack comes after this. Karate means defending oneself with one's own body which has been hardened to be a weapon. Blocking with a body which has the power to smash wooden boards or tiles is attacking in itself. One always blocks with a power surpassing that of the attack. Karate is attacking by blocking and blocking by attacking. This is called *mu hyōshi*, literally meaning "without beat" i.e. there is no rhythm of attack and defense. One can even argue that this is the very essence of *budō*. This principle of *mu hyōshi* is ultimately expressed in the *Shitō* karate rule: "Blocking means attacking."

Moreover not only *budō* but also Japanese culture in general follows the principle of *mu hyōshi*. Nature is continuously moving albeit it sometimes seems as if it is standing still. It is moving in cycles. Living in harmony with a nature which is continuously circulating is a basic concept of the Japanese culture. The circulation of nature cannot be fixed or forced in a certain rhythm. One can only live in harmony with the constantly moving nature by adopting to its flow. This idea of the *mu hyōshi* is the starting point of Japanese culture.

I discussed this topic with O Son-Fa, an outstanding Japanese-Korean cultural philosopher. She pointed out that Japanese Buddha statues always show blossoms which have not yet opened. This is to show that they will open in the future and should be understood as an example for the particularity of Japanese culture to see everything in perpetual motion.

Rhythm and Speed

I am sure every Japanese knows the famous *kabuki* actor[66] Bandō Tamasaburō. His *kabuki* performance follows a certain beat, i.e. it has a fixed rhythm. I thought this to be somehow strange and my view was supported by a musician who told me that Bandō's kabuki performance followed a 16 or 32 beat like western music. The point is that the original *kabuki* had no beat at all. So it is quite easy to understand that Bandō's kabuki is highly appreciated in foreign countries because it is adapted to western auditory habits.

When traveling and teaching abroad I often saw people practicing *kata* or some kind of sports while wearing headphones and following a rhythm. But if there is anything that will absolutely not fit to *budō*, it is rhythm or beat. Because this means fixing things, it can be said to be a deadly mistake and to destroy *budō*. Blocking at "1" (*ichi*) punching at "2" (*ni*) means following a rhythm. This should not be done.

However, one individual beat, *hito hyōshi*, is alright. If one blocks at the same time with the right hand and thrusts with the left hand, or if the blocking hand is simultaneously attacking, this corresponds to the character of *budō* which is to change and to circulate all the time.

A speed that comes out of rhythm is a physical one, it is a sequence that can be perceived. But when one is confronted with an experienced opponent it might happen that one finds oneself suddenly on the ground, or one unexpectedly realizes the back of his fist directly in front of the eyes. This happens when oneself is acting according to a certain rhythm but the opponent's actions have no rhythm or beat.

---

[66] See footnote 25 on p. 26.

The Five Principles of Blocking

Photo 55: Falling Blossoms (*rakka*). Like the earth is taking the falling blossoms, the opponent's attack is solidly blocked with a very slight but powerful movement. This is blocking in the true sense of the word.

My father taught the "Five Principles of Blocking". These principles explain in detail how to turn blocking into an attack. He called these principles "Falling Blossoms" (*rakka*), "Flowing Water" (*ryūsui*), "Bending and Stretching" (*kusshin*), "Change of Position" (*ten-i*) and "Counterstrike" (*hangeki*).

According to the principle of *rakka*, the opponent's attack is stopped out of a simple and basic position with solid blocking, just like the earth receives the falling blossoms without moving or evading them. This kind of blocking is intended to be turned into an attack. The balance of the opponent is undermined, and by getting him under control, a favorable position is adopted for oneself (see photo 55). Of course at the same time the pulled-back hand must start an attack out of the *hikite* position, or the blocking hand (*ukete*) must execute the counterstrike – but not on an extra beat. The counterattack comes at the same time, like a ball thrown against a wall rebounds.

Ryūsui means to let the attack pass like flowing water. The attack is not reversed. But nevertheless also in the principle "Flowing Water" the counterattack is immediate – carried out at the same time with the blocking or pulling hand. In the same way as in "Falling Blossoms" the blocking does not directly harm the opponent but it is changed into the counterattack at the same beat (see photos 56 and 57).

The principle *kusshin* teaches to receive the attack by bending or stretching the own body. This approach allows to totally undermine the opponent's position. But all aspects of the action must be well controlled. This

Photo 56

Photo 57

Photos 56 and 57: Flowing Water (*ryūsui*). The attack is not reversed but left unblocked like flowing water (56). The immediate counterstrike is carried out within the same beat (57).

concerns the own movements and the movements of the opponent, balance and breathing. The counterattack must be carried out on the beat of the blocking (see photos 58 to 60).

In the *ten-i* principle, the aim of blocking can be reached by "opening" the own body and shifting the target of the attack. In this case "opening" means turning the body. By turning the body backwards or forwards to the left or to the right or diagonally the target is removed. It is reasonable to make sure that the action brings the own body into a favorable position. There are eight directions of turning the body (*tenshin happō*) – forwards and backwards, to the left and to the right, forwards diagonally to the left and to the right, backwards diagonally to the left and to the right.

In an ancient, once secret didactic poem on *budō* a saying can be found playing on the word *tachi* meaning "long sword" or "standing": "To stop an attacking sword take away your body." This means that turning the body away is an efficient reaction particularly against an armed opponent who of course will not leave after his first attack. That is why the counterattack has to be made immediately. This shows how in karate the blocking hand is at the same time the attacking hand (see photos 61-65).

The four principles explained above, *rakka, ryūsui, kusshin, ten-i*, correspond to the Japanese sword fighting principle *go no sen*. That means that they are used after the attack: At first the initiative is left to the oppo-

Photos 58 to 60: Bending and Stretching (*kusshin*).

Photo 58: Basic position (*kamae*).

Photo 59: The opponent's thrust is received by bending the body forwards and contracting it like a spring, and adopting a low cat's-paw position.

Photo 60: The counterattack takes place immediately: The body is stretched as if the tension of a spring is relaxed, and a kick is carried out.

Photo 58

Photo 59

Photo 60

nent, then it is taken over and used for a counterattack. This concept is based on the idea of *gasshi uchi* of the *Yagyū* style of sword fighting.[67]

Contrary to this, the last of the five principles, *hangeki*, the "counterattack", is a unique technique of the *Shitō* karate comprising a so-called *aitsuki* or counterstrike. In this counter technique the body is not first withdrawn and then defended. The counterattack is made simultaneously to the opponent's attack. Angle and timing of the counterstrike must be coordinated in a fraction of a second and one must hit the opponent like lightning out of a thunderstorm in spring.

Rakka, *ryūsui*, *kusshin* and *ten-i* could be considered as a kind of fortification warfare including withdrawals and defending, *hangeki* could be regarded to be mobile warfare with the readiness to open battle and total sacrifice. *Hangeki* corresponds to the concept of *kiri otoshi*[68] of the

[67] *Gasshi uchi* literally means: Attack in harmony with the other. – Publisher's comment.

[68] *Kiri otoshi*: Downward cut (with the first and only strike). – Publisher's comment.

Photo 61

Photo 62

Photo 63

Photos 61 to 63: Change of Position (*ten-i*).

Photo 61: Basic position (*kamae*).

Photo 62: Turning the body away with a lateral block.

Photo 63: The force of the recoil is used for the direct counterattack.

Ittō ryū.[69] But for all principles described above the blocking hand is at the same time the attacking hand. So blocking in karate is nothing passive; in fact it is an extremely aggressive attack.

In real life the blocking actions rarely appear in the pure form of one of these five principles. Usually, several ones are combined. Besides this there is an endless number of variations in respect to the way of turning the blocking action into a counterattack.

The Tokugawa[70] clan appreciated as well the *Yagyū ryū* as the *Ittō ryū* because of their extremely developed sword techniques and adopted both styles as official house styles although they are based upon opposed technical principles. And in my eyes it is a quite surprising fact that karate, which was born in the rather remote and peripheral region of Okinawa, developed out of the

[69] *Ittō ryū*: Sword fighting style with the long sword (*odachi*) wielded with both hands. – Publisher's comment.

[70] The Tokugawa were a Japanese dynasty of regents who established the Tokugawa shōgunate (also Edo period, 1603–1867). – Publisher's comment.

Photo 64

Photo 65

Photos 64 and 65: Counterattack (*hangeki*).

Photo 64: Basic position (*kamae*).

Photo 65: At the same time the attacking thrust of the opponent is received and answered by a counterattack.

study of the essence of Japanese sword techniques which are the *gasshi uchi* of the *Yagyū* style and the *kiri otoshi* of the *Ittō* style.

3.3 Learning the Techniques

The Diversity of the Kata Techniques

Karate *kata* consist of many different attack and defense actions and often it is rather difficult to explain their meaning. Because everything is flowing, backward movements may appear as forward movements. Besides this there are quite a lot of hidden techniques, and many actions cannot be understood at all without an historical explanation. It makes me sad to see a tendency to abandon *kata* because their background is not understood and to consider *kata* shortsightedly to be not of practical value. Especially people who think that *kata* are not important, that the only necessary method to practice karate is training or sparring fights (*kumite*), often show techniques with great pride as if they had super weapons directly sent from heaven. People who have studied *kata* are already acquainted with most of these techniques and know that they were invented in ancient times and have been developed by many people during innumerable life-and-death struggles. My father used to say: "There is no limit to techniques", or "Techniques are infinite". I could take this up and say without reservation: "The variations of the karate *kata* are infinite."

Since ancient times warriors have been warned of the three failings called doubt (*giryo*), sluggishness (*kedai*) and conceit (*manshin*). This is doubt about the words of the seniors and teachers, sluggishness and half-hearted commitment to the exercises, and finally arrogance or self-conceit and showing off after reaching good training results.

When we study the innumerable variations of techniques the *kata* include we will probably find not one technique that is absolutely new. Being the head of the Mabuni family I am often referred to as someone who has changed the techniques of the *Shitō* karate. But what I did was only a reinterpretation and new analysis of the *kata*. I did not create new techniques. It is rather unimportant what a single human being has experienced, even in his whole life. During a long history, many outstanding personalities created fighting techniques and passed their knowledge on to the following generations to be improved and enriched. This huge knowledge brought down to present days cannot be surpassed easily. Even I can always find new things in my daily *kata* practice.

Three Principles of the Bujutsu

Kata practice can be useful for several purposes: for health, beauty or self-defense. But whatever *kata* are practiced for, the following rules should be observed:

1. Widen the chest and lower the shoulders.
2. Open the eyes widely and pull back the chin.
3. Concentrate the energies in the "lower cinnabar field"[71] below the navel and adopt a solid stance.

[71] According to the Taoist teachings the lower cinnabar field (Chn. *dantian*, Jpn. *tanden* or *hara*) is the energetic (*ki*) center of the human being. It is situated some inches below the navel. – Publisher's comment.

These rules should always be kept in mind when practicing *kata*. Thrusts and kicks must be filled with energy to such a degree as if one wants to smash a metal bucket. Movements forward and backward must be carried out full of vivid tension as if confronted with a real opponent. If one practices *kata* this way again and again, the spirit of bravery will grow and a healthy body will develop quite naturally. If one practices *kata* just for the health, for a long life or just for looking good it would be superfluous to learn any complicated techniques in addition. But for studying *kata* as a fighting technique, three further aspects are important:

1. The left-right balance
2. Shifting the center of gravity
3. The breathing technique.

For a real understanding of karate these three aspects must be studied thoroughly. I would like to dwell on these points a little bit more. First about the "left-right balance". All techniques the *kata* include are left-right symmetrical. Because the movements are flowing it happens that for example only a technique against an attack from the right is shown. In such a case the whole *kata* should be slowly repeated and analyzed, and the left-right symmetry should be specially trained. Karate techniques should never be imbalanced, tending to the left or to the right side. Keeping the balance is very important. The left hand should function like the right one and vice versa. Of course the same must be said about the legs.

"Shifting the center of gravity" ensures the stability of the body. Without stability one will be finished quickly no matter how clever the technique might be carried out, how nimble the body may be turned. In this regard not the smallest opening should be left to the opponent. That is why the position of the body, the stance and the typical Japanese *budō* kind of walking with the legs slightly bent are so important.

Last but not least in *Shitō* karate the "breathing technique" follows a rule called "five ways and ten forms of breathing" (*goshu jūkei*).[72] The rhythm of breathing is used to sense the energetic structure, the emptiness and the substance. Breathing leads the action and allows understanding of the

---

[72] See p. 209 et seq.

opponent's potential and the moment of his attack. So, by controlling the own breath and analyzing that of the opponent one can thrust with the own "substance" in the "emptiness" of the opponent. Even the best left-right balance, a stable center of gravity and the highest degree of hardening one's body cannot help, if one does not master the breathing technique. This can be compared with a locomotive with a broken boiler. Everything else, such as rails and engine, may be alright, but the locomotive will not move.

Kata practice will become a rich armory if it is properly guided by the three main aspects explained above, that is "left-right-balance", "shifting the center of gravity" and "breathing technique". Of course for a creative study of karate analysis (*bunkai*) and training with partners (*kumite*)[73] are necessary, too. The *bunkai*, meaning observing and exercising actions and body movements analytically, is especially important. If one always practices only the whole *kata* itself some elements will always remain which are not well understood. The *kata* then becomes, so to speak, a "Buddha without soul".

Of extreme importance in a fight is the *maai*.[74] It must be emphasized that in original *bujutsu* it is the *maai*, the harmonious distance in space and in time to the opponent, that decides about victory or defeat. Finally it depends on the *maai* whether a technique thoroughly practiced in *kata* exercises and guided by the three aspects of *bujutsu* explained above is efficient enough to survive or leads to defeat. But this cannot be learned by *kata* exercises alone.

---

[73] *Kumite*: Practical application of the basic techniques (*kihon*) and of the *kata* techniques (with and without their *bunkai*) as partner exercises. – Publisher's comment.

[74] *Maai*: Jpn. Space-time separating two fighters during a short pause (*ma*) in their confrontation. In this moment the mental contact between them is maintained, and harmony (*ai*) is aspired. This term goes far beyond the physical spatial distance between two fighters. Ideally this distance depends on the technical and mental level of the opponent: possible reach, speed of execution, concentration, active or passive spirit etc. For this reason this concept of the "right" (and constantly changing) distance (i.e. large enough to be protected against a fast attack, and small enough to be able to take a decisive initiative) one must find during a fight comprises the feeling of perceiving the danger zone between opponents. – Habersetzer, R. and G.: Encyclopédie des Arts Martiaux. Paris: Amphora 2004.

The Principle of Hikite

Of course the *kata* are the most important elements of karate practice. But there is a close interrelation between *kata* and analysis (*bunkai*). That is why when a partner is available, practice should be focused on analysis and when one is alone it should be concentrated on *kata*. A *kata* sequence may look like a forward action but in a real situation it demands to open and close the body. As in everyday life one always has to adapt to a changing environment. One must always be aware of the opponent's actions. Only this analysis can bring about the understanding of the meaning of the techniques the *kata* contain.

A *kata* is always a model. Of course it is questionable if an advanced student of karate can use the techniques only in the form they appear as part of a *kata*. This can be explained giving the example of the pulling hand (*hikite*). It is a fundamental rule of karate to pull one hand back close to the hip in the opposite direction of the punching or thrusting hand. While one hand is pushing or thrusting the other is pulling.

As shown on photo 5 on page 40, the pulling hand always rests at the hip. During the exercises one may often hear the teacher say, "Keep your left-right balance!" or "Don't let your pulling hand dangle!" That means that the principle of *hikite* is to maintain the left-right balance by a counter-balancing motion and that both hands are always actively used. It does not mean that the pulling hand must be fixed at the hip in any situation. If the function of the pulling hand is well understood, in a real fighting situation it will not matter at all if the pulling hand is resting at the hip or not. In fact, karate is at the same time based on positioning (*kamae*) and on non-positioning (*kamae nashi*). One can even act more freely if one hand is not resting at the hip.

Understanding the Heian Sandan Kata as Fighting Technique

As another example I would like to have a closer look at a certain technique of the *Heian sandan kata* which is a very basic *kata*. The respective sequence is shown in the photos 66 to 69. According to the general interpretation it consists of a side block (*yoko uke*) against the opponent's attack carried

Photo 66

Photo 67

Photo 68

Photo 69

Photos 66 to 69: A sequence of the *Heian sandan kata.*

out on the middle level aimed at the chest area (*chūdan zuki*) (66) and the responding counter-attack with a sword hand (*nukite*) (67). But the sword hand is caught by the opponent. In order to free the arm the upper body is turned backwards (*hineri gaeshi*). The corresponding posture is *kokutsu dachi* (68). Finally a thrust is carried out against the opponent (*chūdan zuki*) (69).

But normally it is almost impossible to block a sword hand without a previous arrangement. But even if the sword hand attack is so weak that it can be blocked, one should never turn the back towards the opponent. The opponent will not wait until the turn is completed and the body is repositioned. He will attack before one has adopted the right position again.

Therefore this *kata* sequence should be interpreted as consisting of two parts (see photos 70 to 72 on the next page). The first set of continuous movements leads from the side block (*yoko uke*) to the sword hand (*nukite*) and represents one complete and independent fighting action. The following turn of the body (*hineri gaeshi*) is a counter measure against a possible try of the opponent to catch and twist one's arm. But this turn of the body must be made in the moment one realizes that the opponent intends to

Photo 70

Photo 71

Photo 72

Photos 70 to 72: A *bunkai* of the *Heian sandan kata*

Photo 70: The opponent uses a grappling technique and twists the arm backwards.

Photo 71: One frees oneself by turning the body. At the same time a counter-strike is carried out.

Photo 72: A joint-locking technique is used to control the opponent.

grab and twist one's arm. When the opponent has already fully applied his joint-locking technique, it is too late. One must always be aware of such correlations. That is why the analysis, the *bunkai* is that important for the understanding of a *kata*.

Of course *kata* analysis does not mean free interpretation. There are some karate books or videos containing such kind of *kata* interpretation which is simply derived from the surface of the *kata* sequences. Here, things are connected forcibly that do not belong together. The Japanese use to call this "bamboo applied to wood".

And in the case of the *Heian sandan kata* the crucial point is to take into account that the opponent never waits patiently for the counterattack to come.

The Gojūshiho Kata, and how to Cope with Unexpected Attacks

Photos 73 to 76 show the *Kururunfa kata* originating from the *Naha-te*. This *kata* is destined for advanced students. It contains a technique to release oneself from a nelson hold[75] when being attacked from the back by hitting the opponent's face with the back of one's head.

In books or videos the stance is explained merely as a *shiko dachi* (a straddle stance where the feet point 45° outwards; this stance is known in *sumō*) following the development of the *kata*. However, it is not possible to make a counterattack from this position. Because this position is very instable there is a high risk to be pulled down by the opponent from the back. In a real fighting situation one would not straddle the legs but open the position with a step forward. It becomes clear that the *kata* must not be explained one-sidedly only with regard to blocking. It must be understood and interpreted as an entity consisting of blocking and attacking. The *bunkai* always has to involve the opponent's actions. This is another example to illustrate why superficial *kata* analysis leads to wrong conclusions.

Photo 73

Photo 74

Photo 75

Photo 76

Photos 73 to 76: A sequence of the *Kururunfa kata*.

[75] Nelson hold: Engl. A wrestling hold. – Publisher's comment.

Photo 77

Photo 78

Photos 77 and 78: The *Kururunfa kata*.

Photo 77: The wrongly interpreted *kata*: From a stance according to the *kata* one can be pulled down by the opponent from behind.

Photo 78: The right interpretation of the *kata*: By making a step forward the opponent has no chance to pull one down. The own position is stabilized and that of the opponent is destabilized.

Photo 79

Photo 80

Photos 79 and 80: The *Gojūshiho kata*.

Photo 79: Basic position with hands at the hips (in the historical context with the thumbs in the belt).

Photo 80: Turning the body.

It must be remembered, too, that each *kata* is the result of the particular local, historical and social conditions on the island of Okinawa. Often a certain sequence can only be understood completely when this background is known. The following sequence of the *Gojūshiho kata* ("54-steps") is an example for this (see photos 79 and 80). The thrust of the opponent is blocked by using the elbow (*chūdan zuki* with *hiji uke*). But in a real fighting situation there is no time to adopt such a position. One cannot explain this *kata* without knowing that the samurai in Shuri used to walk around in this posture called *futokoro de*.

Photo 81 shows myself as a youngster standing in the front row at the right side. My father is standing in the middle. The man standing to the left of him is *Shindō shizen ryū* master Konishi Yasuhiro. The posture I take on the photo is the above-mentioned *futokoro de*. The hands rest on the

Photo 81: The *futokoro de* position.

Photo 82

Photo 83

Photo 84

Photos 82 to 84: Analysis of the elbow block as hidden sequence of the *kata Gojūshiho*. The elbow block is carried out with a turn of the body (82). Without bending it the elbow is drawing a wide semicircle (83). Out of this movement, with the other hand a strike with the edge of the hand is carried out against the carotid (84).

belt, with the thumbs in the interior. It was chosen as the first position for the *Gojūshiho kata* in order to do an elbow block against a sudden attack. Photos 82 to 84 show the analysis (*bunkai*) of the elbow block.

In the *Kōsōkun dai kata* the body position is lowered. This posture is designed to respond to a sudden attack on a road at night. To understand this position it should be taken into account that there were not any street lights in the past and the roads were pitch dark at night. This deep position was chosen to take advantage of the moonlight so that a better sight of the attacker was gained and at the same time the own body became more hidden in the dark. It is easier to look from a dark place into a bright one than vice versa. This *kata* belongs to the classical karatedō *kata* (photo 85).

Photo 85: A posture of the *Kōsōkun dai kata*. The author holds a stone in the right hand.

There is no doubt that the *kata* contain the infinite knowledge of many generations. But this means that we should always keep in mind that they were not created in our times. The social environment has changed considerably. So *kata* include many techniques which may be useless in our days. This is another reason why the *bunkai* is so important. It helps to find out which techniques fit to our present needs.

I want to repeat it again: The totality of karate is incorporated and preserved in the *kata*. Whoever practices karate should always return to the *kata*. Present-day karate is characterized by strongly emphasizing competition and *kumite* and neglecting the *kata* or extremely modifying the *kata* of the old styles in order to adapt them to the needs of competition. So I feel responsible to teach the authentic *kata* and the right interpretations.

The Kata Niipaipo and Haufā

I still practice together with young people in my *dōjō*. When I was younger, I often practiced *kumite* in a rather reckless way; this is normal when one is young and strong. But now, rather aged, I think for *kumite* age and strength of the opponents should correspond.

As a younger person one also wants to use *kata* to express the strength and the flexibility of youth. For those needs the *Naha-te kata Seesan*, the *Shuri-te kata Useishi* (which later became the *kata Gojūshiho* – 54 steps), or the *kata Niipaipo* (28 steps) originating from the Chinese White Crane style[76] were mainly used. My father learned the *Niipaipo kata* from a Chinese master and tea merchant called Go Kenki (1886-1940). This Chinese master belonged to the *Hakkaku ken* school. As long as he lived on Okinawa he was an important member of the Association for Karate Studies, which my father had founded. In Naha, Shuri and other places on Okinawa the *Hakkaku ken* style was called "crane hand" (*tsuru no te*). In present *Shitō* karate it is called *Kakuhō* or crane technique.

After my father had moved to mainland Japan, master Go Kenki supported him in his teaching at the Kansai University. From the crane style the *Shitō ryū* has adopted a *kata* called *Haufā* (white bird). I have modified this *kata* by integrating several traditional techniques. According to the name, movements of a crane are imitated in this *kata*. So it is very attractive for public *kata* performances. In the past it was also called "Scream of the Crane" because it is finished by letting out a battle cry, a *kiai*, resembling the scream of a crane.

The *Niipaipo kata* is very dynamic. The movements need to be wide and free and have to be executed quickly. For this reason this *kata* can often be seen at the great karate events in Japan and abroad. Since the 4th Karate

---

[76] The *kata Niipaipo* (often written *Nipaipo*), original name *Nepai* (28 beats), comes from the southern Chinese style of the White Crane (Chn. Bai-he-quan, Jpn. *hakutsuru-ken* or *hakkaku-ken*). It is not unlikely that the founder of the style, Fang Jiniang herself, has created this *kata*. Go Kenki introduced it on Okinawa. Mabuni Kenwa modified it and made it – with the name *Niipaipo* – part of his style *Shitō ryū*. Kyōda Kohatsu (1887-1968), just as Mabuni Kenwa a disciple of Higaonna Kanryō, adopted it in its original form in his style *Toon ryū*. – Habersetzer, R. and G.: Encyclopédie des Arts Martiaux. Paris: Amphora 2004.

Photo 86

Photo 87

Photo 86: The *Niipaipo kata*. The stretched hand technique which is exclusively part of this *kata* can be associated with the stretched wing of a crane.

Photo 87: The *Haufā kata*. The technique of the hanging or laid-on hand. This *kata* was mainly created as application of this technique.

World Championship in Madrid, it has really been shown often. Unfortunately, the version shown in competitions differs quite a lot from the original form. It seems that I am the only one who knows its original form although it belongs to the *Shitō ryū*.

Recently also the *Tenshō kata*, which is elementary for the *Naha-te*, could frequently be seen. It was created by Miyagi Chōjun, who had founded the *Gōjū ryū*. He developed it based on the *Rokkishu kata* described in the Bubishi.[77] Special about this *kata* is the soft blocking with open hands which is directly turned into a counterattack. This allows even older people to control a stronger and taller opponent.

---

[77] *Rokkishu*: Jpn. "Six Hand Forms". These six positions or techniques of the hand, respectively, that are also considered as the "Six Iron Hands of the Shaolin" are described in the Bubishi. See McCarthy, P.: The Bible of Karate – Bubishi. North Clarendon: Tuttle Publishing 1998.

4 Criticizing Present-Day Budō

4.1 Budō Becoming Sport

Sport or Martial Technique

Recently the process of changing karate into a competitive sport is progressing rather quickly. For *kumite* competitions the different styles do not matter anymore because they follow unified rules. So one never can see which style or school of karate the competitors belong to. It only becomes clear whether they are fighting according to the rules of the Japanese Karate Federation or to full contact rules.

But it is a much more severe problem that there is conflict between *kumite* and *kata*. It is typical for present-day competitions to get points by reducing the distance with a jumped kick (*tobi ashi*) thus surprising the opponent, and to aim at the opponent's weak areas. This surely is rational and efficient. But nearly all *kata* techniques are forbidden! This is because the situations presumed for the *kata* have absolutely nothing in common with the rules applied to *kumite* competitions.

Unfortunately, the *kata*, too, have changed significantly. In the last years I have often met athletes who had specialized in *kata*. But they did this based on western sports theory integrating elements of stretching. This is an even greater problem than the *kumite* competitions. Even if the basic sequences of a *kata* have remained unchanged, the competition *kata* have totally lost the characteristic orientation of the original karate towards fighting. Those *kata* do not teach the body control of *Shuri-te* or *Naha-te* anymore. Watching present-day *kata* competitions, one can see elements of *Shuri-te* and *Naha-te* mixed up, or thrusts and kicks are executed according to patterns of western sports science looking like swings in golf or baseball. Increasingly, *kata* competitions become show-like performances in order to attract the general public.

There is still another problem. It is clear that *kata* oriented towards real fighting cannot simply be performed in sports competitions. If a *kata* would be judged according to martial principles (*bujutsu*) the general public probably would be disappointed because it is not able to understand these principles. Maybe it would make sense to proceed in the field of *kata* in a similar way as in the field of *kumite*. With regard to *kumite* it is very easy to make a difference between martial *kumite* and competition *kumite*. So why not creating new *kata* only for competition-use thus creating a clear distinction to the original *kata*? I will come back to this idea below.

Based on the problems I mentioned above, I would like to go more into detail about the point what karate actually is and how it has become a competition sport.

Competitive Sports and Ritual Games

It was in 1953, one year after my father had died, that I was asked to answer some questions about karate in the radio program "Morning Visit" by the state-owned radio station NHK. The first question was: "Will karate go out into the world?" I answered: "I am sure that karate will be spread all over the world and finally will become an Olympic discipline." 50 years have passed since then but I remember exactly that I have foretold the worldwide spread of karate. Today I still think in the same way, that karate will officially become an Olympic discipline, and all the time this was my wish. But in order to get accepted as an official Olympic discipline, karate must become a sport. If it is not a kind of competition everyone can understand, it is no sport.

All disciplines of present-day sports are based upon the modern western ideas of freedom, equality, democracy, and the capitalist spirit of rationality. In this respect the principle of a free competition market is most important. In detail, the development of sports was aiming first at civilizing the rules, secondly at the standardization of facilities and equipment, and thirdly at guaranteeing equal chances. This also comprised equal rights in competitions and the efficient and rational administration and control of the competitions. The result of this process was the birth of modern sports based on the principle of competition i.e. on the spirit of record-taking, point-collecting and winning. So for all kinds of sports, rules were created, which ensure competition to be based on equality. In addition, point and time systems were created. For competitions like boxing, with results being influenced by differences with regard to the body weight of the athletes, a system of weight classes was introduced. Furthermore, rules concerning age and of course the separation of genders became important. All this was necessary because victory or defeat had to be decided in competitions based on equal opportunities.

On the other hand there already were a lot of games and amusements of a different type in pre-modern times. In Melanesia, for example, there was a tribe called Tangu. The Tangu people played the Taketaku game. For this game, two teams were needed who tried to hit a wooden pole with thrown palm tree branches. But none of the two parties intended to win. They just played until both sides gained the same amount of points. This was neither competition nor sports. In Melanesia equality by nature was a sacred principle. The traditional economic exchange was not based on equal value but on gifts of unequal value. Birthday presents, for example, were gifts that always had to be a unity of object and spirit. Generally, no equivalent was demanded. The whole economic life was based on such giving and taking, following the motto: "Not too much and not too little, not one thing more and not one thing less." If a popular person gets a lot of presents but at the same time gives back the same amount of presents, the relations become balanced in the end. So, the ability to hand out gifts to others was the criterion for popularity in the Tangu society. It was the function of the Taketaku game to confirm the principle of equality. It was a ceremony to celebrate the life of the Tangu people at a sacred time and a sacred place.

Compared to the free market economy of the modern western society, the principle of exchange was absolutely different in the society of Melanesia. The same applies to pre-modern Okinawa or the rural Japan of that time, in which the spirit of giving was typical, too. Like the Tangu society, it was not a competitive society, where the strong used to win and the weak to lose. It was a society of mutual benefit where people helped each other by returning gifts and favors. Of course, in the process of the modernization of Japan a market-based and competitive society was introduced.

Budō, however, is not a competition based on the principles of a competitive society. It is still ruled by the traditional spirit of mutual benefits. In *budō* one understands and develops oneself by "grinding" at and "sharpening" each other. This has nothing in common with a competition of individual abilities for winning or losing. That is why the development of *budō* towards sports is basically limited.

Hagoita – Ritual and Game

In Japan, too, there are traditional games similar to these of the Melanesian people. One is called *hagoita*, which is a kind of badminton and of course not a sport. *Hagoita* is performed like a ritual and it is part of the cultural heritage of Japan. It is played by two persons. One person strikes a shuttlecock so that it flies in the direction of the other. In order not to lose, one must try to strike the shuttlecock back before it hits the ground. But *hagoita* is not a game played to gain a victory over an opponent. What counts is to move the shuttlecock to and fro as often as possible. That is why it will actually just be a mishap if the shuttlecock flies to a point where the partner cannot reach it. In order to turn it into a competitive sport, a well-defined area would have to be determined and a net to be fastened. It makes a huge difference whether one wants to strike the shuttlecock just to become an expert in shuttlecock striking or one wants to make a sport of it.

Recently I saw a scientist in TV comparing the shuttlecock with a dragonfly. The dragonfly eats mosquitoes that often spread diseases. That is why *hagoita* was also a popular ritual to pray for the disappearance of epidemic plagues.

But as described above, *hagoita* is not merely ceremonial. It is at the same time a game aimed at striking a shuttlecock at each other as often as possible. *Hagoita* is enjoyed as peaceful amusement on New Year's Day in public places. Like Taketaku, it is not designed to win or to lose. Instead of a competitive spirit, the only thing that matters is to have fun in striking the shuttlecock at each other. Although at first sight *budō* seems to be something very different, it is guided by the same spirit.

Sports or Budō – What is More Serious?

Some say that *budō* is serious fighting in which one's life is put at risk, while sport is only a leisure activity. But this assumption is wrong. Sport, too, is serious fighting with total commitment. Whatever one looks at in the Olympic Games, soccer, tennis or athletics championships, it is always a fight for all or nothing. The question is whether serious fighting means something different in *budō* and sports.

To create rules and to fight according to these rules to win even for the price to kill each other – this is sport. The origin of the Olympic Games as well as of sports was the ancient Pankration.[78] Pankration meant that people fought with bare fists to the death without time limits or technical restrictions. But this does not mean that there were no rules at all. There was the rule that the opponents had to fight against each other with bare fists until one of them surrendered or died. So the only criterion clearly determined was the question of victory or defeat. Of course this is quite different from modern sports, which is governed by the ideas of humanism. But ancient sport was the source of the modern one. One killed each other, but in a fair way, just as sport.

But what is victory in sports, can be defeat in *budō*. And vice versa defeat in sports may become victory in *budō*. The duel between Miyamoto Musashi and Sasaki Kojirō on the island of Ganryū-jima mentioned above is a good example.[79] If their duel had been sports Musashi would have lost already because he had broken the rules by coming too late. And the unfair production of the longer sword during his way to the island would clearly have been an infraction of the principles of equality and equal opportunities. But *budō* is no competition in terms of equal opportunities and thus it cannot be judged in an objective manner by everyone. Furthermore there are no forbidden techniques. Such a kind of serious competition cannot be accepted by a sports festival like the Olympic Games. All techniques

[78] Pankration, Greek. "All Powers": Sporting duel in ancient Greece combining elements of fist fighting and wrestling; almost everything was allowed (only scratching and biting were prohibited) to disable the opponent. Since 648 BC Pankration was part of the Greek Olympic Games. – Publisher's comment.

[79] See p. 81.

contained in the karate *kata* presuppose a serious fight in terms of *budō*. They would all be banned.

It is quite clear that the *kata* and *kumite* competitions of the Japanese Karate Federation are held according to the rules of modern sports. The Japanese Karate Federation was founded under the guidance of the Japanese Association for Physical Education and naturally followed the modern Olympic ideals. Spiteful remarks characterizing the *kata* competitions as "dancing karate" must be put up with. These *kata* are just the result of a process of modernization. Of course, *budō karate kata* would look quite different.

The full contact karate arose as an antithesis to this modern karate. But it is not that much a negation of the *kata* of modern competitive karate but rather a negation of *kata* in general. It is based on a new rule which allows all punches and kicks except for those directly to the face but prohibits all kinds of throwing, joint-locking and ground techniques. Like the complex technique of *vale tudo* (everything is allowed) of the Gracie *jūjutsu*[80] it is a negation of the modern and a return to the ancient sports. I do not criticize this. But for me it is by no means a return to the original karate.

I think it is just time to reconsider what is sport and what is *budō*. It is way too simple to say, "If it goes along with an all-out commitment and the opponents try to kill each other it is *budō*." The same applies to the statement: "Tradition is *kata* practice."

Separation of Sports and Budō

Basically, the official participation of karate in the Olympic Games would be something very good because many people would learn more about it, and so it would promote the worldwide spread of karate.

But if no clear differentiation is made between competition and *budō* there will be confusion. Both exist in parallel and should not be mingled.

---

[80] Gracie *jūjutsu*, also known as Brazilian *jūjutsu* (also *jiu jitsu*) is a martial art developed by the brothers Carlos Gracie (1901-1994) and Hélio Gracie (1913-2009). Gracie *jūjutsu* has particularly proven to be very effective in free fight combats (*vale tudo*). – Publisher's comment.

After all there are always people who are not interested in competitive sports and who only want to study karate as *budō*.

In the world of *jūdō* there once were severe debates between the followers of *budō* and those of sports about whether colored *jūdō* suits should be introduced or not. Especially westerners had claimed that colored *jūdō* suits could make judgment easier. From the point of view of sports, this demand is justified because everyone should be able to judge about victory or defeat with his own eyes. The point of view of the representatives of Japanese *budō*, who argued that the white color would express the Japanese spirit and the spirit of *jūdō*, was not acceptable to the advocates of modern sports. Additionally, for competitive *jūdō* a system of weight classes has been introduced.

The Japanese Karate Federation, too, has tried different things in order to create a complex system of rules for *kumite*. So karate becomes more and more bound to the principle of competition, and exercises in many karate clubs, particularly at schools and universities, are only designed to get points in *kumite* competitions. The present development of karate is obviously tending rather one-sidedly towards competition and sports. If karate is practiced as a competitive sport, one will sooner or later reach physical limits. Hearing words like "active" or "retired from an active career", one must automatically think of sports. Young people can fully deploy their physical energies and their life may be filled with sports. But what will they do if their career in competitive sports has come to an end? Will it be possible for them to study *budō* karate for the rest of their lives? Are there enough experts left who are able to ensure the continuation of such traditional karate? From this point of view, the Japanese *budō* today is in a deep crisis.

Sundome and Full Contact

The *sundome* rule[81] of the Japanese Karate Federation led to a repetitive pattern in competitions: The opponents try to hit each other by surprise at a weak point using a jumped kick (*tobi ashi*) from a well measured dis-

[81] *Sundome*: Jpn. Stopping the punch shortly before the impact on the opponent (*no-contact*). – Translator's comment.

tance. Blocking is absolutely neglected. But even in the case of full contact karate not all blocking techniques are of interest because the face does not need to be protected since hitting the face is forbidden. But in any case, whichever rules are followed, *kata* techniques are hardly used, no matter how much they may have been studied. *Kata* techniques include attacks against the face, kicks against the joints, joint-locking and throwing techniques, and also sword-hand attacks against the eyes. There are *kata* to defend oneself against several attackers at the same time and others against armed opponents. The rules of the Japanese Karate Federation as well as those of full contact karate generally exclude all *kata* techniques because they are considered to be based on situations of real fighting. Using *kata* techniques means breaking the rules and is considered to be a foul. In original karate there is of course neither *sundome* nor something like full contact. And it goes without saying that both are not part of the *Shitō* karate since its beginnings. People of my generation who learned karate before it became competitive do not care about the difference between *sundome* and full contact at all. For sure the same could be said about the old Okinawa masters and the old *jūjutsu*. "Hit, not hit?" No one cared about this question at that time. If no real punches and kicks are used how can one practice blocking? Whether a thrust should be stopped close before it hits the opponent or should hit him with full force was for the first time discussed among the karate students when the development towards competitive karate began. This debate about *sundome* or full contact actually started when Japan entered the period of high economic growth[82] and more and more big karate contests were held. But this was not a debate about karate in general but about karate as a competitive sport. The topics of the debate were the rules for competition.

Provided that *kata* are practiced regularly and studied analytically there is nothing to criticize about participation in competitions, trying to give one's best according to a set of rules. But the competition must be clearly defined as such. That means, if someone practicing full contact karate also studies attacks against the face and blocking such attacks, he will nevertheless be able to keep the face out of the actions in case of a competition.

[82] The end of the 1950s. – Translator's comment.

But it is quite different if someone only practices for full contact competitions with the face considered as a taboo zone. If the ultimate question is: "How to win within a framework of complex rules?" the understanding of what is essential is already lost. Imagine an examinee who prepares for the examination choosing the stuff to be learned according to whether it might be asked in the examination or not. Sure one does not prepare for questions like: "How many toes belong to a frog's foot?" because such a question would most probably never be asked. But in general one should not avoid learning something just because it will not be asked in an examination.

In *budō*, the rules are made by oneself. This implies to strengthen one's spirit and one's morality. If someone is only interested in winning according to rules others have established he might become a simple "thug" one day.

4.2 Modern Competition and Budō

The Assessment of Competition Kata

As explained in the last chapter it would be rather easy to solve the problem of the *kumite* competitions. The problem of *kata* competitions is more serious. The mind-set of a person performing a *kata* cannot be a criterion of judgment for a competition because it is a very subjective aspect. – Sometimes I ask myself whether my father, supposing he were still alive, would win anything in such an international *kata* competition.

It is not surprising that the *kata* performed in competitions have been reformed. Especially in competitions abroad, *kata* performances are the actual highlights. The response of the audience, the shouting and applause influence the decisions of the referees. In general, the *kata* shown in the competitions are very far from their original interpretations, the actions are pompous and the movements carried out extra slowly. All athletes perform like this because it is the only way to win. Of course it cannot be denied that these athletes have practiced very hard, and the *kata* they are performing are difficult to master. But *kata* that prove to be successful in competitions are almost useless as fighting techniques. That is why I think the old original *kata* should be left as they are and special *kata* should be created for competitive use. The demands of sports and *budō* simply do not go together.

I have already advanced this opinion in an interview for the magazine *Gekkan Karate Dō* in 1998 and was asked by the surprised journalist: "As head of a traditional karate style, do you really think it is right to create new *kata*?" Yes, I think new *kata* for competitive use should be created to preserve the *budō kata*. The fighting situations presupposed for the traditional *kata* are really too far from the rules of competition. To give an example: Ten traditional techniques could be integrated into a new *kata* and the performance could be limited to five minutes. This could also be judged easily by the referees. I even guess the best would be to combine *kata* and *kumite* competition and to judge the competitors according to their overall performance in both disciplines. Besides this, competition could also comprise *bunkai* performances by two partners in order to demonstrate the understanding of the techniques contained in the *kata*. So, even techniques which are not part of *kumite* competitions could be shown. Furthermore this would be an opportunity to prove that the competitors are able to maintain the state of *zanshin*[83] throughout their performance. This is a state of body and mind continuously enabling the practitioner to react to an opponent's attack. So, even after the own action is finished, one maintains a high level of caution and does not allow to loosen oneself energetically. Of course, maintaining such an attitude until the end, i.e. until both partners have accomplished their techniques correctly, requires mutually respectful behavior.

Even analytical *kumite* with three opponents attacking one after the other could be introduced. To control their attacks it would be very important to master body turns. The attacking persons would need to cooperate in a well-coordinated way and even to harmonize their breathing.

Such *kata* and *kumite* performances and competitions could be appreci-

[83] *Zanshin*: Jpn. Mental state in *budō* characterized by inner calmness, alertness and readiness. – Publisher's comment.

ated. This would allow integrating many techniques of the original karate into the framework of competitive sports and could help to solve many of the problems mentioned above.

Is Modern Karate Really a Progress?

There is another much more severe problem my father was already confronted with when *kata* were step by step used for competitions. To call something a sport, everyone must be able to understand it objectively. It must be something comprehensible that can be controlled. This is the same principle modern science is based upon. Studying things with a critical approach, filtering out only clear facts, analyzing its pieces, measuring them and finally reintegrating them – this way of thinking is called "reductionism" and it is the starting point of modern science. These ideas appeared in Japan for the first time in the second half of the 16th century in a period called Azuchi Momoyama.

In the past, the Okinawan karate masters or the senior students (*sempai*) normally did not explain anything. They only said: "Do it like this. More like this. Look, this way…" Of course this was not very clear. They never explained by using words. They did it by showing movements. Fixing terms for single techniques such as *seiken zuki* or *yoko uke* only began in my father's era. Expressions used in our days like: "He is good at kicking in the medium level (*chūdan geri*)" were not known on Okinawa. Normally one directly referred to the hand, like: "He knows how to use his hand" or "He has a good hand for this or that *kata*."

The point is that there is no limit to the variations of techniques and there is no technique that can be used only for one purpose. The side block (*yoko uke*), for example, is carried out differently according to the various conditions. It depends on the opponent's technique, his position and one's own position, or the ground the fight takes place on. That means that there is not only one *yoko uke*. At least it can be said that it is never the same because a technique is unique at a certain time and in a certain place.

After the war, the systematic and detailed verification, classification and naming of the karate techniques began under the supervision of the Japanese Association for Physical Education. This was set as a condition to become member of this association. With the old and vague methods and terms of the Okinawan epoch, karate could not gain appeal among the broader public. And without explanations understandable for everyone, karate could not be spread internationally. Classifying the *kata* and segmenting them into separate single techniques made it possible to explain karate with simple words easy to understand, and to develop a clear and logic training system. Karate was modernized. The "pre-modern, pre-logic, unclear teaching and guiding methods" were abolished. But there are times when I ask myself whether this was really a progress and not a fatal regression.

Flowing Techniques – Consciousness Going Ahead

When entering a karate *dōjō* as a newcomer one has to learn the basic thrusts, punches, kicks and blocks and to exercise them again and again. In the original Okinawan karate, training began with *kata*. No one had an idea of what was a punch or a block. This did not even come into mind. Nothing but *kata* were exercised. There was *Passai* training or *Kōsōkun* training, etc. It might sound strange but actually one *kata* was understood as one technique.

The practice was based on a holistic approach focused on the free flow of attack and defense actions. In our days, even *dan* grade seniors can be seen doing stereotypical blocks or counterattacks, exactly the way they have learned it. But they have no idea of what could be the next action, how the movements could be modified. If one isolates one particular technique out of a set of flowing movements and gives prominence to it, in other words: pauses, this is called in *budō language* "to reside or to settle" (*i-tsuki*). This is like the "cheese" posture when getting photographed. But in *budō* this kind of remaining or "residing" means death.

In front of Buddha statues one can often hear people say that the statue looks lively. Buddha statues created by famous sculptors normally do not show fixed postures. In fact they show a moment of motion and change. If they appear to be fixed, motion has come to a halt. If one is familiar with *budō* one can understand this easily. The same phenomenon can be studied in Japanese calligraphy (*shodō*). Passages in the text where the flow of mind was interrupted can be recognized immediately.

When a movement is not fixed, not remaining or "residing", the mind always goes ahead. In order to understand this idea let's think of reading with a loud voice. People who are good at it, like news presenters, do not look at the words, the mouth is just speaking. Their eyes are always one or two sentences ahead. The mouth movements follow the movements of the eyes. That means they follow the mind. In this way a good reading flow is ensured. People who are not that well-trained are voicing the words the eyes are just seeing. The movements of the eyes and the movements of the mouth coincide. This leads to halting reading.

The mind is in permanent motion, it always changes. If the movements of the body follow the mind the motions will be flowing ceaselessly. This continuous changing and moving is very important, and for sure I do not exaggerate to say that this is the starting point of all Japanese martial arts.

My father wanted karate to be adopted as an element of the national physical education and therefore made a lot of efforts to systemize the techniques. But in his book published in 1938 *Introduction into Attack and Defense Techniques in Karate Kempō* he stressed the principle of change and of unlimited variability of techniques contained in the *kata*. Of course, as a far-sighted, deep-thinking first-class *bujutsu* master his concern was also that karate as *bujutsu*, as system of fighting techniques, would not get lost.

After my father's death the Japanese Karate Federation was founded, which promoted the development of karate into competitive sports. For this purpose it developed detailed standards. This standardization concerned even the slightest details. Exact distances with the precision of one inch were defined as well as the angles between the different parts of the body. For example, with regard to the side block (*yoko uke*) it was determined that the fist had to be kept at shoulder level and that a space of about one fist's width between breast and elbow had to be maintained. By defining a technical system understandable for everyone, in fact a new sport was created to be spread democratically. But from the point of view of *budō*, karate became, so to speak, a dead body characterized by "settling or residing".

In the performance of competition *kata* this sometimes leads to pure showing-off, to put it frankly. *Kata* become mere show. *Kime*[84] are made in a dramatic way. But this *kime* is something absolutely different from the *kime* in *bujutsu* because it is not used from the point of view of real fighting but of that of showiness. Such boasters' poses are a symbol for the complete congealment of the forms. *Kata* executed in this way have literally lost their vitality. Authentic martial karate *kata* are the complete contrary of such a congealment. The problem is that such *kata* would probably appear as incomprehensible and impenetrable to the public.

Learning in the Flow of the Practice

The book *Kasshiyama* by the famous Matsuura Seizan (1760-1841) includes a story about Yagyū Munenori[85]. Once Munenori accompanied the third ruler of the Tokugawa family, Iemitsu, to visit a *nō* theater[86] performance. The main actor was the famous Kanze Sakon. Iemitsu who liked the martial arts, watched Sakon dancing the role of Taira Tomomori[87] and

[84] *Kime*: Jpn. Short focusing of the mental and physical energy in the *hara* (cf. footnote 36 on p. 36) or at the point of impact of a punch. *Kime* is an explosion-like projection of the inner energy (*ki*) perfectly directly towards the target. In general *kime* is accompanied by a *kiai*. – Habersetzer, R. and G.: Encyclopédie des Arts Martiaux. Paris: Amphora 2004.

[85] Yagyū Munenori (1571-1646) was a master of sword fighting (*kenjutsu*). He was the son of Yagyū (Sekishūsai) Muneyoshi (see p. 69 et sqq.) and the father of the *Yagyū ryū* founder Yagyū Mitsuyoshi. Munenori was the official sword master at the court of the Tokugawa shōgunate. He is the author of several works on his martial art. – Ibid.

[86] *Nō*: Jpn. Lyric theatre style that emerged in the 14th century. Traditionally, only male actors played and danced and were responsible for the musical accompaniment. In most cases the leading actor (*shite*) wore a mask. Usually the traditional themes were taken from Japanese or Chinese mythology or literature. During the Edo period (1603-1868) it was a privilege of the samurai to act in the *nō* theatre and to visit it. At that time the *nō* actors had the heritable status of samurai. – Publisher's comment.

[87] The Taira (also known as Heike or Heiji) were one of the most important samurai clans in medieval Japan. Their political ascent was topic of the book "Heike Monogatari" that is attributed to Hamuro Tokinaga. – Habersetzer, R. and G.: Encyclopédie des Arts Martiaux. Paris: Amphora 2004. – Taira no Tomomori (1152-1185) was the son of Taira no Kiyomori and one of the clan leaders and commanders of the Taira during the Gempei war (1180-1185). – Publisher's comment.

"The Ghost of Taira no Tomomori at Daimotsu Bay". Multicolored wood-block print by Yoshitoshi Taiso (1839-1892).

got the impression that he was perfect in mastering the *naginata* (a pole weapon with curved blade on the end; see figure) and his movements did not show the slightest fault or weakness. To assure himself, he ordered Munenori to tell him if he could spot a moment when Sakon's movements would allow the idea: "This was careless enough for me to hit him."

But Sakon was performing with the *naginata* as if he had totally become one with the role of Tomomori and did not even fail for a second. But at one moment of his performance, when he came close to the right corner of the stage, Munenori slightly smiled at him.

After the performance Iemitsu asked Munenori to give his judgment. He answered: "His artistic performance is good. His spirit is strong. He did not show any weak point to attack. But when he came to the right corner, he might have been a little bit careless."

When Sakon came back to the dressing room he asked: "Who was this man close to the Shōgun?" After he was told that this had been the leading sword master of the Tokugawa family, Yagyū Munenori, he nodded, deeply satisfied, saying: "Yes, I noticed this man. I felt all the time that he was watching me closely. So I tried harder than normally. When I approached the right corner I had to take breath for a moment. And in this very second he showed a little smile. Suddenly I lost my energy and felt very tired." When Sakon came close to the edge of the stage the flow of his mental energies was stopped and his movements "resided" for a moment. No wonder a master of *bujutsu* like Munenori realized this immediately. When Iemitsu was told about this he was deeply impressed by the abilities of both men.

In sports the basic positions are learned first. For example, in tennis, the beginners at first learn how to hold the club and how to handle it. The same applies to baseball. In karate, too, basic exercises are practiced in the beginning. In *kendō* the first topics are body positions, stances and aiming. This approach is considered as normal in our days.

But in the *Yagyū ryū*, body positions, stances and other basic elements were learned in a flowing training. Contrary to present *kendō* practice, "flowing" was in the center of everything. The same can be said about the old karate. Everything in nature is "circling" interdependently. "Circling" means moving and changing. "Flowing" is the expression of this continuous change.

The Reductionism of Sports

The essence of Japanese *budō* is to get unified with the energies of the earth. This is the starting point of all ideas and body movements in *budō*. The basic question in this context is how the human being can borrow as much energy as possible from nature. In a certain sense this is also the idea of an "absolute higher force".

In contrast to it, "reductionism" is the principal idea of body control in western sports. It is based upon a mechanical understanding of the world. The human being is considered a mechanism, a kind of robot. This mechanism is to generate maximum energy. The idea is that this energy is exclusively generated by the body. Sports physics and sports technology based on "reductionism" are progressing in large steps. The results of sports science are more and more introduced also into karate training. Scientific methods help to harden parts of the body rationally and efficiently and to produce maximum abilities. But this is of course not "Japanese spirit combined with western technique" but "western spirit and Japanese technique". That is why now, even in karate *kata*, body control and body movements are governed by the principles of sports.

Photo 88: Tennō Mutsuhito (*Meiji tennō*) (1853-1912) was the 122nd *tennō* of Japan. "*Meiji*" ("enlightened rule") was the era name (*nengō*) of his reign (1868-1912). Photograph from 1873.

This change of patterns already began in the Meiji period[88]. Striving for a "rich nation with a strong army", the imperial army was trained according to the German model. From time to time even nowadays one can see in TV or in newspapers German or Russian troops parading like robots with straight backbones, marching in goose step, the legs lifted high without bending the knees. This way of marching is a typical example for showing how western patterns influenced the original Japanese body control through the military education which in Japan was also part of the curriculum of general schools.

In the early Shōwa period[89], about the end of the 1920s, Miki Nisaburō, who lead the karate club at the Tōkyō University, came to Okinawa to

[88] In 1868 in Japan the Meiji era began. This new historical stage began with the accession to the throne by the young Mutsuhito. It was characterized by a rupture with the feudal past of the country. By Imperial will Japan became a modern country, the most advanced in the Far East. – Publisher's note.

[89] The Shōwa period (literally "Period of Enlightened Peace") was the time of the reign of Emperor Hirohito (1926-1989). – Publisher's comment.

show the masters his *kata*. But they judged: "This is not karate!" This episode illustrates the problem. On mainland Japan, those who carried the development of karate as a driving force were university students and other progressive intellectuals who at the same time were the pioneers of westernization and modernization and somehow let karate be influenced by western body culture. That is how the modernization of body control in karate began already in times when it was still represented by my father and master Funakoshi.

Competition Karate Returning to Ancient Patterns

The change from *budō* into sports is a very severe problem also concerning *jūdō* and *kendō*. But in contrast to karate both were already mature when the waves of modernization rushed upon them. To a certain degree they had the means to defend themselves. They were technically and psychologically solid. The term "residing" (*i-tsuki*), for example, stems from *kenjutsu*. Compared to *jūdō* and *kendō* the history of karate is still rather short.

Karate appears to me like a child, which was left behind too early by my father and master Funakoshi, a child who struggled to the utmost and survived not knowing what had happened to its body. It did not have the means to understand its own situation. Children cannot perceive their environment from a wide perspective and by remaining reserved and distant. If one has no words one cannot think in an abstract way.

Also the fact that competitive karate appeared on the scene in the shape of "karate for real fight" or "*budō* karate" shows how difficult it is for karate to find its right way. So it appears to be a child of modernization different from all the rest of the family.

The value system of democracy and capitalism of the post-war era changed the whole society in a way never seen before. In karate these changes brought about that the karateka were striving for stoic behavior and extreme performances. As a result they returned to Pankration-like ancient sports.[90] In this sense karate was most severely hit by the impact of

[90] Cf. footnote 78 on p. 105.

modernization. This is a point I would like to be thought over thoroughly by everybody concerned with karate. How could such a radical change happen? And even those not related to karate should be inspired to think about the question what modernization actually is. 60 years after the end of the war and after the breakdown of the cold-war structures, modernization as well as Americanization again becomes a topic of public discussion – and, as everyone knows, this is not only a problem of karate.

4.3 The Unity of Soul, Body and Technique

Testing the Abilities Before Kumite Came into Use

In the recent years of booming "fight techniques", new complex fighting systems have appeared, which like the ancient Pankration follow only the one rule that "everything is allowed". An acquaintance who had seen such a tournament in TV said: "The eyes of the fighters look really frightening", and he asked, "Do they look the same in *budō*?" Of course they do not. I must repeat that Pankration and *budō* are absolutely different. Pankration and *vale tudo*[91] are based on rules. So they belong to sports although there may be only that only rule that "everything is allowed". *Budō*, however, was developed as a self-defense technique. It is not actively aiming at killing the opponent as such "fight techniques" do. Karate is not made for people who like fighting and are looking for it. This is already shown by the fact that "all karate *kata* begin with blocking and end with blocking". Master Funakoshi Gichin once commented in this context: "Karate is difficult to be explained and taught by using words. It must be shown in reality. Special about karate is that one cannot make it competitive or economize it. The essence of karate will emerge when there are no protective clothing and competitions."

Budō and sports differ because the original aims were different. *Budō* was not created for competition like sports, demanding immediate active and determined attack. *Budō* was made for the purpose of self-defense and

[91] Cf. footnote 80 on p. 106.

one cannot make a competition with self-defense techniques. The essence of *bujutsu* is counterattacking out of defense (*go no sen*). In competitive sports this is punished with deduction of points. In *jūdō* one can often see competitions in which athletes get cautioned because they do not attack and retreat to a defense position.

In original karate there was no competition at all, not even what is now called "free *kumite*", that is *randori* competitions which allow the free use of techniques. In my father's era something like this was strictly forbidden. Master Funakoshi too did not allow this according to what he had learned from his teachers. I already mentioned a case at the Tōkyō University at the end of the 1920s. The karate club had suggested a kind of "real fight karate" including the use of protective clothing. Master Funakoshi angrily rejected this and made the person responsible to resign.

However, in Okinawan karate it was possible, too, to pit one's strength against each other. Young people who practiced karate made real-fight exercises called *kake tameshi*. Students who wanted to check themselves in such a test fight had to apply for and to ask witnesses to attend. One of the witnesses would act as referee. Then they would meet at an appropriate place in the streets, surrounded by their fellows. At that time there were no street-lights. So, when the sun had set, the opponents had to fight in the light of the lanterns held by the bystanders. The referee stopped the fight according to the situation and gave advices like: "You should practice this and that a little more..." Finally the technical abilities were discussed among the fellows.

My father, too, was often invited to such test fights and asked to serve as a referee for his friends. But the *kake tameshi* were not competitions like today. It was serious, real fight and "everything was allowed" but an opponent was never beaten up inexorably. Both opponents served each other to study their own weak and strong points. It was not "competing against each other" but "cooperating with each other".

Harmony instead of Competition

If the opponents only intend to smash each other, to win a victory over the other, this can of course not be called "cooperation". To create cooperation, both sides must let the other act. So mutuality becomes decisive. Both partners serve each other and make full use of the techniques offered by the opponent. In such a fight the whole personality should be invested. It is not about becoming glorious. If it is a good cooperation, both sides can display their abilities and share the glory. While fighting the opponents sharpen and polish each other. They entrust and reflect each other. That is why watching the opponent means watching oneself. The self is reflected and sharpened by the opponent.

The more both act in such a mood the more they can reach a state of energetic correspondence and connection (*aiki*). This is far from the experience of competition for winning a victory. In fact it is the essence of human relation. To practice this in the reality of everyday life means turning the law of war into the law of peace, changing "fight" (*bu*) into "civilized or cultural value" (*bun*).

There is a term for mutual harmonizing called *taiwa* which was fixed by Kiichi Hōgen who left the oldest Japanese script on the art of war. He lived in the Gempei period, from the end of the 11th to the end of the 12th century, at the edges of mount Kurama in the north of Kyōto. It is very probable that the great Tengu mountain ghost[92], who was said to have taught Ushiwaka-maru (as Minamoto no Yoshitsune[93] was called in his childhood) the martial art of *ninjutsu*, was in reality this Kiichi Hōgen.

In his writings there is one sentence which the founder of *aikidō* Ueshiba Morihei liked to cite: "In confrontation harmonize! 5 plus 5 equals 10. But 1 plus 9 also equals 10. And so does 2 plus 8." He wanted to say by this that it is not important who is stronger but that even in competition, what counts is cooperation. And I and people like myself can only agree. But taking the standpoint of modern sports of "winning or losing" it is probably very difficult to get an idea of what this sentence might mean.

---

[92] See footnote 173 on p. 191 et seq.

[93] See p. 9.

"There is no First Attack in Karate"

In biographies of fighters and warriors one often can read episodes about fights and bravery. But one will hardly find such things about the old Okinawan *budō* masters. For example, there were no fights or even quarrels reported about master Itosu, who was my father's teacher, and whose whole life was dedicated to karate. As a *budō* master he was a man of noble character and high moral values. Yamaoka Tesshū (1836-1888), a great sword master who lived at the end of the *Edo* period, was said to have not used his sword to kill a human being even once. He became famous as founder of a sword fighting style[94] aiming at "winning without weapons or even without fighting at all" (*mute shōryū*). This attitude that means that one does not intend to use a weapon and to hurt the opponent is identical with the spiritual principle (*shin*), while the will to win is based upon the principle of techniques (*gi*) and of the body (*tai*).[95] The unity of these three aspects is the basis of each classic martial art.

Current confusion in karate is also caused because people don't know anymore to make a clear distinction between the spiritual aspect (*shin*) with the physical aspects (*gi* and *tai*). The maxim "there is no first attack in karate" must be explained in a psychological and a technical sense. But today, one only considers the physical aspects *gi* and *tai*. This is due to a way of thinking rooted in dualism. In the world of dualism one only thinks in contradictory terms like "victory an defeat", "right and wrong", "yes and no", "cold and warm", "confused and enlightened". From this dualistic point of view the maxim "there is no first attack in karate" is irrational because in order to defend justice and other higher values attack might be

---

[94] *Ittō Shoden Mutō ryū. Mutō*: Jpn. Without sword.

[95] *Shin-gi-tai*: In the practice of a classical martial art (*budō*) *shin*, *gi* and *tai* designate the three elements that enhance effectiveness. *Shin* is the spiritual contribution, *gi* the contribution by the technique and *tai* the contribution by the bodily aspects. Often the terms are also interpreted as heaven (*shin*), earth (*gi*) and human being (*tai*). These three aspects form a unity. It is impossible to influence one of them without influencing the other ones. Their integration is the expression of mastery on the Way (*dō*). Yamaoka Tesshū modified this expression into "*shin-gi ittai*" ("spirit and technique are one"). – Habersetzer, R. and G.: Encyclopédie des Arts Martiaux. Paris: Amphora 2004.

necessary. Sometimes it is required to intervene either immediately before (*sen no sen*) the outbreak of violence or far in advance (*sensen no sen*) in order to avoid such an incident in the family or between acquaintances.

That is why the maxim "there is no first attack in karate" is normally explained as a psychological advice: "One does not learn karate because one likes fighting, but because according to the ethics of the warrior one wants to finish the fight quickly." Furthermore: "One does not use karate techniques for private quarrels."

But I think there is a spiritual dimension too with respect to this maxim. People who study karate should also get mental and spiritual education and understand the whole practice as a kind of *kōan*. *Kōan* are used by Zen priests mainly of the Rinzai sect to guide their disciples on their ways to enlightenment (*satori*).[96]

Hakuin Ekaku (1686-1769) who reformed Rinzai Zen Buddhism in the beginning of the 18th century created the *kōan*: "What is the sound of one clapping hand?"[97] There are no rational answers to such meditation sayings. Which sound could the clapping of only one hand cause? Actually such a sound should not exist. So, the Zen disciple is to think in a sitting meditation position (*zazen*) about a sound that normally should not exist. But he must give an answer to the Zen master. There are some who simply repeat a prayer like: "Holy Buddha adored above all".[98] Others dare to hit the master's cheek with the flat hand.[99] Because there is no fixed rational answer to a *kōan* it is important what is transferred on the mental level. The priest judges only the spiritual condition of the disciple. Even if the answers of two disciples were the same, one may be accepted and the other rejected with the words "*nama satori*!" ("pseudo enlightenment!") accompanied by a kick. To my mind the motto "there is no first attack in karate" and thus karate itself is like a *kōan* a practitioner has to think about all life long. That is why karate could be called "Zen in motion" (*ugoku zen*).

---

96 This *kōan* is a paradox appearing as a riddle. – Translator's comment.

97 *Sekishu no onjō?*

98 *Namu shaka muni butsu.*

99 ...based upon the belief that one is now entitled to such a behavior because one has become enlightened and thus independent of one's master. However, this often turns out to be an error. – Translator's comment.

Painting by Hakuin Ekaku depicting Linji Yixuan (Jpn. Rinzai Gigen), the founder of the Linji school of Chán Buddhism which in Japan became the Rinzai school of Zen Buddhism.

II

The Spirit of Budō

1 The Essence of Budō

1.1 The Difference between Budō and Violence

Taking Life, Giving Life

Budō literally means the "way of *bu*". The *kanji* with the reading *bu* consists of the elements "spear" and "stop", the whole character carrying the meaning "to stop a spear". Hence, the meaning of *budō* would actually be "the way to stop a spear". In general, however, the character for *bu* is interpreted as indication for an attack, i.e. as "using the spear". But the original sense is evidently of defensive nature.

Of course not only karate but all kinds of *budō* were by origin methods to kill, or more precisely, fighting techniques to kill people. This is what the ability to fight (*buryoku*) and violence (*bōryoku*) have in common. But there is also a great difference. The same ability is on the one hand as *bōryoku* illegal and excessive use of force or on the other hand as *buryoku* used to stop violent action. This is the main point to discuss with regard to *budō*. In his book *Introduction into Attack and Defense Techniques in Karate Kempō* my father wrote: "If you let your fists dance and your legs fly to cause harm and pain to people without any reason, this will not be *bu* but *kyō* (crime)." And he also wrote: "If you fight for a proper aim this will be bravery (*yū*). If you give yourself to the evil this will be crime (*kyō*)." Undoubtedly one cannot go the way of *bu* unless the essence of *bu* is understood and accepted as self-defense.

As is generally known, traditional Chinese medicine teaches that there are energy pathways, the so-called meridians, through which the life energy (*ki*) circulates. All diseases are explained by Chinese medicine as changes in these energy pathways. If they are blocked and the energy flow stagnates the "*ki* starts to suffer" and one falls ill. If the pulse diagnosis called *myakushin* indicates changes in the flow of energy, the related vital or acupuncture points (*tsubo*) are determined and used to fill the weak points or deficiencies (*kyō*) or to discharge energy excess (*jitsu*). For example, in order to cure a tonsillitis a point at the top of the forefinger called *shōyō* is pricked with a needle. This point on the epidermis is cautiously pierced in

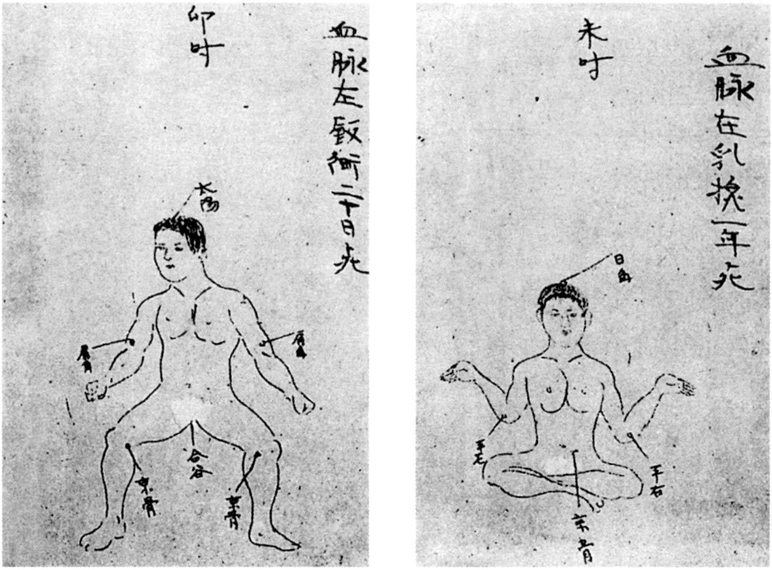

Figures from the *Bubishi* showing vital points as targets to attack.

a way not to injure blood vessels although slight bleeding may occasionally happen. In most cases the fever decreases quickly.

The vital points called *tsubo* can be found all over the body. Because they are points of influence they can also be considered as weak points. So, by influencing the meridians one can as well vitalize as kill. It is a method to heal and at the same time a method to kill. In other words if this method cannot be used to kill it cannot be used to cure. Killing and vitalizing are like the two sides of a medal. When I was a middle school pupil in Ōsaka, I attended a one-year course in *jūdō* chiropractic at master Konishi Yasuhiro's in Tōkyō. What he had taught me with respect to the vital points proved to be very useful in later years.

My father had inherited from master Itosu old secret writings about Chinese *kempō* called *Bubishi*.[100] On many illustrations one can see joint-

[100] See McCarthy, P.: The Bible of Karate – Bubishi. North Clarendon: Tuttle Publishing 1998. A German edition of the *Bubishi* with focus on historical aspects and on the martial techniques is: Habersetzer, R.: Bubishi – An der Quelle des Karatedō, 3rd ed. Chemnitz: Palisander Verlag 2009.

Figures from the *Bubishi* showing fighting scenes.

locking, grappling and throwing techniques, thrusts and kicks. The script shows whether the left or the right person won the fight. Besides this it is shown how according to the kind of attack, the death of the opponent will occur within a certain period of time, that is, on the same day, in 20 days or after one year. When I saw this I could understand that it was explained here how to hit the vital points of the opponent with precision. Expressions like "one-year-killing" or "three-years-killing" represent techniques against the vital points of the opponent, which result in death in the corresponding period of time.

Today hardly anyone is interested in studying the meridians. But original karate was a universal fighting technique to be used to give or take life.[101] This is a very important aspect. Whether karate becomes a method of giving life or killing depends on the own attitude of mind. That is why the mental and spiritual momentum is so important for karate. Fighting techniques without mental and spiritual rules are nothing but techniques for brawls, and mere violence.

---

[101] *Kassatsu jizai jutsu.*

Karate and the Spirit of Respect (Shurei)

If being asked what the mental and spiritual rule of karate actually is, I can answer without hesitation: "This is expressed by the character *rei*!"[102] This *kanji* is part of the word *shurei*, which is well known in Japan because of a historical sight on Okinawa recognized as national cultural treasure. It is the *Shurei no mon* which is a rebuilt gate of the Ryūkyū kings' palace in Shuri.[103] This building (see photo 89), which represents the old Ryūkyū culture, is also depicted on the reverse of the 2,000 Yen notes. On a signboard above the gate it is written *shurei no kuni*. That means "land where the rituals are respected". This script is an important symbol of the Okinawan people and has a deep spiritual meaning to them. The spirit of *shurei* is enshrined in and transmitted by karate, the *budō* which originated and developed on Okinawa.

Master Matsumura Sōkon, also called Bushi Matsumura, who accomplished the *Shuri-te*, left a scroll written in his late years with the title *The Seven Moral Rules of Bu*[104]. The text begins with the following words: "The Seven Rules of *bu* are: Violence is forbidden. Master the military profession. Protect human beings. Achieve merits. Pacify the people. Harmonize the society. Increase material wealth. This is what the holy men were praising. This is what the book is about." The first statement that *bu* prohibits violence is in the very center of the whole work and expresses the spirit of the Okinawan *shurei*.

Already for a long time there have been three ritual expressions of respect and gratitude in karate called *san rei*. There is one *rei* towards the gods, one towards the teachers and one mutual *rei* called *sōgokan no rei*. Every training in *dōjō* begins and ends with this expression of respect: *shinzen ni rei*[105] *– sensei ni rei – o tagai ni rei*. The gratitude towards the gods is not only religious in the narrow sense. It is also an expression of thankfulness

---

[102] *Rei*: Character referring to the lexical field of "rite, respect, thankfulness, and politeness". – Translator's comment.

[103] The gate was constructed between 1527 and 1555, and reconstructed in 1958.

[104] *Bu no nana toku.*

[105] Also *shōmen ni rei*; the meaning of both salutations is the same. – Publisher's comment.

Photo 89: *Shurei no mon*, one of the gates of the castle of Shuri, the residence of the kings of the Ryūkyū kingdom.

for the gift of life we got on our planet earth that is blessed with sunlight and water.

The thanks to the teacher are not only directed towards the ones who are just guiding our training but also towards their teachers and all the others who contributed their energy in favor of the development of karate. Furthermore we need opponents to try and develop our technical abilities as well as we need teachers, because they help us to learn from our own errors. And it does not matter whether the opponent is a beginner or an advanced student, a junior or a senior. One should be able to learn from everyone. Me too, I still learn from the often surprising questions of my students. I must feel gratitude and show my respect to this. My father addressed even younger students, attaching the honorable *san* to their names and used an extra polite style of speech. The old masters like Funakoshi treated their students the same way. This is *rei* towards the students.

Finally the mutual *rei* is not only addressed to the fellows of the *dōjō* but to all the people who contribute to our karate training, who help that we can meet and practice together, to the parents who allow and finance our training, the wives who must spend the evenings alone when we are exercising in the *dōjō* and to our friends who help us in our work with great understanding. It is the meaning of the mutual *rei* to thank all these people.

No one who practices karate must ever forget to show his respect for the spirit of *shurei*. Unless one expresses one's respect in advance one does not have the right to endanger his opponent by swinging his fists and legs against him. Karate even demands to show respect particularly towards an opponent one intends to harm.

Master Funakoshi Gichin is said to have always told his beginners that all the movements in the karate *kata* deliver the following message: "I swear in the light sent by the gods of this world that I do not want to fight. But I also cannot escape. So, why not drop it? But if you insist I am going to withstand." This is the reason why all karate *kata* begin with blocking and end with blocking. They teach without words the maxim "there is no first attack in karate" which also conveys the spirit of *shurei*.

The Meaning of the Karate Techniques

As explained above, under the rule of the Shimazu clan from the Satsuma fief in southern Kyūshū the Okinawan natives were forbidden by pain of death to own weapons. So, under very oppressive living conditions, in many life-and-death struggles, they developed and systemized a variety of self-defense techniques which finally became karate. It is clear that they could not fix their secret technical knowledge and ideas in a written form.

In contrast to karate, for sword fighting an excellent written heritage exists due to the fact that the sword styles of the noble houses where protected by the central government of the Tokugawa and by other lords. There are, for example, Miyamoto Musashi's (1584-1645) work *The Book of the Five Rings* (*Gorin no Sho*)[106] and the *Book about the Rules for Warriors of the Noble Houses*

[106] Miyamoto, M.: The Book of Five Rings. Boston: Shambhala 2000.

(*Heihō Kaden Sho*)[107] written by the great sword master Yagyū Munenori (1571-1646). These books were written in a very elaborate and rich style. The technical and spiritual aspects could be explained by using a clear and metaphysical language since the samurai could understand such a language because they were educated in Confucianism and Zen Buddhism.

It is sad to say, but there are no written records of karate to describe its essence so brilliantly as the old books on sword fighting or *jūjutsu* do. But we received from our ancestors, the old masters of karate, the *kata*, which they have created with their blood and their hearts, putting their whole souls into them. To build the *kata*, they combined a lot of well-proven techniques, removing their weaknesses, stressing their strengths. In doing so they arrived at a perfect expression of their fighting techniques and the corresponding spiritual contents.

Compared to the *kata* for sword fighting or *jūjutsu*, karate *kata* are longer. They are a sequence of scenes designed like a little drama. A long karate *kata* can include more than 70 different actions. Sword fighting or *jūjutsu kata*, however, are only single attack or defense actions. They are not dynamic forms like karate *kata* but static models. In fact, for the two *kata* types even different *kanji* are used.

This specific character of karate *kata* must be well understood. Karate was created and developed in the Tokugawa period and was not protected and promoted by the ruling system like sword fighting. Instead it was highly suppressed by the officials. The technical and the psychological and spiritual knowledge could not be put down in a sophisticated language as it could be done for sword fighting. In order to explain the techniques to the students by using *kata*, to demonstrate what was to be observed in particular and what was not done correctly, one needed rather long sequences of actions. The old masters could not describe the techniques with written words or pictures and had to express them in the *kata*. This needed a lot of time, brains and effort. Furthermore, the *kata* had to become a means to teach without words not only the technical aspects but also the psychological and spiritual abilities to turn the methods of killing into methods of saving lives.

---

107 German edition: Yagyū, M.: Der Weg des Samurai. Anleitung zum strategischen Handeln. 4th ed. Munich: Piper 2004.

Photo 90: Funakoshi Gichin (1868-1957).

The misleading prejudice that karate compared to *kendō* or *jūdō* was a rather gross method of fighting, something simple used for "real fights" or street fights, is caused by the fact that there is no written tradition. From the beginning of the Meiji period after 1868 it was not necessary anymore to study karate like a secret science. After my father had moved to mainland Japan to spread karate, he did a lot to put the techniques and spirit of karate into words. To reach the levels of other kinds of Japanese martial arts like *kendō* or *jūdō*, karate, too, needed suitable words to be explained to the average people, being easy to understand and convincing. In my father's books as well in the writings of master Funakoshi these efforts became evident.

But in the juvenile stage of karate, time was too short to be spent for this purpose. After the outbreak of the Greater East Asia War in 1941 Japan was painted in the uniform color of war, and a country in the state of war is no suitable place for karate.[108] After the war, under allied occupation, karate was totally forbidden until 1951. In 1952 my father died. He was soon followed by master Miyagi (1953) and master Funakoshi (1957). Shortly before he died master Funakoshi had just finished his last article for the magazine *Nihon Shūhō* and the last words he has ever written are: "To love the fists and apply techniques is a process shaping the human character and teaching what is right and just. This is the true aim of *budō*. The fist and Zen are one (*ken Zen ichi*). To master the way of karate we must strive for the utmost and even go into religion. So, devote yourself to the faith (*kenkyo tare*)! This is the way we fellows talk to each other."

[108] See footnote 9 on p. 15.

“Karate is Zen in motion.” My father had had this idea already in his years on Okinawa. This was a few decades before master Sō Dōshin (1911-1980), who after the war had founded the *Shōrinji kempō*, voiced the idea “Fist and Zen are one”, which he had derived from the word by Zen master Takuan (1573-1645) “Sword and Zen are one”.

The reasons for the early death of my father can surely be found in the circumstances of life in the post-war years, the lack of food and the overwork. If he had lived longer and would have had the time to explain the mental and spiritual aspects of karate methodically, the karate of today would be quite different. But unfortunately this did not happen.

The “Superhuman Techniques” of Ueshiba Morihei

After his death Ueshiba Morihei (1883-1969), the founder of *aikidō*, was called “god of *budō*”. There is probably no other personality in the world of *budō* about whom more mysterious stories are told. Among the many heroic stories is the one about his fight against the famous *sumō* fighter Tenryū Saburō (1903-1989), who after resignation from Japanese *sumō* had gone to Manchuria to found his own style of *sumō*. It is said that even by applying all his energies he was not able to move Ueshiba Morihei even a little bit.

At another occasion master Ueshiba fought at the same time against several *kendō* masters who could not hit him with their bamboo swords even once.

Master Ueshiba was a close friend of master Konishi Yasuhiro from Tōkyō, who also helped me very much. Once, master Ueshiba met the outstanding boxer Tsuneo Piston[109] Horiguchi (1914-1950) in master Konishi’s *dōjō*. He was said to have blocked a deadly punch by the boxer in with his little finger only and then brought him down to the ground.

Master Motobu Chōki (1871-1944), too, who was well known in real fight circles as “Motobu the monkey” (Motobu Sāru), had an encounter with the same boxer. He could block endless series of Horiguchi’s punches. Like master Ueshiba he was already a relatively old man. Their strength could not have been mere physical power.

---

[109] Piston: Engl. nickname. – Translator’s comment.

Master Ueshiba's explanation of *aikidō* was very religious and mystical. It is widely known that he was under the influence of the religious teachings of Deguchi Onisaburō.[110] For him *aikidō* meant to a high degree to practice a kind of Shintō. His son Kisshōmaru, the later head of the house of Ueshiba, wrote a biography on the founder of *aikidō* titled *Aikidō Kaiso Ueshiba Morihei Den*. In this book he describes an episode from 1924 when Ueshiba accompanied the religious leader Deguchi on one of his journeys to Mongolia. At that time he truly walked on the line of death and experienced enlightenment.

> *Once, when the squad was marching through the mountains, they suddenly came under heavy fire from the mountain shadows to the left and right. The attack was focused on the sedan chair in which the religious leader Deguchi was carried. One bullet had already grazed it. But master Ueshiba went in front of the sedan in order to protect his religious teacher. Later he told: "I could not go away even one step. So, I had to evade the bullets by moving my head and my body aside. I stared at the bullets coming from the left and from the right side. I sensed them intuitively but very clearly. A moment earlier than the bullet came I saw a white light flying up to me. And just when I had turned my body aside the bullet whistled by. I already often had experienced similar things, but in that very moment the essence of* budō *was revealed to me in a quite natural way. I understood that I can sense my enemies' intentions to kill intuitively, and that I can do this the better, the clearer and calmer my soul becomes."*

Since this adventure the spiritual aspect became dominant in master Ueshiba's explanation of *budō*. With respect to the martial techniques he was a direct student of the famous *jūjutsu* master Takeda Sōkaku (1848-1953). Takeda represented a martial art called *Daitō ryū Aiki bujutsu* which in the 16th century became the house style of the Aizu branch of the Takeda clan that was taught only secretly to the members of the lord's family and the

[110] Deguchi Wanisaburō (Onisaburō) (1871-1948). Japanese monk, member of the Ōmoto kyō sect founded by Deguchi Nao (1836-1918). This sect is based upon the teachings of Shintō, Buddhism and Tibetan shamanism. It taught the existence of a universal God becoming manifest in the whole Nature by the pulsation of the life energy (*ki*). Master Ueshiba Morihei joined the sect in 1922. – Habersetzer, R. and G.: Encyclopédie des Arts Martiaux. Paris: Amphora 2004.

higher ranking samurai.[111] It was a complex martial art in which the notion of *aiki* played a special role.[112] Only in the Meiji era the *Daitō ryū* for the first time became known beyond the borders of the Aizu region. This was the merit of master Takeda. He was said to have flung around several opponents at once by using a special throwing technique or stopped all by kicking the leg of only one of them. It is also said that he was able to snatch away at the same time all the bamboo swords of a number of opponents who had attacked him.

One of his disciples was Sagawa Yukiyoshi (1902-1998), who became a famous master, too. In July 1998 the magazine *Karate Dō* was published as a special edition about me and the *Shitō ryū*. To honor master Sagawa, who had just died at the age of 95, it also included an article written by him and photographs of his performances. While he was still alive one of his students Kimura Tatsuo wrote a book about him and published it at Kōdansha publishers with the title *The Invisible Force* (*tōmei na chikara*). In this book he tries to show that in contrast to master Ueshiba, master Sagawa was focused on the technical interpretation of *aikidō*. He cited master Sagawa with the following statements: "*Aikidō* is a technique to make the opponent powerless", or "*Aiki* is by no means incomprehensible. It is rather something very reasonable. All my techniques include a moment of *aiki* used to destabilize the opponent. After his balance is undermined, I am free to apply my techniques. For a long time I have been studying the problem how to react when one is held in a way one cannot move at all.

---

[111] The Aizu ruled the Aizu region, an area northeast of Edo (Tōkyō), situated in the western part of the present prefecture of Fukushima. – Translator's comment.

[112] *Aiki*: Jpn. "Unification of the energy (*ki*)". State of mind and attitude aspired by every practitioner of a martial art by concentrating on the center of his "vital energy" (*hara*). The concept refers to the release and the control of this inner energy (which is part of the cosmic energy) the fighter can use in a fight, if required, by projecting it outwards (*kime*). In a greater context *aiki* is as well a physical as a mental attitude enabling the practitioner to win without fighting – this is possible by focusing the energy concentrated in this way on a potential opponent. In this case it is said that the attitude is "charged with the *kiai*". If this energy is used in an explosive and dynamic way it is said that the fighter "lets out the *kiai*" – this can be done without a noise or in the form of a short and powerful cry accompanying the action (cf. footnote 36 on p. 36). – Habersetzer, R. and G.: Encyclopédie des Arts Martiaux. Paris: Amphora 2004.

Photo 91: Ueshiba Morihei (1883-1969).

Finally I came to the conclusion that the *aiki* one uses in such situations is something physical. From this moment *aiki* was no longer a secret to me. But what counts is to continue to study such things." Master Sagawa stressed the rational aspects of *aiki* and showed that any kind of technique could be explained as a natural phenomenon and that there is nothing mystical to search for.

There is an exercise in the *Daitō ryū* that helps to understand what *aiki* is. It is called *aiki age*. Both wrists firmly gripped by the opponent are at the same time raised and pulled away. If with this exercise one has thoroughly learned the *aiki* technique one can make the opponent powerless and unable to resist in the very moment his hands are touching oneself whatever technique he might use to attack.

The Main Principle of Karate: The Body Follows the Mind

When I was talking about this problem with the editor of this book[113] he said: "Master Mabuni, you yourself made strong foreigners and 5th or 6th *dan* grade fellows look the fool, didn't you? Could you show me how it works, are there any special techniques?" Actually there are no such techniques but I said: "Ok, let's try. Pull my arm as strong as you can." The editor is in his 30s and has been practicing since his 20s and holds a black belt, but not in *Shitō ryū*. Although he tried with all his power to pull my

[113] Yokoyama Masahiko, the publisher of the Japanese edition. See afterword, p. 224 et seq.

arm he did not manage to move or twist it even a little. One may call this the "power of *ki*", "energy of life" or "technique". These are only words but all of them are right. I am already in my 80s. My height is 1.58 m (5 ft 2 in). So, physically I am not superior at all.

I mentioned above that the thrusts and kicks in karate make use of a method called "falling tree" (*tōboku hō*). I am not an expert in natural science but I understand that exploiting the natural fall to earth or gravity to the maximum degree in order to gain speed and power for one's own actions finally means nothing else but "to become one with earth and borrow power from the earth". In his book *Introduction into Attack and Defense Techniques in Karate Kempō* my father wrote: "The essence of *budō* is spirit. The techniques are only its reflection." So, as already explained above, the most important maxim of karate is that "the body follows the mind".[114] To become one with earth and to generate power from it, one must unite oneself with the earth mentally and spiritually. This sphere of mental unity is the same as the sphere of "emptiness" (*kū*) which is a central topic in Zen Buddhism. That is why karate can be called "Zen in motion". And, as shown above, it is no accident that karate means *empty* hand. But that is not all. In Zen one gains inner silence by uniting mentally and spiritually with the earth. In karate the body is acting out this unity to express the *bu*[115]. In my opinion *aiki* is basically the same. Master Ueshiba offered a religious and mystical explanation while master Sagawa understood it as a technique. For both, *aiki* was finally part of the sphere of mental unity. But with regard to this unity of spirit and technique master Ueshiba was more conscious of the mental and spiritual aspect while for master Sagawa the technical aspect was dominant. However, the only difference between them are the words they used to describe this.

Budō is rational technique but this rationality does not necessarily correspond to western ideas of rationalism. It is not easy to explain *aiki* with words. It is always possible to express scientific problems objectively by means of formulas and figures so that any results can be calculated. But

---

114 See p. 112 et sqq.

115 *Bu*: The ability to fight; actually to defend oneself. – Translator's comment.

I do not think that it would be of any use to try to understand the *aiki* rationally as causal relation in a similar way.

1.2 Beyond the Natural Movements of the Body

Reacting to Natural Changes

In recent years karate became more and more defined by sports science and reduced to data. Training programs are calculated and chances of winning are analyzed. But even practicing ten thousand times with the *makiwara* how to hit the opponent properly or practicing hard in order to reach a certain striking speed or to destroy an increasing number of tiles will not be sufficient for the confrontation with a real opponent, because he will move and change all the time.

This is similar to someone trying hard to prepare for a university entrance examination. Finally he manages to develop his academic abilities to a degree that even his teachers are convinced that he will pass. But there is still no guarantee that he will be accepted by the university he has applied for. For example he could become ill shortly before the examination. His father's enterprise could go bankrupt or some other unexpected things could happen so that he would fail the examination.

There is a force connecting cause and effect. In Buddhism it is called karma[116] or fate (*en*). According to the idea of karma, a good cause is connected with a good effect, and vice versa a bad cause with a bad result. The ability to smash a pile of ten tiles with one strike may be helpful to knock someone down. But whether one can overthrow the opponent in reality depends on the karma. The Kannon sutra explains the power of Kannon who is the goddess of mercy. This power is the karma:

---

[116] Karma: Sanskrit. Law of causality according to which all actions, words and thoughts dispose of a density and a dynamic force expressing themselves in the course of successive existences (Samsura) until the karma is completely consumed (destroyed) which leads to the final liberation (Nirvana). This religious and philosophical concept comes from Hinduism (Upanishads) and has been adopted by Buddhism and Zen Buddhism. – Habersetzer, R. and G.: Encyclopédie des Arts Martiaux. Paris: Amphora 2004.

If someone wants to hurt you
And pushes you into a great firepit –
If you think of the power of Kannon
The firepit will change into a pond.
If from the peak of the mount Sumeru
Someone would push you down –
If you think of the power of Kannon
Like the sun you will stand firm in the sky.[117]

There are lots of similar verses in the sutra. Maybe some of the readers will consider this to be ridiculous. The sutra states that the goddess Kannon creates the relation which as karma connects cause and effect. Because of this power one should believe in this goddess. This power connecting cause and effect could also be called the "in-between" (*ma*) or "luck" (*anbai*). This sounds a bit vague. But it is actually something very reasonable. Maybe the following examples can help to understand this.

Japanese temple carpenters are able to hit the nails exactly in the middle of the plank without taking measure in advance. If one would check this one would find the intervals absolutely the same. Even of 100 nails there will be not even one that has missed the right position. Once a joiner who makes saw handles told me he could realize even the slightest deviation of a fraction of an inch only by taking a handle in his hand. The amateur may think this to be almost supernatural but for a professional joiner or carpenter this is quite normal.

Most of us can remember the day they rode a bicycle for the first time. One had tried and tried and jealously watched others who already could handle it. But then suddenly one mounted the bike and started riding as if it was not difficult at all. This cannot be explained in a rational manner. One does not learn cycling by explanations such as: "Do it this way, do it that way..." If anything, this would be rather disturbing.

[117] *Ke shi kō gai i suiraku da kakyō nenpi kannon riki kakyō henjō chi. / Wakuzai shumibu ininsho suida nenpi kannon riki nyochi ko kū jū.*

"God-like" Techniques, and the Falling Dewdrop

In Japanese there is the expression "mental state of a falling dewdrop" (*rakuro no ki*). It describes the moment a dewdrop is just getting off the tip of a leaf to fall down. This happens without any deliberation. The dewdrop does not plan to fall in a certain moment. It just falls. This is exactly the same with the moment one is riding a bike for the first time. When this happened one may have felt the bicycle, which had always been something separate, now becoming a unit with oneself. This moment, when one feels: "Now it's time!", this almost supernatural timing is called *rakuro no ki*. If one ever has fully experienced this sensation one will realize that what up to now was only accidental was in truth a necessity. That is what master Sagawa had in mind when he said: "If one understands *aiki* rationally one will understand that there are no supernatural techniques at all."

Nevertheless all this is not easy to understand. In a *budō* encounter one is confronted with a living opponent. So, it is always something mutual, something relative. It is not easy to find the absolute within this relativity, but that is what it is all about.

The name of the goddess of mercy Kannon is written with two characters. One means "to see, to look or to watch" and the other means "sound". Hence the meaning of the word is "to see a sound". But this special character for "to see" indicates a certain aspect of seeing: observing and comprehending by looking from an elevated position.[118] This expresses the idea that the goddess Kannon sees and understands the various phenomena of the human world from the point of view of an absolute world transcending the five senses (*gen, ni, bi, setsu, shin*), transcending even will, consciousness and thought. The view of Kannon is the view of *budō*. Also the "seeing" of Miyamoto Musashi was not the mere physical one but rather the "comprehending" one of Kannon.

The so-called supernatural techniques are born out of a moment which can be understood by the view of the goddess Kannon as the "falling of a dewdrop". To "see" and "understand" a fight with a continually changing opponent during which one is also permanently changing with the view

[118] The seeing of the stork or the crane. – Translator's comment.

of Kannon, one must distance oneself from the own self and transcend even the duality of cause and effect. To put it symbolically: The soul must become one with heaven and earth. This is the aspect of the *shin* in the martial arts. If there would be only this aspect, *budō* would be exactly the same as Zen. But in *budō* out of this unity of the soul with heaven and earth one must move the body (*tai*) and display the techniques (*gi*) in order to express the ability to fight (*bu*). When *shin*, *gi* and *tai* are interacting harmonically, the "supernatural techniques" (*kami waza*) can emerge.

After these explanations it might become clearer that the only difference between the masters Ueshiba and Sagawa is the more or less stronger accentuation of the mental or the physical-technical side of the relation.

The Magic Experience of the Control of Gravity

A rather long time ago I visited Mexico. After this visit I was invited to attend a national contest in the USA. There I met a Japanese who took part in the competitions and we talked a little afterwards.

He told me that he was hardening his hands with a hammer every day. His hands had even become bigger in doing so. He finally added: "Actually, I do not know very much about karate. But with such hands I can knock everybody out." But if one uses the fists against an opponent, there is no guarantee that the cause of an extraordinary strong punch will result in a deadly strike. The opposite case may happen: following the karma, a rather slight punch or kick can be devastating for the opponent. In boxing there is the so-called "lucky punch". What counts is to positively influence one's fate, the karma.

Master Motobu was able to block the punches of Piston Horiguchi because he had what is called *mi kiri*. That means that he was able to assess the overall situation, to foresee what would happen next and to make quick and clear decisions on this basis. So he could avoid the normally "logical" result of being hit by the young and powerful boxer. It is a truly miraculous moment when a strike that seems to be absolutely deadly does not result in a deadly effect but perhaps even in a completely different one. Such a moment does not occur twice. One must perceive such a moment clearly and strike or block. One may use a throw, a joint-locking technique or block a thrust. There is always a point where one can neutralize the opponent's power. In case of a thrust the moment immediately before the opponent's arm is fully stretched is essential. This is the exact moment for the counterattack. In any case one must prevent the opponent of reaching the result he was expecting. To put it more concrete: The center of the space both opponents are occupying is the center of gravity. This must be controlled. I mentioned above that one day the editor of this book had tried to push or pull my arm. But he could not move it because I controlled the center of gravity in the space occupied by the two of us. I had the control to manipulate this center of balance or gravity with my arm. Of course all this is not easy to be explained with words.

I think that the above-explained is valid for the *aiki*, too. The *aiki* is exactly the moment or point of controlling the center of gravity. By manipulating it, one gains control over the own movements and the opponent's movements. If one can manage this, the number of opponents to be confronted with will not matter at all.

Once master Takeda Sōkaku was asked: "Can you reach *aiki* even when you are in the air?" So, five or six fellows had to lift him up. Then, from above he pressed them together and only by kicking the leg of one of them, he finally managed to control them all. In the book *The Secret Japanese Jūjutsu*[119] there is an illustration showing master Sagawa with such a technique which is based on the control of the center of gravity in the space occupied by oneself and the opponents.

No matter how big or strong a building may be, if the center of gravity that keeps the balance is hit, even a little impulse can make it collapse. But if the balance is not undermined, the building can withstand even the strongest earthquakes.

So, the aim is to find the center of balance, to control and to break it within a fraction of a second. If this problem is understood and one wants to learn how to control the center of gravity, theoretical studies will surely not be enough. As in case of the "luck" (*anbai*) of the carpenter, the karate practitioner needs to learn it on a bodily level. In the beginning of this

[119] *Hiden Nihon jujutsu* by Matsuda Ryūchi.

process one is in a state in which body and soul are still not united. By learning karate step by step the body learns unconsciously to move in the right way. The original Okinawan karate provides the methods enabling this process of learning.

Ambling, and the Parallel Punch

Above I tried to explain that there is no rhythm or beat in karate. Now I would like to ask the reader, how he normally walks. Everyone would admit that we naturally walk swinging our arms from the left and right of our bodies in opposite directions while alternately the leg of the opposite side is stepping forward. Already the little children are taught that this way of walking is the proper and healthy way. Also at sports events or school ceremonies people normally march moving arms and legs alternately. Moving arms and legs parallel in the same direction is laughed at as being "unnatural and foolish". But in the past this was the natural way to walk. Marching with legs and arms moving alternately was introduced as part of the Meiji reform (*Meiji ishin*) according to the German model. Before the reforms, arms and legs were moved at the same time in the same direction.

Ethnologists call this kind of walking *nanba aruki*. Today it can be seen in the *kabuki* and *nō* theater or in *bon* dances. *Nanba* is a basic figure in traditional Japanese art showing the right half of the body with the arm and leg stretched forward. The peasants took this position holding the hoe in the dry fields. This posture is specifically Japanese and one cannot find it in Korea or in China or elsewhere. If one walks in the western style with Japanese clothing it would loosen because the hips are twisting.

Furthermore traditional Japanese footwear forced Japanese to touch the ground first with the tip of the foot and use a shuffle style of walking (*suri ashi*). The toe strings of the *zōri*[120] and *geta*[121] keep tight only by ambling.

[120] *Zōri*: Jpn. Sandals made of rice straw, with two thongs (*hanao*) for attaching them to the foot; the thongs are led between the big toe and the other toes. Generally *zōri* sandals are worn together with *tabi* socks having a separated big toe. – Habersetzer, R. and G.: Encyclopédie des Arts Martiaux. Paris: Amphora 2004.

But ambling did not become common in order to adjust to a certain clothing consisting of *kimono* and *geta*. The clothing developed in order to correspond with the common way of walking. Recent research proved that walking with *geta* is healthier and less exhausting because the toes must hold the toe strings and the leg steps forward in a natural way with the tips of the toes touching the ground first. Wearing shoes one cannot but touch the ground first with the heels.

From the point of view of *bujutsu*, ambling causes each half of the body to move in the same direction and position. So, for example to evade a sudden sword attack immediate reaction is possible. If the whole half of the body does not react at once the sword might hit the leg in spite of an evasion maneuver.

Of course ambling does not allow to run as fast as it would be possible with alternate arm and leg movements. The hips must be lowered and one moves with a shuffling walk. Although it might not be evident as in the case of the *budō* exercise of the "falling tree" (*tōboku hō*), by ambling, too, one is unconsciously lending power form the earth. Messengers in feudal Japan (*hikyaku*) ran in this way with a relatively low speed but they could manage distances between 120 and 180 miles each day. Using present marathon style running one could not achieve this.

In karate the *nanba aruki* principle can be found in the *jun zuki*[122], a punch with the fist on the same side of the body whose leg is in front. This is the basic method of a fist attack in traditional karate. But to the beginner the alternate or counter thrust (*gyaku zuki*), where the other leg is in front, always seems to be easier to learn. But not only beginners feel a bit uncomfortable with the *jun zuki*. Nowadays even for breaking tiles and wooden boards, the *gyaku zuki* is preferred. But this is not the actual karate punch but rather one that belongs to boxing or kick-boxing where

---

[121] *Geta* are Japanese wooden sandals with (rounded) rectangular profile. Small transversal wooden rods are mounted below them in order to ensure a certain distance to the ground. *Geta* sandals are attached to the foot the same way like *zori* sandals. Traditionally, *geta* sandals are worn together with a *kimono*. – Habersetzer, R. and G.: Encyclopédie des Arts Martiaux. Paris: Amphora 2004. See also photograph on p. 52 (young Mabuni Kenei and his father).

[122] In *Shōtokan* karate this technique is called *oi zuki*. – Publisher's comment.

the body is moved according to the principles of sports. This is symbolic for the erosion of karate. In present karate, the principles of body control and the individual movements belong more and more to the principles of western sports.

Today ambling makes Japanese feel ashamed and moreover would not be rational because they wear western clothing and western shoes. This problem points to the fact that culture is something very complex. It includes various ways of clothing, food, housing, spirituality and body control which correspond to the historical, geographical, racial and ethnical peculiarities. Karate is not an exception. It has developed in the context of a great culture, and now becomes more and more a kind of modern "physical culture". Meanwhile it is an urgent task to say clearly how modernization did influence karate.

The Release of Power in Budō and Sports

The alternate positioning of arms and legs, making a movement forward with the arm while the leg of the same side of the body supports backward can be considered as the main principle of sports, no matter if it is baseball, tennis, golf or whatever. According to the natural law of action and reaction, the firmer the stance the stronger the counter motion will be. The swing for the counter motion is generated from a turn or twist of the hips. The centrifugal force generated from the turn of the body is used like a pendulum. This is also typical for boxing and kick-boxing.

From the point of view of mechanics this is the most efficient method to generate speed and power. But in *budō*, which is an element of Japanese culture, power is lent from nature and not generated by moving against it with full force. Naturally, for lending energy, action is needed to cause reaction or motion. But the way the first motion is produced is different in *budō* and sports. This is very difficult to explain. As well in case of *jun zuki* as in that of *gyaku zuki* the supporting leg not only stems against the ground, but for a short moment the knee muscles are relaxed and power is released. For a very short time the body is attracted by the gravity and falls. The body is left to the effect of gravity and the force of gravity released in this way is used for the punch. This movement is barely seen from the outside. It is commonly called "to take the knees out" (*hiza o nuku*). By this technique of "taking the knees out" one falls towards the center of gravity of the space occupied by the two opponents. The explosive dynamic energy required for the punch is not generated by turning the hips as done in sports but by lowering them. This is connected with the sensation that the center of gravity is always in front of the hips. It is the same sensation that accompanies ambling: In order to advance one first has to move the hips forward, and the body follows as if pulled by them. That is the principle of the "falling tree".

Under philosophical aspects, under the aspect of *shin*, one could say that by abandoning the body the self is negated thus becoming one with the earth. In this case there is neither subject nor object.

The Crab Walk, and "Taking the Knees out"

Watching experienced karate students performing *kata* it looks as if they were moving only arms and hands while their legs seem to be hovering over the ground like a cloud. By moving this way in a real fight, the opponent cannot foresee one's movements. An expert fighter is truly "hovering" unexpectedly into the opponent.

In the *Kōsōkun kata* of *Shuri-te* and the *Sūpārinpai kata* of *Naha-te* there is a jumped double kick (*nidan geri*). In *kata* competitions the karateka always tend to jump very high. But actually it should look as if one suddenly rises or emerges out of a firm stance. In fact the karateka himself is feeling as if he is rising up to the surface instead of jumping using the own power. People who can do this can already control their center of gravity freely. But in order to be able to do so one must already master the technique of the *hiza o nuku*.

The famous grandmasters of *sumō*, the *Yokozuna*[123] Taihō Koki (born in 1940) and Kitanoumi Toshimitsu (born in 1953), always "took their

[123] *Yokozuna*: Jpn. Grandmaster of *sumō*. This title has been awarded since the 17th century. Until now, about 70 *sumō* masters obtained this eminently respectable title. – Habersetzer, R. and G.: Encyclopédie des Arts Martiaux. Paris: Amphora 2004.

Photo 92: Motobu Chōki practicing the *Naihanchi kata*.

Photo 93: The 27th *Yokozuna* Tochigiyama Moriya (1892-1952) adopting *shiko dachi*.

knees out" in a very spectacular way. Out of a position with very lowered hips[124], the *shiko dachi*, they adopted after the ritual stomping, they could raise their legs alternately very high without any movement of the upper part of the body.

The technique of the *hiza o nuku* can be practiced and be made conscious by means of an elementary *kata* of the *Shuri-te* called *Naifanchi* (*Naihanchi*). For this *kata* one adopts a special stance (*naihanchi dachi*) which allows to walk like a crab (*kani aruki*) to the left and to the right so that the head does not rise and remains always exactly on the same height. This *kata* clearly proves the importance of the *hiza o nuki* in karate. To my knowledge there is no other martial art but karate where this technique is systematically taught.

For this reason the first *kata* the old masters used to teach was the *Naifanchi* and the disciples had to practice it in muddy paddy fields[125]. The outstanding master in real-fight karate, Motobu Chōki, is said to have known only this *kata* that is so important because it teaches correct walk-

---

[124] ...and with almost horizontally positioned thighs; see photo 93. – Translator's comment.

[125] Most of the year paddy fields use to be submerged in water. – Publisher's comment.

ing as the basis of all *kata*. And master Itosu purportedly used to say: "Walking is *Naifanchi*." Of course this does not mean that walking should always be like crab-walking. Walking with the "knees taken out" must be adjusted to suit everyday life.

Japanese *budō* is a cultural heritage created by the spirit of the Japanese people who always strived to be one with nature. Karate developed as a pure martial art of the empty hand during 300 years, in a special environment without weapons, under the rule of the lords of Satsuma. It became a *budō* art which reached the highest level of body control by allowing body and mind to become one with the earth thus mobilizing its energies.

Even people with lack of confidence with regard to their physical and fighting abilities can experience the mental and spiritual unity with the earth and enjoy its inexhaustible virtues, if only they practice the old *kata* of the Okinawan karate carefully.

2 Victory or Defeat

2.1 Their Famous Fights

Ōyama Masutatsu's Report

I am often asked to tell some heroic stories about the life and great fights of the founder of the *Shitō* karate. But not only my father, master Funakoshi or master Miyagi, too, were very gentle and kind people who actually did not like fighting. My father used to say: "Never talk about karate outside the *dōjō*." On occasions when people were drinking alcohol it was especially dangerous to talk about karate because one never could tell whether someone might get the idea to provoke a fight and to say: "Let's see who is stronger!" As a policeman on Okinawa, my father managed to arrest criminals with the help of karate several times. But he did not use it for personal aims even once. Me too, I was often asked: "It is incredible, are you really a karateka?!" Of course I do not hide it but I do not look as if I would do karate.

Not a single heroic story is handed down about my father's teachers Itosu and Higaonna. One of the last disciples of master Itosu was master Chibana Chōshin, who founded the *Kobayashi ryū*.[126] He was said to have a very gentle way of moving and speaking, like a woman. And master Itosu, too, used to call him with his boyhood name and to utter rather female sentences like: "And don't hang around. Go straight home!" Master Itosu and master Chibana were just *bushi* with well-balanced characters.

When I was younger, I often did martial arts demonstrations together with master Ōyama Masutatsu[127], the founder of the *Kyokushin-kai* karate.

---

[126] *Kobayashi ryū*: "School of the little forest", Okinawan karate style founded in 1920 by Chibana Chōshin (1885-1965). It belongs to the *Shōrin ryū* branch. "*Kobayashi*" is an Okinawan reading of the characters for "Shaolin" ("small forest"). – Habersetzer, R. and G.: Encyclopédie des Arts Martiaux. Paris: Amphora 2004.

[127] Ōyama Masutatsu (1923-1994) was a Korean karate master who lived in Japan since 1938. His original name was Hyung Yee. After having studied *Shōtōkan* karate in the *dōjō* of Funakoshi Gichin, and later *Gōjū* ryū karate with Sō Neishu, he founded the style *Kyokushin-kai* (originally called *Ōyama ryū*). Ōyama was famous for his fights with bulls. Since 1951, in about 50 of such fights he killed three bulls with his punches, and with his "sword-hand" he deprived several others of their horns. – Ibid.

In our later years we met from time to time to dine together in the restaurant Kandagawa in the north of Ōsaka. He was five years younger than me and died already some years ago. Recently one of my students showed me the autobiography of master Ōyama titled *Wind and Fist.* It includes an episode about my father that became an incentive for him to dabble in "killing bulls":

Looking for a Challenge

When I hear this I must think of an episode regarding Mabuni Kenwa who had founded the Shitō karate. Mabuni came from Okinawa. Okinawa belongs to Japan but in mainland Japan the people from there were treated like strangers. Once he was visited by a high ranking Japanese government official. Mabuni prepared the bath for him. When the official sat in the bathtub he said the provoking sentence:

"What about finding out who is the stronger one?" When Mabuni heard this he started to break fire wood with his flat hand exactly with the spot where a big bruise could be seen. When the official realized this he said: "It looks as if you want to frighten me?!" So, he got a helpful lecture.

In autumn Okinawa is afflicted by typhoons. Then powerful rainstorms are ravaging the island. Mabuni used to take a tatami *mat to withstand the rainstorm. He did this to strengthen his ability to resist. He is said to have stayed in this posture for up to two hours. Because of such exercises nobody was stronger than him. His thrust was so devastating he was even said to be able to knock down a bull. [...]*

And I asked myself: "But could Mabuni and the other masters really do this?" And so I had found my challenge.[128]

Well, I do not know whether my father really did ever knock down a bull. A long time ago a member of the Okinawa fellowship in Ōsaka told me: "Your father is a real expert. He can jump up out of his seat and kick the

[128] In order to understand why master Ōyama was inspired by the mentioned episode to kill bulls one must take into consideration that Ōyama Masutatsu was Korean by birth. So, in the nationalist Japan of that time he had to try hard to gain recognition, and for this reason Mabuni Kenwa as a native of Okinawa was a particular example for him. The fact that Mabuni Kenwa commanded respect of the arrogant Government official by demonstrating his force inspired Ōyama Masutatsu to try to earn respect in the eyes of the Japanese by demonstrating his force, i.e. by his fighting with bulls. – Translator's comment.

ceiling." I answered that I had never seen my father doing this. But I assume that he was able to do so. Nevertheless, he did not do it in front of my eyes. Unfortunately there are not so many people left in the world of the *Shitō ryū* who personally knew my father. But everyone I asked about him confirmed that he was a warm-hearted and gentle person who never showed off with his abilities.

A Lack of Heroic Stories

Master Funakoshi was challenged three times to a duel by Toku Sanbō (1886-1945), the roughneck of the *Kōdōkan*. Funakoshi always refused, stressing that karate was not made for this, but Toku did not listen and insisted. So, he complained about Toku "causing problems" to his teacher Kanō Jigorō. Even after Toku insulted master Funakoshi in public, calling him a coward who evades fighting, Funakoshi did not respond at all. In the past it was normal that the great masters not only in karate but also in *kenjutsu* or *jūjutsu* evaded fighting when they had reached the state of mental and spiritual unity with the earth called *isshin*. They embodied the principle of harmony so that open conflict could not occur in the sphere surrounding them.

Master Miyahira Masahide of the *Shōrin ryū* who was respected as one of the masters of the Okinawa-te (*ti-bushi*), is said to have complained about the lack of chances for real fighting in karate despite endless years of practice, "I don't understand which purpose karate is learned for. It's just a waste!" I guess he had not realized how his character had changed as the result of such a long time of study on his way to the essence of karate. In the end of such a development a personality emerges that does not need karate as a means for fighting. To my mind such a development of human character should rather be highly appreciated.

Also stories on famous fights in the world of sword fighting in most cases tell about the spiritual aspects, the expression of the *bu*, the ability to fight without direct physical involvement. Miyamoto Musashi is a good example for this, too. When he was young he fought with great passion. His famous battle with the Yoshioka clan and the fight with

Sasaki Kojirō[129] on the island of Ganryū-jima were episodes of his youth. But after this fight (he was just 28 old) he dedicated himself thoroughly to the development of the *Nitō ryū*.[130] It is well-known that in his later days he abandoned worldly life to retire in the Reigandō grotto in the mountain Iwato in the vicinity of Kumamoto. There he practiced Zen, completed his famous *Gorin no Sho* and created a statue of Fudō Myō Ō[131]. This statue was a portrait of Musashi himself. The sword in his hand became a symbol of the Buddha. This showed how much he was imbued by the spirit of Zen Buddhism.

Miyamoto Musashi practicing his *Nitō ryū* using two *bokken*. Multicolored wood-block print by Utagawa Kuniyoshi (1798-1861).

In contrast to the world of sword fighting, there are scarcely any reports of famous fights or any other heroic stories about karate. Of course, this can be explained with the special situation on the Ryūkyū islands under

[129] See p. 81.
[130] Also called *Niten ichi ryū*. Sword-fighting technique with two swords, described by Miyamoto Musashi in his book *Gorin no Sho* (*The Book of Five Rings*). *Niten* ("two heavens") was also Miyamoto's pen name. – Habersetzer, R. and G.: Encyclopédie des Arts Martiaux. Paris: Amphora 2004.
[131] Fudō Myō Ō (Sanskrit: Vidya-raja), also called Acala or Acalanatha: Jpn. Deity; one of the five powerful Bodhisattvas that are conjured up by *kuji-kiri* (finger postures of the clasped hands with magical effects). This bodhisattva is designated as "eternal and imperturbable diamond", and his attitude of mind corresponds to the *fudōshin* in the martial arts (see p. 220 et seq.). He carries a sword (*ken*) as symbol of the victory of the knowledge (*myō*) over falsity, and a lacing for tying up the demons. – Ibid.

Photo 94: Statue of Fudō Myō Ō at the temple Okuno-in on mount Kōya in Japan.

the rule of the lords of Satsuma. Karate was a martial art to be taught only to people with moderate character, and lessons were held only at night, at hidden places and in absolute secrecy. The knowledge of the masters and the stories they had to tell were transferred only verbally. Even about the masters who lived 100 years ago nothing is known in detail, simply because there are no written records. The situation is quite different with regard to the masters who founded modern sword fighting or *jūdō* almost at the same time. But in the Shōwa period that began in the middle of the 1920s, writers and other intellectuals began to write down and publish the verbally transmitted material about the masters of karate. In my personal library there are, for example, books like *The History of the Ryūkyū Karate* that was written in those days, or *Biographies of Famous Karate Fighters* published recently. In these books one can find the same episodes with different interpretations and different lessons to be learned from. Even the facts may be rather different. And in the memories of the disciples the lives of the masters are often dramatized and romanticized.

There is a story about master Funakoshi who refused his nephew Kabuta to become his student. He explained his decision saying: "He is a crude person. When drinking he becomes violent. He is said to waste his time with fighting. Why should I teach karate to such a guy?!" – Today everyone can learn karate if only the fees are paid correctly. In the past, karate lessons were for free. But the students were chosen rigidly. So, the main reason for the lack of heroic stories about the past time masters of karate is the fact that they without exception did not like quarrelling or fighting. Ruffians who loved violence had no chance to enter their circles.

My father as well as master Funakoshi had started karate practice to improve their physical condition. For this aim my father practiced every day. Not only karate, every kind of *budō* demands many years of exercise in order to become a real expert. Today we often come across people who only want to learn karate to become stronger in fighting. Often such people are not patient enough for a long time of practice and quit after a few months.

Matsumura's Fight with his Bride

Master Matsumura Sōkon was the real founder of the *Shuri-te*. Already as a young man he received the honorary name "*Bushi*" Matsumura that preceded him like rolling thunder. He was considered to be a holy man of the fist. People said that there had never been anyone equal to him and that even in the future there would be no man like him. But he is also remembered as a man, who in his entire life had only once fought with another person. This person was his future wife Ume.[132]

There are a lot of stories about this event, some of them surely a bit exaggerated. I want to relate one version of the story that appears to be rather likely.

In the beginning of the 19th century, when master Matsumura was about 17 or 18 years of age, the western powers started to exert pressure on China and Japan. The atmosphere in the area became strained and nervous and also on Okinawa a feeling of change began to spread. In Shuri and Naha and everywhere common people like peasants, craftsmen and merchants, even the women in the noble families started to practice karate. In nearly every household one could find *makiwara*.

At that time a rumor reached the ears of Matsumura from Shuri that

[132] In most publications Matsumura's wife is named Yonamine Chiru. Publisher's comment.

the mayor of Yonabaru had a very beautiful 15 year old daughter called Ume. She was not only blessed with beauty and reason but also said to be quite good in fighting. Her father was reported to have offered her saying: "The man who can win a fight (*kake dameshi*) against her will be allowed to marry her." It goes without saying that men came from everywhere to challenge her. But nobody could win. Because the mayor was also a representative of the central Tokugawa government, it was a desirable aim to have his daughter as bride.

Matsumura thought: "She may be a strong fighter but finally she's only a woman", and he, too, put his name on the list to fight against Ume. Ume thought: "I suppose, tonight against Matsumura Sōkon, said to be the strongest in Shuri, this will be my last fight. – However, if I am prepared to counter his attack with *ai uchi*[133] I might even get a little chance to win." This way, arranging her mind she straightened her collar, fixed her helmet and went to welcome Matsumura. The very moment they encountered each other to fight, Matsumura attacked her with a kick. But while his right leg was still swinging through the air a thrust of her left fist fully struck him in the face. Thus, for Matsumura the affair ended with total defeat only because he had been too careless. It is basic knowledge in *bujutsu* that kicks are only efficient against weaker opponents. Because they are slower than thrusts or punches, they cause openings (or weak or empty points) (*kyō*) on the attacker's side.

That is why for example the *Gojūshiho kata*, which is the *kata* of the highest level in the *Shuri-te* practice, does not include kicks. The same can be said about the *Naha-te*. Its most superior *kata*, called *Sūpārinpai*, includes only one kick (*nidan geri*) as a final *sutemi* attack (a so-called sacrifice technique).

How could Matsumura assume Ume to be a weak opponent? That he was so clearly defeated only resulted from his arrogance and carelessness. Her victory was a victory of her spirit, her readiness for a life-and-death

[133] *Ai uchi*: Jpn. Simultaneous action of two opponents who hit their targets at the same moment. It is assumed that the winner is he whose body and spirit are sufficiently strong to better cope with the opponent's strike. – Habersetzer, R. and G.: Encyclopédie des Arts Martiaux. Paris: Amphora 2004.

fight. After a number of sleepless nights, worn down by shame, he decided to go and see Ume again. He asked her for a second fight. Of course, she knew that she had not won because of her power and abilities and she also knew that Matsumura would come again. So she was prepared to accept his wish. Her father was asked to supervise the fight as referee. This time Matsumura came mentally well prepared. Very carefully he reduced the distance and then his right fist struck her left breast like a lightning. Because he expected her to jump half a step to the side, he let a second thrust follow with his left fist against her right breast. Again Ume intended to hit his face with a simultaneous strike (*ai uchi*). But Matsumura could evade the counterattack by jumping back in time. Because Ume was technically and physically inferior, she had no other chance but to use a *sutemi ai uchi* technique as she had done in the first fight, that is taking full risk and throwing her whole body into a simultaneous strike. But this time Matsumura's attack had been aiming at her breast, a weak point of the female body. So, she could not choose her counterattack freely. She could not respond without her breasts being hit again. And they were already quite swollen. Just in this moment the mayor's voice ordered: "Stop fighting!" Thus, the case was decided. Matsumura had well remembered the essence of the law of the warrior: "If you know yourself, even in a hundred fights you will not come in danger." By anticipating her actions he had acted according to the *sensen no sen* principle.[134]

But there is another version of the story according to which Ume matched him fully or was even stronger than Matsumura. She purportedly had blocked his attack and allowed him to stand up and go after paying respect with a short *rei*. But then Matsumura looked at his *kimono* and saw a hole just in the solar plexus area and understood that she could have killed him with her sword hand thrust (*nuki te*) which had struck as fast as a lightning without that he had even realized it. He would have lost his life if Ume would not have stopped in time. – To tell the truth, this version seems exaggerated to me. Anyway, the fight resulted in a marriage between Ume and Matsumura. Soon after, just at the age of 20, he passed the examination for government officials in the kingdom of Ryūkyū.

---

[134] See p. 174 et seq.

Matsumura and the Bull they Called "the Killer"

Matsumura got the post of the Second Chamberlain of the 17th king of the 2nd Shō dynasty (1470-1879) of the Ryūkyū Islands, Shō Kō[135], who was referred to with the honorific *Ushu gana shii mee*. This corresponds to the Japanese expression *kami sama* meaning "Your Highness"[136] that was used to address the head of the ruling Tokugawa family in Edo. The official function of Matsumura in the Ryūkyū kingdom was similar to that of the Japanese sword master Yamaoka Tesshū in Edo.

King Shō Kō ruled as a very farsighted man willing to take the initiative for progress. In this regard he was a match for Shimazu Nariakira, the lord of Satsuma, or for the higher officials of the central government in Edo, who strived for the opening of the country. But he was also the first king of the Ryūkyū Islands to resign officially before he died. He suffered from a disease called *kami daari* in Okinawan dialect today it would probably be diagnosed as manic depressive psychosis or vegetative dystonia. After his resignation he was named "silly Shō Kō". Matsumura became the chamberlain of his son Shō Iku and also of the following king Shō Tai. So, until the time of the Meiji reforms he served three successive Ryūkyū kings. And from all these years there is only one heroic fighting story reported and this is the one about his fight against his later wife Ume. But there is another episode worth to be told.

This is a well-known story about his fight against a ferocious bull which sustained his reputation as "*Bushi*" Matsumura. I would like to relate it by removing any embellishment that covered the story over the years.

Matsumura was in his mid-20s and King Shō Kō had just resigned. Because of typhoons and drought there was widespread hunger on the Ryūkyū Islands. More than 4,000 inhabitants had already starved to death. Suddenly, on an early summer-like day in May the old king appeared in the castle of Shuri. He gave orders to three ministers of the new king to plant sago palm trees to fight starvation and organize a great *bon* festival to

[135] Shō Kō (1787-1839) reigned from 1804 to 1828.

[136] These words can also be interpreted as "Your Holiness" since *kami* also means God. – Translator's comment.

King Shō Kō. Painting by Mo Choki; 1837.

raise the spirits of the people. And a fight between Matsumura and a wild bull should be the highlight of the celebrations.

A village called Nakanishi was chosen as festival ground. It was close to a small bay and in an area where strong fighting bulls were easy to find. One was called "the killer" because he had never lost a fight against a man in the years of his career. Amongst the bulls he was something like a *yokozuna*[137]

[137] See footnote 123 on p. 148

in the world of *sumō*. He was so strong and so wild that he had already injured many a cattleman and many of his fellow bulls. The owner was already fed up with this terrible animal which could neither be used for farm work nor for bullfights. The old king thought the festival would have a great appeal to the people if he could make Matsumura fight against "the killer". Everyone thought the old king to be again in a state of confusion. The three ministers sent for Matsumura to come to the palace. In fact Shō Kō would demand nothing less of Matsumura than to "sacrifice his life for his country". Everyone expected Matsumura to refuse and quit his post. But to everyone's surprise he accepted the order without any objection. When the ministers asked him why, he answered: "I was granted so many favors by the old king, so that it is my obligation to be loyal and protect my lord's dignity." The son of the old king, Shō Iku, was said to have had tears in his eyes when he was reported Matsumura's words.

The news of the fight between Matsumura and the undefeated bull spread quickly all over Okinawa. More and more voices were critical of the old king. In the Shuri castle the idea was born to let the "killer bull" disappear in silence or let him die a "natural death". But Matsumura prevented this and kept his decision for the "honor of the old king and the honor of the new king". Finally the day of the fight arrived. The festival began at 2 pm. At noon already 30,000 people had gathered. The whole population of Okinawa was about 150,000 in the beginning of the Meiji period. So, one in five of the population, or half of the inhabitants of Shuri and Naha had come to the festival place at the little bay.

Master Matsumura appeared in a black and white suit. He wore a white, brimless hat and a white *kimono* made of abaca fabric, a white belt, and a black *haori* wrap. People could see an iron fan in his right hand. Everyone was holding their breath, realizing that he was "dressed for death". Matsumura and "the killer" were coming face to face. One could only hear the sound of the wind coming from the sea. The bull, lowering his neck, was taking the posture to attack, his hoofs stamping the sandy ground. For a while, the opponents were staring at each other with hostility. Matsumura was slowly raising the iron fan above his head, like a sword in the *dai jōdan* position. Then he started walking step by step towards the bull. When he had reached the dangerous "point of no return", the bull suddenly lost his will to fight. His tongue hanging out of his mouth, he started running to escape. The whole place went wild with excitement.

Later Matsumura said to the old king who looked very satisfied: "This was only luck. I guess so many people at one place did frighten even the killer bull." But only he, his wife and the owner of the animal knew the real reason for his victory. For a certain time, every day Matsumura had been going secretly to the house of the cattle owner. While wearing the clothes he would wear in the fight, he hit the bull in the cowshed straight between the eyes as if he was practicing thrusts with the *makiwara*. He did not strike with full force. But of course his iron-like fist proved results. In the first week the bull had raged, pulling fiercely the rope attached to his nose. After 10 days he gradually became more peaceful, and after 20 days he immediately let his tail hang down and surrendered as soon as he saw Matsumura's face. A few days later it took only the smell of Matsumura to show his readiness to subdue by bending his legs.

From now on Matsumura came every day to hit the bull with the iron fan until the bull was so terrified that he felt pain already when he was slightly touched with the fan. The day of the festival, with an audience of 30,000, the bull was so excited that he did not recognize Matsumura at first glance. But than he realized: "Oh dear! This terrible guy again!" and he immediately submitted to Matsumura.

This story is told in a number of versions. The main points are always the same. The question may come up to why master Matsumura was ready to fight against the bull in this way. It is worth thinking about. When some of his disciples later heard the story they spoke disparagingly behind his back: "Master Matsumura is not such a great man anymore. He was simply not convinced of his own strength to knock down the bull with empty hands." But I think that Matsumura rather wanted to show that if one wants to win without fighting, as the law of the warrior recommends, one must try hard and must not be lazy.

Knocking down a Raging Bull

30 years later Matsumura, his assistant Itosu and some other students went out to watch a bull fight. Matsumura was already 58. On their way home they all of a sudden came across a wild bull which had managed to break free from his owner. Master Matsumura and his disciples instinctively jumped behind some pine trees at the side of the road. But they could not let the bull rage around. He could easily have killed people with his sharp horns. The bull had to be stopped. So Itosu took the task, jumped in front of the bull and hit a full strike between his eyes. When the groaning bull was staggering, trying to keep standing, Itosu took the horns and turned them until the bull collapsed.

First master Matsumura praised Itosu's courage and steel fist but then he blamed him, saying: "I can tolerate that you sacrificed yourself for your country like this only because you luckily managed to keep the bull down. But you could have gotten hurt in this fight which you carelessly engaged in contrast to the law of the warrior. You could have even lost your life. This would have been a much greater damage to your country and could not be forgiven."

Master Itosu apologized saying: "Yes. I understand. If you had tried to really fight against the bull with empty hands 30 years ago you would not have been allowed to lose, too."

This episode, too, exists in a number of more or less colorful versions. But it is a matter of fact that master Itosu eliminated a public danger knocking down a bull with one strike.

Master Matsumura had accepted the king's unusual order to fight the bull for making the festival more attractive because he wanted to show his loyalty. Going to the cowshed every day, hitting the killer bull's head was a practical application of the teachings of Sun Tzu's *The Art of War*: "He who is skilled in war always finds himself in an invincible position and, at the same time, he will be sure to miss no military opportunities to conquer the enemy. Thus, a victorious army is one that will not fight with the enemy until it is assured of the conditions of winning, while a defeated army is one that starts the fight first and expects to have victory later."[138] Attacking the enemy directly may also provide a chance to win. But if one loses, not only the own honor will be violated but also – according to the sense of honor of the samurai – the honor of one's lord. In contrast to master Itosu, Matsumura was not suddenly confronted with the bull. He had the time to position himself in the sphere of not-losing and to carefully prepare a certain victory. As a result, the honor of the king was saved and the mood of the people suffering from hunger improved considerably. Moreover, neither Matsumura nor the bull was hurt. Both could leave the arena on their own feet. This fight also revealed the deep meaning of the basic maxims of karate: "There is no first attack in karate" (*karate ni sente nashi*) and "attacking out of defense" (*go no sen*).

As I have already said, in karate, unlike other kinds of *budō* such as sword fighting, there are almost no stories about great fights or heroic actions. But the mere fact that such stories do not exist tells us a lot about the character of the great masters of karate, and it was no accident that this martial art was called "the fist of the noble" (*kunshi no ken*).

2.2 Not to Lose Means Winning

Victory Without Struggle

Next to Miyamoto Musashi there was another great sword fighter. His name was Tsukahara Bokuden (1490-1571).[139] The following story about this master has also been included in the *Meiryō Kōhan*.[140]

Bokuden was already an old man when he was involved in a quarrel with a masterless samurai (rōnin) during a sea passage. The rōnin provoked

---

[138] Part 24 from Sun Tzu's The Art of War (Chinese/English). Beijing: Shang wu yin shu guan, 1996. – Translator's comment. – Sūn Zǐ (i.e. master Sūn), also Sun Tzu or Sun Tsu, Chinese military strategist who lived in the 6th century BC. His book *Sunzi-bing-Fa* ("Sūn Zǐ on the Art of War") is the oldest known text on martial arts and military strategy and has amongst other things strongly influenced the theoretical foundations of different quanfa styles. Of its originally 82 chapters 13 have been preserved. – Habersetzer, R. and G.: Encyclopédie des Arts Martiaux. Paris: Amphora 2004. – English edition of the *Sunzi-bing-Fa*: Sun Tzu: The Art of War. Filiquarian 2007.

[139] Tsukahara Bokuden was considered as *kenshi*, "sword saint". Just like Musashi he had the reputation to be invincible. – Publisher's comment.

[140] Collection of tales about the "sagacious and good ones". – Translator's comment.

the master in a more and more aggressive manner. But Bokuden did not want the other travelers to be dragged into this affair. So he pointed to a small island and said: "Maybe we can fight there." Just when the captain was maneuvering the ship close to the island, the drunken, brawling *rōnin* drew his sword and jumped off the boat. While the ruffian was splashing through the flat waters to the shore Bokuden gave the captain a signal to steer the ship away. When the *rōnin* realized this he furiously yelled: "Hey! Now you are running away! What a coward! Let the ship come back! Come back!" Bokuden burst of laughter: "I am sorry, but your lordship is still unharmed, and to me, the unworthy servant, nothing has happened either. This is what I call 'winning without fighting' (*mute shōryū*)!"

Perhaps this story was invented by later generations but nevertheless it expresses the essence of *budō* quite well. Not only karate, but *budō* in general is aimed at defending oneself. So, it could be said that a victory is won over the opponent if self-defense has been successful. And if there is no other way one should practice it the way Bokuden did.

A Victory by Running Away

There are countless stories about famous personalities of *budō* in Japan who instead of fighting preferred to run away. These stories reveal a lot about the mind and spirit of the Japanese.

One of them is about Yokoyama Sakujirō (1862-1912), who held the 8th *dan* in *Kōdōkan jūdō* and whose nickname was "Yokoyama the Demon". Once he took a walk with Ōsaki Kumao, an 8th *dan* master in Japanese chess (*shōgi*).

Without any special reason they were approached by a building worker who yelled: "Hey, you bastards!" Evidently he was looking for trouble. Ōsaki was also a soldier and practitioner of martial arts. He immediately took a firm fighting position thinking: "If he wants trouble he'll get it!" But to his surprise Yokoyama the "demon" said: "Come on, let's leave!" grabbing his sleeve and dragging him away. Yokoyama who was also respectfully referred to as being one of the "four heavenly kings of the *Kōdōkan jūdō*" could have tamed one or even two wild men at once without any efforts. But a victory over a building worker would not mean any honor for him. Furthermore, he could have unnecessarily injured this man. And it could not have been fully excluded that also his friend Ōsaki was injured in such a conflict. Therefore Yokoyama did not have to reflect very long on this matter. His body just left this place spontaneously. He had no fear. He did not run away because he had to. He ran away because he could do it. And his reaction came as quick as a lightning.

Matsumura Sōkon and the Big Guy

I would like to return to the great fighter of the old Okinawa, Matsumura Sōkon, and tell another relatively well-known story about him.

He was then 41 years of age. It was a day in autumn when a young man in his early 20s came to him asking to be accepted as his student. He was tall, more than 1.80 m (about 6 ft)[141], with a strong stature. Matsumura was already a famous man and many young men wanted to become his disciple. But he chose his students very carefully. While the young man was begging, Matsumura noticed that there was something ill-bred in him that he did not like. He grumbled a few words and finally refused his wish. The young man left with a rather angry face.

A few days later master Matsumura went home from his service in the castle of Shuri together with two of his disciples. Suddenly they were ordered to stop by a group of about 10 young men who had waited for them in ambush. The place where this happened is today the road behind the Shuri high school. "Oh, am I seeing master Matsumura?" The young man who had stepped out of the group and said this was taller than the others. Matsumura thought this voice reminded him of someone. Calmly he answered, "Right, I am Matsumura." When the moonlight let the young man's face emerge more clearly Matsumura recognized him as the big guy who had visited him a few days ago. "If you want to pass you must crawl between my legs!" As if by command, the men started to surround Matsumura. His students stood silently aside and watched the scene. "If you

[141] ... i.e. by Okinawan standards he was a real giant. – Publisher's comment.

say so." Master Matsumura nodded and without objection kneeled down in front of the young man. While sitting on his knees he bowed his head down to the ground. Suddenly, the tall guy seemed to be puzzled because he did not understand what master Matsumura was really intending. But then he straddled his legs to let him crawl through. He looked very strained. Sweat was running from his forehead. In the moment Matsumura put his hands on the ground to crawl on all fours he could not stand the tension anymore and jumped back shouting: "Ok, ok, I got it. You are free to go." Angrily he spat on the ground. He was panting with a pale face, his shoulders trembling. Matsumura took a quick look full of contempt at the stunned young men. Then he shoved his equally stunned students and left the scene as if nothing had happened.

Both students who went behind the master had to struggle to control their emotions. But finally they could no longer restrain themselves: "Master, what we were just seeing, was this really "*Bushi*" Matsumura? Wasn't it just terrible being humiliated that way?" The other one added: "Right, even if there are so many enemies you must not allow them to bring such a shame and humiliation on you and force you to creep like a dog." Matsumura listened to their words with a gentle smile. But they went on saying: "Master we understand, that we were wrong about you. We never were humiliated so much in all our lives. We want to finish the relation with you immediately. Goodbye." They left, filled with anger.

Of course the other students heard about this matter soon. So did Matsumura's wife Ume. She is said to have told the students: "Look, you should understand that Matsumura has just won without fighting." Of course, he could have chosen to fight. One strike would have been enough to knock out the tall gang leader. Then he would have knocked down four or five of the others and the rest would surely have run away. But he was accompanied by two inexperienced disciples. There was the risk for his students to be injured. He would have had to protect them. So the situation was more difficult as if he had been alone. But even if he had been alone, fighting against so many people would not have left him much room for modesty. Probably he would have had to injure a few of them. Maybe one of them would have even come to death. His king would never have forgiven such a behavior. This is why he chose "winning without fighting".

But again this was not a deliberate decision but a natural and spontaneous reaction to the situation.

From the early Han period in China[142] a similar story is reported. In an ancient chronicle (in Japanese: *Jūhachi Shinryaku*) an episode is mentioned about the famous general Hanshen who also chose to "crawl between the legs of the enemy". Like master Matsumura, he did not do this because he was frightened of the enemy. Just in the contrary, it was a very courageous act in order to get all the persons concerned emotionally moved.

Matsumura was in the mental state of emptiness (*kū*) when he was facing the dangerous situation. He had made himself empty and clean so that he could act like a mirror in which the tall guy could see his own paltriness. This made him lose his mental balance. Moreover the young ruffian left his weakest point unprotected to master Matsumura who was one of the greatest fighters of his times and while becoming conscious of this, a question was arising from the bottom of his heart making him tremble: "What on earth will he do now?" – This is meant by "winning without fighting".

There is a saying in Japan that "when reaching 40 years of age one is passing the hill of uncertainty". But in reality one never really reaches such state. One cannot become empty-minded like master Matsumura only by mastering the right techniques. That is why the masters of *budō* trained their souls.

The "Miyamoto Musashi of the Ryūkyūs"

Master Matsumura traveled twice to China and twice to the Satsuma province in southern Japan. There he studied the Chinese *kempō* and the *Jigen* sword technique. The last time he was sent to China as envoy he was already 51 years old. Sea journeys to China were very risky at that time. People used to say, "A journey to China is a journey to death." The sailing ships were made of wood and had a tonnage displacement of less than 100 tons. If they were caught by a typhoon they were almost condemned to wreckage. During his last passage, they were attacked by a terrible storm

142 2nd century BC. – Translator's comment.

although it was not the typhoon season. The ship was heavily shaken by rainstorms and close to capsize several times. Despair was spreading among the travelers. Everyone started preparing for death. Some were sniveling, some were crying loudly. Only master Matsumura was motionless, sitting in the cabin on his heels in the formal *seiza* style, reading sutras in front of a small Kannon statue, which he always carried about with him. Luckily in the end they escaped shipwreck and they were drifted to the shores of Satsuma. When the people there heard about what had happened on board they said: "This man is enlightened. He is beyond life and death. This man is the Miyamoto Musashi from the Ryūkyū islands."

Master Matsumura like Miyamoto Musashi committed his later years of life to the way of Buddha and reached the state of emptiness (*kū*). His soul had become one with heaven and earth. He was seeing, hearing, thinking and acting in this state of heart and mind. His life had become *bu*[143]. This state of heart and mind made him ready, for example, to crawl through the straddled legs of that ruffian. Being criticized and despised by his own disciples will not have troubled him; it was as if he had absolutely forgotten about it one moment later.

This spirit of the "fist of the noble men" (*kunshi no ken*) was transmitted from master Matsumura via master Itosu to my father. That is why the *Shitō* karate must preserve and transmit it to the generations to come. In his book *Introduction into Attack and Defense Techniques in Karate Kempō* my father has explained this spiritual heritage in a very clear manner.

> *Originally karate was not a technique for attack. While practicing kata it is easy to understand that the "receiving hand", i.e. blocking, has priority. The attack is defended with sufficient energy. But karate is not only a self-defense technique. In social life, the spirit of karate and the inner strength make a person behave gently towards others. People who practice karate want to develop this emotional state.*
>
> Kendō, *too, is not a method to kill other people with a sword. It is a method to control one's own needs and wishes. In the same way karate is a means for mental and spiritual education to control one's own desires and promote a*

[143] *Bu*: Jpn. Ability to fight. At the same time, the syllable *bu* has the meaning of "emptiness" or "nothingness". – Translator's comment.

spirit of modesty. It is not the actual meaning of karate to punch and kick around recklessly to frighten people and fight in the streets.

Sometimes one can see karate students who are very proud to show off the power of their fists by entertaining the public with smashing tiles and crushing wooden boards. Of course it is necessary to strengthen the fists. But using this to shock and threaten people is vulgar and undignified from the point of view of the karatedō.

The martial arts originally aimed at the education of body and mind. They are means to build the human character. Once a famous man said: "Nothing is worse in the world than a man of bujutsu *who pretends to be a man of* bujutsu.*"*

Among my numerous students there are some who were proud of having swung their fists in front of other people or having smashed tiles and boards in public. But not one of them made real progress in the world of karate. Some others are not eager to do kata *exercises. Of course strong fists are desirable. But it is much more important to practice* kata. *In the past, practice and teaching were done at secret places. Moreover, those who practiced karate avoided places where many people gathered. [...]*

But what counts most is the mental and spiritual aspect. No wonder that I mention this in connection with the smashing of tiles. Of course this needs a lot of physical practice. But to smash something like a wooden board or a tile, much harder than the hand, a lot of mental training is needed, too. In our age of science it might even be useful to study this problem with scientific methods. I am sure, among the readers of this book there are many who truly want to understand and study karate.

In our country, those who practice karate have been called "nobles" or "honorable men" (kunshi) *since ancient times. They are regarded to be people of high character like the warriors* (bushi) *or the well-educated men* (shinshi).

2.3 The Absolute Will to Win in the Yagyū Ryū

Sword Fighting and "Mental Cleansing"

In the original martial arts which have no rules, real competition meant killing each other, and fighting for victory or defeat meant life-and-death struggle. Because every fight consists of attack and defense one can say that the starting point of all kinds of martial art was the creation of a method of martial fighting (*heihō*), in which attack and defense are united. As explained above, the martial concept of the Tokugawa family was based upon two absolutely different methods. One was founded by Yagyū, the sword master of the Tokugawa family. The other was the *Ittō ryū*.

Yagyū Munenori took over the post from his father Muneyoshi, better known as Sekishūsai, to become the highest ranking sword-fighting teacher of the Tokugawa family at a time when the clan head Tokugawa Ieyasu, one of the three unifiers of the country, was already more than 50 years of age.[144] Ieyasu made his choice after Yagyū Sekishūsai had revealed to him the unparalleled technique of *mutō dori*. Ieyasu was impressed to such a degree that by all means he wanted Sekishūsai to become the highest counselor for martial techniques at his court. Sekishūsai rejected the ruler's request for reasons of his old age and suggested to appoint his son Munenori instead. First, Ieyasu hesitated for a while. Then Lord Kuroda Nagamasa offered Munenori a fief of 150 *koku* rice[145] a year to become his sword master. But Yagyū Munenori refused and answered: "Only if I serve at the Tokugawa court the *Yagyū* style will survive." And finally the Tokugawa decided to appoint Munenori as sword master.

But why did Yagyū Munenori believe that his martial art could only thrive in the environment of the Tokugawa clan? The Yagyū style is by nature the "life saving sword". The sword technique created by Munenori's father Sekishūsai was not designed to kill people but first of all to defend oneself. Munenori was devoted to the Zen priest Takuan (1573-1645). Takuan had been a disciple of the Zen priest Shunoku from the Daitoku-ji temple who had characterized the *Yagyū* style as "sword of peace". According to Munenori's judgment, a sword style like this was neither appropriate for Toyotomi Hideyoshi whose policy was aiming at the invasion of Korea[146] nor for the mighty war-loving lords like the Date, Maeda, Shimazu, Mōri or Uesugi.

---

[144] The other two unifiers of Japan were Oda Nobunaga and Toyotomi Hideyoshi. Tokugawa Ieyasu has completed the work of his predecessors by installing a stable central government after a long period of ceaseless civil wars, thus creating the fundament for a long period of peace. – Habersetzer, R. and G.: Encyclopédie des Arts Martiaux. Paris: Amphora 2004.

[145] A *koku* was a measure of the quantity of rice an adult person usually eats during a year. In 1669 the *koku* was defined with 180 liters of dry rice grains. – Publisher's comment.

[146] Toyotomi Hideyoshi (1536-1598), Japanese commander and regent (*kampaku*). He tried two times to invade Korea, in 1592 and in 1597, but he failed in this attempt. – Habersetzer, R. and G.: Encyclopédie des Arts Martiaux. Paris: Amphora 2004.

The essence of the "life saving" technique of the *Yagyū ryū* consists of letting the opponent act and finally reaching victory by following the opponent's actions. Contrary to this technique there is another one called the "killing sword". With this technique one can win by suppressing the opponent's actions. This is typical for the *Ittō ryū*.

After Munenori had become the shōgun's highest counselor for martial techniques he propagated his method of mental and spiritual purification and eliminated from the sword fighting practice all fixed body positions (*kamae*) and partner exercises (*kumite*). In contrast to this, for the *Ittō ryū*, which was designed to prepare for the fight in the battlefield, in particular *kata* with blunt or wooden swords were practiced. In this context Sekishūsai wrote in his treatise *Motsujimi Shudan Kōden Sho*: "One learns how to use the "killing sword", exercising with fixed body positions (*kamae*). To learn how to use the "life saving sword" *kamae* are not needed. This sword technique will emerge after fixed positions (*kamae*) have been totally abandoned and practice has become freed from fixed positions."

Sekishūsai's son Munenori taught how not to be caught by a vicious circle of position and counter position like in the children's game called "catch the weasel" in which one has to lay the hand above the opponent's hand. After one of the opponents has adopted a good position the other has to adopt a better one. If one cannot find a gap to attack the opponent one changes the body position and tries to open it. But if one transcends life and death, if there is no opponent in front of oneself anymore and even the "self" has disappeared, there will be no fear even when confronted with 10 or 20 enemies, and the chances for victory will emerge quite naturally. Munenori called this principle "water of the big western river" (*seigōsui*). "Big river" in this context corresponds to a metaphor of Zen Buddhism meaning "boundlessly wide western sea". Zen master Baso Dōitsu (709-788) is said to have created this metaphor when he told a disciple: "When you have swallowed up the whole water of the western sea there will be nothing I can teach you anymore." The disciple is reported to have been enlightened on the spot. The point is that his abdomen had to be boundlessly big and empty to take in all the "water of the western sea". Such a mental state is described by the term *seigōsui*. Munenori explained: "The state of *seigōsui* comes when everything else has disappeared."

Yagyū Yoshiharu from the 4th generation of the Owari branch of the Yagyū family wrote in his treatise *Inryūsho*:

> *The soul is placed in the abdomen* (hara), *in the back* (senaka) *and in the "water of the big western river"* (seigōsui). *One must not tighten the belly or stick it out but rather keep it relaxed so that the power can spread over the back of the body. To prevent abdomen and back from getting stiff, one lets the soul sink into the whole body as if it would sink into water so that there are neither places where power is concentrated nor places totally emptied of power. This state of the soul is called* seigōsui. *This mental and spiritual state corresponds to a "proud and straight posture" similar to the shape of a slightly curved sword* (tachi). *Thus, the whole body is not simply empty. The emptiness is totally filled. It is filled with life. When the soul has sufficiently filled the emptiness one can respond freely and flexibly to any event the moment it occurs.*

The founder of the Owari branch of the Yagyū family, Hyōgosuke, is said to have been a friend of flowers and the seasonal change of the blossom landscape. To his mind, the spirit of enjoyment of the flowerage was in the flowers but at the same time not in the flowers. The famous painter Tokuoka Shinsen (1896-1972) uttered a similar opinion. When he observed falling cherry blossoms in order to paint them, these blossoms, when hitting the ground, made a sound he could hear. – But is it physically possible to hear the sound a leaf of a cherry blossom makes when hitting the ground? Of course it is impossible to hear this sound with the ears. But there is a certain mental and spiritual state that makes this sound perceivable to the "heart" (*kokoro*)[147]. This is a state of mind and spirit where one can "see" the whole life of the flower, its growing and decay. In the very moment one becomes aware that the life cycle of this blossom and the cycles of the boundless universe are finally one, one is able to create a good painting, the painter explained.

In this spirit the sword-like body position called *tsuttata mi* is the straight position of a mentally purified body in the state of "emptiness".

---

[147] *Kokoro* (also *shin,* Chn. Xin): Jpn. Heart, spirit, soul, and consciousness. According to Japanese and Chinese concepts *kokoro* – and not the intellect – is the seat of the true "substance" of the human being, his essence. – Habersetzer, R. and G.: Encyclopédie des Arts Martiaux. Paris: Amphora 2004.

The "Life Saving Sword"

The *Shinkage ryū*, which was taught by Yagyū Sekishūsai was invented by Kamiizumi Nobutsuna.[148] This style originates from the experience of an endless circling called *morobashi*. The word *morobashi* means that body, soul and sword become one spherical structure that follows the movements of the opponent and acts in a freely circulating manner. From a technical point of view, the opponent moves first. One responds with a counterattack from the defense position of *go no sen*, i.e. the defense that anticipates and advances the counterattack of the opponent. This approach is continued, and one finally "wins by letting the opponent act". One does not win by exerting pressure on the opponent but by letting him act as he likes. This is the principle of the "life saving sword" of the *Yagyū ryū*. The idea of Yagyū's sword technique is also expressed in the term "adapt to the attack" (*gasshi uchi*). It symbolizes the technical principle of letting the opponent act and strike freely, and to win by following the movements and strikes of the opponent.

In contrast to this the *Ittō* style is characterized by hitting or cutting downwards (*kiri otoshi*). Unlike the *Yagyū* style one does not try to evade the attack. One also does not turn into the attack or react flexibly in other ways. After having noticed the starting point of the opponent's attack, one directly jumps into it, trying to terminate the fight by a simultaneous exchange of strikes (*ai uchi*). So, the *Ittō* style teaches the victory by direct attack. In his book "*The Secrets of Sword Fighting*"[149] Chiba Shūsaku (1794-1855) wrote:

> *In normal sword fighting lessons one is taught to anticipate the opponent's attack. The own attack precedes that of the opponent. This is called* sensen. *Meeting the opponent one thrusts or hits immediately and directly. Blocking or receiving and stopping the attack is not in the foreground.*
>
> *There are other schools where the principle* sensen no sen *is strived for. In contrast to the above-mentioned method, one does not hit or thrust immediately, but by anticipating the opponent's thrusts and strikes one lets them come*

[148] Cf. p. 69 et sqq.

[149] *Kempō hiketsu.*

and blocks or sweeps them or strikes them off. But one does not lose the spirit of attack or of anticipation (sen no ki) *and wins out of a defensive position with a counterattack, i.e. with* go no sen. Sensen no sen *is another way to express the principle of the* go no sen.

Having a closer look at the terms *sen* (preceding), *sen no sen* (anticipating by preceding the other) and *sensen no sen* (anticipating by preceding the other who himself tries to precede) it can be understood that they do not express the "before" and "after" of physical time but the problem of mental control of anticipating and preceding. So, we get one more explanation of the term *go no sen*.

At first glance the *Yagyū* style and the *Ittō* style seem to represent totally opposite principles. But with a closer look one can see that finally as well behind the *Yagyū ryū* principle *gasshi uchi* (adapting to the opponent's attack) as behind the *Ittō ryū* principle *kiri otoshi* (cutting with the first strike) the basic principle of *go no sen* is hidden. This is the highest ideal of sword fighting, and it also determined the strategy of Musashi in his famous fight against Kojirō.

Our ancestors developed the martial arts to this extremely high level under the conditions of real fight, always putting their lives at risk. And I think what they achieved deserves great respect.

Mutō Dori and the Point of Origin of Karate

Some time ago I watched a documentary in TV about the *Yagyū ryū*. At the end of the program one of the interviewed persons who had practiced *kendō* when he was a student, was asked to demonstrate what he thought to be the essence of the *Yagyū* style. The interviewer – who was a *kendō* practitioner, too –, raised a bamboo sword with both hands high above his head into a striking position and just in this moment his "opponent" grappled his arms so that he could not strike anymore. This was the *mutō dori* – the kernel of the *Yagyū* style created by Yagyū Sekishūsai.[150]

[150] Cf. p. 69 et sqq.

The *Yagyū* style was actually a rural fighting technique originating from the Yamato province. The decision of Tokugawa Ieyasu to choose this style as the official Tokugawa house style and to assign the heads of the Yagyū family to become highest counselors for fighting techniques to his court was made because Ieyasu was so impressed by the *mutō dori* principle.[151] When Sekishūsai and his son Munenori were performing in front of Ieyasu, Munenori was holding a wooden sword in the middle position, its tip pointed to the eyes of Sekishūsai. Then he started to slowly reduce the distance. Suddenly Sekishūsai jumped forward. In the very moment Munenori was expected to let the sword rush down with a terrifying *kiai* he was already deprived of his sword, lying on the ground on his back. His sword, pointing to his own throat, was in the hands of his father. Ieyasu had attentively observed the whole action and was sure not to have missed the decisive moment. But still he did not understand how this had worked. So, he took a sword, but this time a real one, and placed himself in front of Sekishūsai. Just when Ieyasu was raising the sword above his head, Sekishūsai grabbed Ieyasu's fists that were holding the sword, pinched them and blocked the movements of the lord so that the latter was unable to act.

Sekishūsai developed the principle of *mutō dori* by working with a *kōan* he had received from his teacher Kamiizumi Nobutsuna. Once Nobutsuna was sitting in the garden of the Myōkō-ji temple in Owari absorbed in writing characters in the sand. Suddenly he was attacked from behind by a mad man with a sword. But he managed to wind off the sword and knock the man down without a weapon. Incited by this experience he thought this should be developed into a reliable technique of a "non-killing but life saving sword". He instructed his most trustworthy disciple Sekishūsai to carry out this task. In the introducing of the chapter about the principle of *mutō* of the *Heihō Kaden Sho*[152] he wrote:

---

[151] When Yagyū Sekishūsai and his son Munenori showed Lord Ieyasu for the first time the *mutō dori*, Toyotomi Hideyoshi was still the ruler of the country. The battle of Sekigahara that changed the balance of power decisively in favor of the Tokugawa took place six years later, on 21 October 1600. See also footnote 144 on p. 171. – Publisher's comment.

[152] Text on family traditions in martial arts. Besides Yagyū Munenori as its most important author, already his father Yagyū Sekishūsai and his father's teacher Kamiizumi Nobutsuna had contributed to this work. – Publisher's comment.

The mutō *principle does not always mean to take away the opponent's sword. Neither it is about taking away the opponent's sword for covering oneself with glory. If one is attacked with a sword in a moment when one has no sword, this is* mutō. *It is not the crucial point of this principle to show how to take the opponent's sword away or the like.*

It follows an explanation of some of the main aspects of *mutō*:

That the opponent does not want his sword to be taken away does not mean that it must be taken away in any case. So, it is also mutō *if one leaves the sword to someone who does not want it to be taken away because the one whose sword is not taken away and who is cautious that his sword is not taken away will forget to strike with the sword and therefore cannot kill people. In the end one will win if one is not struck dead. So,* mutō *is an exercise for not being struck with a sword at a moment oneself has no sword.*

Mutō *is not only a technique to take away a sword. Using different instruments as weapons is also* mutō. *If one wants to take away the opponent's sword without having a sword one can use anything at hand by turning it into a weapon. One can even win with a fan. This is based upon a mental attitude which is the* mutō. *One can also gain control over an opponent and win with a bamboo staff.*

Mutō *does not simply mean to go straight forward and take the opponent's sword away. It also does not mean to have the intention to struck him down. But if the opponent comes to strike with his sword, one must take the sword away, because there is nothing else one can do. But to manage this, the distance must be well controlled. If one knows the distance within the opponent's sword cannot reach him, there is no need to fear it. If the own body comes within the reach of the opponent's sword, then one has to take it away. Winning means to control the opponent. This is the main point.*

Mutō *means to reach a mental state that allows to fight with empty hands as the only weapon against an armed opponent. The sword is long, and the hand is short. That is why one must come close enough to the opponent's body that one can be struck by the sword. So, one must take care that the sword will miss one's body. Then one must try to bring the own body under the hilt, and with a turn of the body one pushes the sword down. Of course the* mutō *technique will only work if one comes close to the opponent's body and follows his movements.*

This reads like an explanation of karate. Indeed, *mutō dori*, the climax of the *Yagyū* style as sword technique for self-defense, as "not killing but life saving sword", is, so to speak, true karate. The old Okinawan masters had developed karate in a situation of deep crisis. Under the Satsuma rule they were bereft of their swords and had to withstand the enemy's ferocious *Jigen* sword technique without weapons. So by historical accident, karate developed from a starting point, a basic principle similar to the *mutō dori* which represented the essence of the unparalleled *Yagyū* sword style.

Yamaoka Tesshū and the Mutō Dori

The great sword-master of the *Ittō ryū*, Yamaoka Tesshū (1836-1888), too, finally reached the mental and technical level of *mutō* and developed the *mutō ryū* on this basis. Thus, also the *Ittō* style, which is based on a technical principle completely contrary to the *Yagyū* style, was approaching the ideal of the *go no sen*, the attack out of the defense, finally reaching the sphere of *mutō* and leading to a kind of *"muto karate"*, i.e. to fighting without weapons, with empty hands.

In a treatise[153] Tesshū wrote the following can be found:

> Mutō *means that one has no sword outside the soul* (kokoro). *The soul unites the three worlds which are the past, the present and the future. In this unity of the soul the interior and the exterior have become one. If in such a state one is confronted with an enemy, there will be no enemy in front of oneself, and oneself will not be in front of the enemy. This miraculous state of non-location in which the self does not leave any traces is called* mutō.

In another treatise, *Lies and Truth in the Art of Sword Fighting*,[154] he wrote: "The true essence of the correctly transmitted sword fighting art is not contained in a special rule. One simply leaves the initiative to the enemy and gains the victory." This, too, corresponds to the principle of the "life saving sword" of the *Yagyū ryū*, i.e. the straight position (*tsuttatsu*) reached by mental and spiritual purification and abandoning all fixed body positions

[153] *Ittō seiden mutō ryū heihō jūni kajō kōyakusho.* The twelve martial arts rules of the *mutō* corresponding to the correct transmission of the *Ittō* style in colloquial language. – Translator's comment.

[154] *Kempō shingi ben.*

(*kamae*). This means that a posture of readiness (*kamae*) is adopted without really adopting it (*kamae atte kamae nashi*). The precondition for being able to do so is the ability to totally stop one's thoughts (*kyoshi tankai*). In this context, the famous master of sword fighting Asari Matashichirō should be mentioned, too, who was one of the greatest technicians of the *Ittō ryū*. He became famous because of the so-called "soundless *kamae*" (*oto nashi no kamae*), a posture that cannot be perceived.[155] Again it can be seen that finally the *Ittō ryū* also leads to the *mutō* although according to its technical logic it is totally in contrast to the *Yagyū ryū*.

However, this is quite reasonable. When fighting with a sword, unlike in fighting with empty hands one cannot adopt at the same time a defense posture and an attack posture. Attack and defense follow each other, and each with its appropriate posture. This is another restraint. Furthermore, fairly often weapons are not at hand, e.g. while sleeping or sitting in the bathtub. If one only knows how to fight with weapons, one will not be able to defend oneself in such a situation.

So, in order to acquire a fighting technique which unites defense and attack actions, as well fixed fighting positions (*kamae*) as the sword or other weapons must be given up.

From the point of view of the soul, the best way of self-defense is not to fight at all. This does not mean to just run away but rather to sense danger and leave or keep away from dangerous places. For a soul that has become one with heaven and earth it is no longer necessary to carry a sword. One has become one with the world, and the world is *mutō*.

Karate and the Yagyū Ryū

In my opinion, with respect to the technical logic, karate comes closest to the *Yagyū* style. The *Yagyū* style is like karate a fighting technique mainly for self-defense. In karate the idea and technique of the *mutō dori* principle has been developed to highest levels. In the technical as well as in the psychological respect, karate evolved out of the essence of sword fighting.

[155] See p. 181 et sqq.

It might be said that the beginners in karate are demanded to understand things which are the essence of what very advanced students in sword fighting experience. In other words the karate beginner is suddenly exposed to the ideas and techniques which correspond to the essence of sword fighting and therefore should be understood correctly even if it is not easy to be understood. Being confronted with the spiritual and technical essence of sword fighting does not make the understanding of karate easier. And this is all the more difficult because nothing of the old karate has been handed down in written form. So, for the understanding of karate, the old styles of sword fighting should be studied. Compared to other styles, the explanation of the *Yagyū* style is particularly rich in terms and expressions. Being the house style of the Tokugawa Shōguns, a lot of formal requirements had to be observed. Thus the mental and spiritual aspects of sword fighting were deliberately developed in close cooperation with Zen priests so that a complex metaphysical and psychological teaching system was created.

Karate is a martial art without weapons in which quick progress is possible. But there are also people studying it for reasons of its obvious efficiency in order to turn it into a means of street fighting. That is why in the past students were chosen so carefully. Master Nakayama Hiromichi (1873-1953) wrote in his book *The Sword Saints in the Shōwa Period*:[156] "Karate is the empty hand as a sword." And this is exactly what karate is about. The hands and feet of the karate fighter are as dangerous as a sword. This is not a mere metaphor. According to its ideas and techniques, karate literally replaces the sword that is missing.

The reason for Ieyasu to choose the *Yagyū* style as the house style for the Tokugawa family was not only because he thought *mutō dori* to be the ideal and essence of sword fighting. Moreover he thought it to be a way of leading the warriors into a world of everlasting peace where the sword was not needed anymore especially because the use of firearms had already become widespread. So, the *Yagyū* style was a fighting technique that suited on the one hand as a means to rule this new age and on the other hand to enhance the physical and mental abilities of the samurai of that time.

I believe that karate, the starting point of which corresponds to the *mutō*

---

[156] See footnote 89 on p. 117.

dori principle of the *Yagyū* style, is a "fist of peace" and "life saving fist" that in our days, with increasing national and ethnical conflicts after the collapse of the cold war structures can contribute to build a world in which we can live peacefully together. In this context our age needs karate more than ever before. But here I should repeat that the "life saving fist" (*katsunin ken*) is at the same time a "killing fist" (*satsunin ken*). After years and years of hard and difficult practice one reaches a martial level where one is able to kill. But when this level is reached, the "heart" (*kokoro*) understands the insignificance of killing and the importance of saving the lives of the others. Such a state can never be reached by simply thinking or sitting on the office desk. It emerges from concrete practice. One learns a physical technique that is connected with risking one's life. And in the end one really kills the self by overcoming the ego.

The swing is a good a metaphor for the "life saving fist" and the "killing fist". A swing consists of two long ropes hanging down for example from a high branch of a tree, their ends fixed to both sides of a log. This construction can be used to swing and fly to the branches of another tree, for example in order to suddenly attack an enemy from a distance. This, by the way, was also part of the practice and fighting tactics of the ninja. The upswing symbolizes the striving for the "fist that kills people". For this purpose one uses everything – body, mind and soul. At the climax one has reached this goal, but the "victim" is the own self. In this very moment the swing begins to return abruptly. The backswing symbolizes the negation of the previous goal, and now one is on the way to the "fist that saves lives" and thus to the true destination of karate.

2.4 The "Soundless Kamae"

The Satori of Yamaoka Tesshū

Shortly before the breakdown of the Tokugawa government in 1868, when the joint forces of the southern lords were approaching Edo, the capital was in danger of being destroyed in a sea of flames. In this situation Yamaoka Tesshū managed, with courage and prudence, to convince the

Photo 95: Yamaoka Tesshū.

chief of the general staff of the attacking troops, Saigō Takamori, to enter into negotiations with the commander of the Tokugawa government troops Katsu Kaishū. As a result the castle of Edo was peacefully surrendered.

The man who saved Edo was also a master of the sword. Yamaoka Tesshū (1836-1888) had been the favorite disciple of master Chiba Shūsaku (1784-1855), who had founded the *Hokushin Ittō ryū*. Tesshū was already widely feared when he was only 20 years of age and called "iron demon" (*oni tetsu*)[157]. He was not only good at sword fighting but also intellectually and spiritually outstanding. Just 15 years old he wrote the famous *20 Rules of Moral Education*. But however outstanding he might have been technically and mentally, there was one sword master he was not a match for. This was Asari Matashichirō, who was the teacher of Tesshū's own teacher Chiba Shūsaku. Asari was praised as "the man without enemies". For the first time Tesshū met him in the *dōjō* of master Chiba. Before the bamboo swords had even touched each other, Tesshū was already totally defeated. He then decided to become a student of master Asari, too.

Asari was famous because of his acting out of the defense (*go no sen*). He used to let the opponent act first and then struck him down. His fighting posture was called "soundless *kamae*"[158]. The term "soundless *kamae*" is known from the novel *The Great Buddha Pass*[159] by Nakazato Kaizan (1885-1944). The hero of this novel was Tsukue Ryūnosuke. His secret

[157] *Oni*: Jpn. Demon; *tetsu*: Jpn. Iron. *Tetsu* is a wordplay with his first name that is composed of the *kanji* for *tetsu* (iron) and *shu* (boat). – Translator's comment.

[158] *Oto nashi no kamae.*

[159] *Dai bosatsu tōge.* A novel comprising 41 volumes that had been published since 1913 over a period of about ten years. Although it remained incomplete it belongs to the most

sword technique was referred to as "soundless *kamae*". The historical model for this character was the 19th century samurai Takayanagi Matashirō. In the treatise *The Secret Knowledge of Sword Fighting* by Chiba Shūsaku, it is written that Takayanagi Matashirō defeated an opponent in a fight with bamboo swords without even touching him, and that one of his disciples called Matashirō's technique "soundless *kamae*". But nowhere else in the martial arts literature the term "soundless *kamae*" appears again. But of course one cannot simply draw the conclusion that it was nothing but the invention of a novelist.

In the *Ittō* style there is a fighting posture called "*kamae* of the misty or blue look"[160]. This posture is commonly also called "soundless *kamae*". Tesshū understood that this "soundless *kamae*" was neither a posture nor a technique but a state of mind. He gratefully remembered his father in law, Yamaoka Seizan, always admonishing him: "It's not the techniques that brings about victory, it is the morals!" He understood that he had to train his mind in order to really understand this and finally to understand how Asari Matashichirō could have defeated him so easily. So, he decided to study Zen with the famous priest Seijō. He always walked the 20 miles[161] to the Ryūtaku-ji temple in Izu to see his teacher. Later he also went to the Kenchō-ji temple in Kamakura, where under the guidance of Zen priest Ganō he had to meditate about the saying: "Everything comes out of emptiness" (*honrai muichi motsu*). This saying meant: "If one is afraid of the enemy one cannot win. As long as the sword of Matashichirō remains in your soul, worries about life and death will also remain there. But a warrior who is thinking about life and death is not a true warrior." Despite all his efforts Tesshū still felt that he could not rival Matashichirō. After 10 years had passed, his body and soul still became tense when he just saw Matashichirō. Even in the Meiji period, after 1868, when he had already opened his own *dōjō* and personally served the Meiji Tennō as a chamberlain, he did not manage to overcome Matashichirō's "soundless

voluminous works of world literature. – Publisher's comment. – The Great Buddha Pass is a pass in an altitude of 2,057 m (6,749 ft) near the city of Shioyama in the prefecture of Yamanashi. – Translator's comment.

[160] *Kasumi sei gan no kamae.*

[161] 20 Japanese miles are about 50 statute miles. – Publisher's comment.

kamae". Tesshū was now the sword master of the Yamaoka *dōjō* and also a man of high morals, fully trusted by the Meiji Tennō. He was able to outclass every other sword fighting expert of the country. But when he met the old master Matashichirō he still felt paralyzed. Awake or asleep, the tip of Matashichirō's sword would always twinkle under his eyelids. He practiced tirelessly. He was even seen sleeping in the *dōjō* with his bamboo sword (*shinai*) in his arms. For Tesshū, Matashichirō's sword had become a meditation riddle, a *kōan*, in itself. Once he traveled to the Tenryū-ji temple in Kyōto, where he asked the priest Tekisui for advice. The priest answered: "You are in this situation, because you are wearing misty glasses. But your eyes are fresh and clear. So, if you take off the glasses you will be free to see the moon as it really is." Finally he gave him a *kōan*: "Neither sword nor lance will help you. The power that reaches the heavens lies in the fate and in the light of the flames of the lotus."

One morning, 23 years after having become Matashichirō's student, Tesshū was practicing *zazen*.[162] Suddenly his whole being was enlightened as if struck by lightning. In this moment the face of Matashichirō disappeared from his mind where it had been imprinted. Even after he stood up and took the bamboo sword, the image of Matashichirō's face did not appear again before his inner eye. After Zen priest Tekisui confirmed the enlightenment of Tesshū, he immediately went to see Matashichirō. When the old master saw Tesshū coming, he nodded with understanding and with tears in his eyes he said: "It is good that you have understood the things so deeply. This is what is called *musō ken* (the 'sword of imagination', and at the same time the 'sword of not-thinking')[163], the essence of what our old masters have taught us. Now, there is nothing I could teach you anymore. Yamaoka, this was well done. Thank you."

After his experience of enlightenment Tesshū called the branch of the *Ittō* style he was teaching *mutō ryū*.

---

[162] This is said to have happened in a morning of March in 1880. – Habersetzer, R. and G.: Encyclopédie des Arts Martiaux. Paris: Amphora 2004.

[163] On the one hand, *musō ken* is the sword of the master as a threatening image in the mind of the opponent, and on the other hand it is the capability to erase this image by not thinking. – Translator's comment.

“There is no Kamae in Karate”

The “soundless *kamae*” made Tesshū suffer for 23 years, the man whom the commander of the Tokugawa forces Katsu Kaishū called “Japan’s greatest warrior and its faithful servant”. But nobody knows what the “soundless *kamae*” actually is. It is not depicted anywhere and no technique carrying this name is known. So, it should be asked what it actually is.

Since ancient times there has been the maxim that “in karate there are *kamae*, and at the same time there are no kamae”[164]. In *kumite* or other competitive situations one normally approaches the opponent choosing a certain fighting posture (*kamae*). There are *kamae* with the hands raised or others with arms hanging down at the sides (*shizen tai*). There are many kinds of *kamae* such as the “hook stance” (*kake no kamae*) or the “cat-paw stance” (*nekoashi kamae*). This seems to be contradictory to the statement that “there is no *kamae* in karate”. In fact this is not a contradiction. There are some karate teachers who try to explain this problem by saying although there is no *kamae* in karate there is *kamae* in the soul (*kokoro*) of the *karateka*. But this explanation does not seem to be really helpful.

There is an old song saying: “The human heart is easy to fall victim, don’t let it be captured by your wishes.”[165] That means that it is also not good when the soul is captured or fixed. As Zen master Takuan said, in order “not to be conquered by a wishful heart” the “immovable wisdom” (*fudōchi*) must be firmly anchored in the soul, because it is this wisdom in the depths that can take the soul home when it got lost, i.e. that is able to calm and cure a confused heart.

It is known that Yagyū Munenori, who served at the court of the Tokugawa family under the Shōguns Ieyasu, Hidetada and Iemitsu as the highest counselor for martial techniques, was deeply devoted to Takuan[166]. On

---

[164] *Karate wa kamae atte kamae nashi.*

[165] *Kokoro koso kokoro mayowasu kokoro nare. Kokoro ni kokoro kokoro yurusu na.*

[166] Takuan Sōhō Zenshi (1573-1645): Buddhist monk of the Rinzai-shu tradition of Zen Buddhism. He was also a poet, a painter, a calligrapher, a master of the tea ceremony (*chadō*), and a master in sword fighting. He is famous for his writings on the relationship between Zen and the martial arts of his time, in particular with respect to the *kenjutsu*. In 1608 he became abbot of the Daikoku-ji temple of Kyoto. On request of the Shōgun Tokugawa

request by Munenori Takuan wrote the treatise *On the Divine Essence of the Immovable Wisdom*[167]. He explained in it that the soul of a human being should not be bound or fixed to one thing. If the soul is caught by one thing it cannot turn to others.

The thousand-handed Kannon might well have one thousand hands. But if she were devoted only to the one that holds the bow, the remaining 999 hands would become useless. If the soul is caught by the view of the blossoms when one is looking at a tree, one cannot see the leaves. But if the soul is not fixed one can see the whole tree. The thousand hands of the thousand-handed Kannon show that one can act at the same time with thousand hands if only the soul is filled with the "Immovable Wisdom" (fudōchi).

If the attention is caught by the enemy's sword, the soul is fixed, too. So one looks out only for the sword and does not pay attention to other things. If one concentrates the attention on the eyes one forget the legs. If the soul is fixed on the right one forgets the left. This is not the way to defeat the enemy. But if the soul fills the whole body attention will be present wherever it is needed.

If during a sword fight one of the bystanders calls "Tajima!"[168] *in a decisive moment and you will start thinking about who might have called this and why, or much worse, you look around, possibly answering something, in this very moment you will be hit by the enemy. Only someone who, except perhaps dropping a little "hem", is not paying any attention to such an interjection, not thinking about it at all, only such a person is able to adapt to all circumstances.*

If one is asked during a Zen exercise who or what Buddha is one can answer anything. One can even say Buddha is a dog or a plum blossom. But one has to answer without first thinking about it. People who start thinking about how to answer this question are full of worldly desires that cause suffering. When someone learns dancing in the beginning he thinks about everything – how to stretch the hand correctly, how to move the legs, or how he might look in the

---

Iemitsu he went to Edo (Tōkyō) and founded the temple Tōai-ji in Shinagawa. On demand of his disciple and friend Yagyū Munenori he wrote a letter (*taiaki*) that indeed was a real instruction for the practice of the martial arts in the spirit of Zen (*Fudōchi shinmyō roku*). In this document he developed the concept of the *mushin*, and in particular he underlined the relationship between the spiritual (*ri*) and the technical (*gi* or *waza*) aspects. His famous aphorism "sword and Zen are one" (*ken Zen ichi*) is the essence of these considerations. His teachings also influenced the research of his contemporary, Miyamoto Musashi. – Habersetzer, R. and G.: Encyclopédie des Arts Martiaux. Paris: Amphora 2004.

[167] *Fudōchi shinmyō roku.*

[168] Geographical designation for the north of the prefecture of Hyōgo, but it is also synonym of Munenori. – Translator's comment.

eyes of the partner. But once he is a good dancer, he will dance for himself as if he were alone. Then, the soul is not fixed anywhere. This is the highest level of the art. And the same can be said for sword fighting.

One of the central terms derived from this doctrine is called *happō yabure* meaning "broken in eight (or actually in all) directions", i.e. full of holes and thus leaky. In a state like this the soul does not remain at one place. That is why it is only halfway thinking to accept the idea that there is no *kamae* in karate but there is *kamae* in the soul. One must go further to reach the spheres where one can realize that "there is neither *kamae* in karate nor *kamae* in your soul". The state can be described by the *kanji* with the meaning "nothingness" or "emptiness" and the Japanese reading *mu* or *bu*. "Studying" this character thoroughly i.e. writing it down or contemplating it in the state of total inner silence one can experience the essence of the way of karate physically. In an old poem one can read: "See the moon in the Hirosawa pond. It reflects itself and the water reflects it. Both do this without any intent."[169] The same state is described with the expression "there is no *kamae* in karate".

The *Bubishi* includes the "Eight Principles of *kempō* (*kempō hakku*)" The first one says: "The human heart should be like heaven and earth." This means that heaven and earth and human beings have the same origin. Human beings are one with all things. That is why our heart, our soul can become one with heaven and earth. If one is enlightened to a degree that one reaches the spheres where the heart has become one with heaven and earth, one will no longer be agitated when confronted with an opponent and think about how to prepare the encounter: "He will probably attack me from this direction. So, if he acts this way I will react that way... But if he comes from the other direction, I will react like this..." Furthermore, one does not need to react with too much tension: "Yes, come on! I shall beat you!" or pretending to be totally indifferent in showy manner: "I don't

[169] *Utsusu tomo mizu wa omowazu utsuru tomo tsuki wa omowanu hirosawa no ike.* – In the Heian era, the Hirosawa pond had been constructed by the grandson of the emperor Uda (887–897) as part of a temple garden. Meanwhile the temple is in ruins, but the pond still exists. Hirosawa no Ike is a widely admired lake, and numerous poems have been dedicated to it. – Publisher's comment.

mind where the wind is blowing from." In the state of mental and spiritual unity with the world, the soul is purified and calm. So, one reacts mentally to the mental actions of the opponent and physically to his physical actions. All this can happen as an incredibly small action in an extremely short moment. I suppose that Asari Matashichirō's "soundless *kamae*" was such a state without any kind of *kamae*.

The Simultaneous Withdrawal of Both Opponents

If the opponents confronted are both embodying the "soundless *kamae*", the capacity to fight (*bu*) will reach its utmost level. In this way *bu* becomes *bun* (cultural value). Harigaya Sekiun (1592-1662), who founded the *Mujū shinken ryū*, called an encounter of this kind *ainuke*[170]. When the enlightened Tesshū came to see Matashichirō – this was an *ainuke* experience.

Of course, history has many other examples of fighters who met without fighting – both at first glance mutually realizing their potentials, after drawing the swords immediately unsheathing them, thus deciding the fight by merely facing each other. There is an example for this kind of encounter between Kamiizumi Nobutsuna and Taki Gosho. Once they met, one holding his sword in the upper position the other in the middle. Then, after facing each other for more than 30 minutes, they bowed respectfully and left. In the middle of the 19th century, Shirai Tōru and his teacher Terada Munenori had a similar encounter. So did Shimada Toranosuke and Odani Nobutomu, who were both teachers of Katsu Kaishū. They all unsheathed their swords and went away without fighting.

The trial match (*gokui shiai*) between Harigaya Sekiun and his successor Odagiri Ichiun (1629-1707) was very typical in this context, too. Such trial matches were used to decide whether a disciple was ready to become classified as a "master". There were three such trial matches between Sekiun

---

[170] *Ainuke*: Jpn. Situation of confrontation of two opponents in which a fight has become impossible because the energies (*ki*) of them have suddenly united. The opponents are in the state of perfect spiritual harmony (*aiki*), and for this reason there can be neither vanquisher nor vanquished. – Habersetzer, R. and G.: Encyclopédie des Arts Martiaux. Paris: Amphora 2004.

and Ichiun, which all were finished by mutual retreat (*ainuke*). Ichiun remembered one of these fights: "The day of the *ainuke*. I have no idea what Sekiun is planning. He pulls his prayer beads out of his pocket, approaching me. Then, he lights an incense stick and bows to me." This reminds me of the scene when Matashichirō was noticing Tesshū's *kamae* and with tears in his eyes acknowledged his accomplishment.

According to the ideas of Thomas Hobbes, in the human society everybody is everybody's enemy and the world is a place of eternal fighting.[171] Sekiun called a state of mind oriented towards fighting and demanding to fight only driven by the idea of victory and defeat depreciatory as "animal spirit". A warrior who is only interested in victory or defeat, strength or weakness, behaves like an animal.

The Utmost Spheres of Bu Are Beyond those of Zen

As long as one clings to the idea of victory or defeat one cannot really gain a victory over the opponent. The same applies to sports. The former coach of the baseball team Giants, Nagashima, was convinced that the ball would always fly to places where no catcher is if only one put one's soul into the ball. That is why he always stood at the batter's box when he was still an active player. And his conviction proved to be true in reality again and again. Fukuda Masanosuke, the "Father of Japanese Tennis", who was an active athlete particularly in the Taishō period, i.e. in the years before and after World War I, left the following "tennis rule":

---

[171] Thomas Hobbes (1588-1679): English philosopher. In his philosophy Hobbes adopted the mechanistic and natural-scientific methodologies to political science and social studies. His concepts are based upon theories of the Natural State and the Treaty. In the Natural State the human beings are determined by the instinct of self-preservation as part of the human nature and hence by insatiable striving for power ("homo homini lupus" – "man is a wolf to man"). The inescapable consequence of it would be the war of everyone against everyone if the human beings would not transfer all of their power to the "Sovereign" by absolute renunciation of the natural right. Only through the foundation of the state in this way (the Treaty) the arbitrariness of the individuals not bound by rules can be overcome by the law-giving power, and thus peace can be ensured. – Brockhaus Enzyklopädie in vierundzwanzig Bänden. 19th ed., vol. 10. Mannheim: F.A. Brockhaus 1989.

This ball is only this single ball, it is absolutely unrepeatable. So you must put all of your mind and all of your body into this single stroke. One ball, one stroke. This technique must be refined. Strengthen the body and develop the mind. Give your whole self for this single stroke. – This is what I call the soul of tennis.

This attitude expresses an extremely developed mental state. Also in sports, which is a world of victory and defeat, there are first-class athletes who manage to surpass the sphere of victory and defeat and reach the state of the "absolute within the relative". They abandon the struggle for victory or defeat in order to win, because the more one wants to win the less one really wins in the end. But if both opponents reach the sphere of mental and spiritual unity with the world, becoming able to carry out techniques and move the body within this sphere, they finally cannot but achieve the ability for "mutual retreat" (*ainuke*). The opponents are merging with each other. There is no me and no opposite anymore, no winning and no losing. No matter how much time is passing by, none of both can beat the other. This is the highest level of fighting (*bu*) which turns the "animal" fighting into peace. With respect to this I think that the highest level of fighting (*bu*) exceeds Zen, because there is a contribution to peace, which can only be provided by *budō*.

There are many karate teachers who complain about the change of karate into sports and think the integration of Zen into karate practice to be a remedy. Others suggest including religions like Shugendō or Shintō.[172] But

---

[172] *Shugendō*: Jpn. "Path of Training and Testing"; a way for gaining knowledge by asceticism. Folk religion influenced by Chinese Taoism and Japanese Shintō and Mikkyō. The roots of this system of beliefs can be found in the esoteric Tendai-shu and Shingo-shu Buddhism. Shugendō is based upon the ascetic practice as determined by the Shingon monk Shōbō (Rigen Daishi, 832-909). The Shugendō emerged in particular in the 12th century amongst the Hijiri and the Yamabushi, ascetic mountain monks. The ascetic techniques comprised mountain climbing, meditation, exercises below ice-cold waterfalls (e.g. praying, meditation, *mudra* hand attitudes, *kata* techniques). Through the Yamabushi some Shugendō knowledge became part of the *ninjutsu*.
Shintō: Jpn. "The Way of the Gods". The only native religion of Japan before Buddhism spread there. It is based upon a shamanism in which the *kami* (natural powers and higher beings) are worshipped. The mythology of Shintō is very complex. The Sun Goddess Amaterasu plays a central role, and she is also the basis of the legitimization of the Japanese emperors (*Tennō*: Jpn. "Son of Heaven"). – Habersetzer, R. and G.: Encyclopédie des Arts Martiaux. Paris: Amphora 2004.

master Itosu wrote in his *Ten Lessons* in 1909 that karate does not come neither from Confucianism nor from Buddhism, Taoism or Shintō.

In sword fighting there were indeed always close relationships between sword masters and Zen priests. This was for example true for Yagyū Munenori and the Zen teacher Takuan, as mentioned above. Like Kamiizumi Nobutsuna, Tsukahara Bokuden or Asari Matashichirō, many a sword master reached enlightenment under the guidance of Zen priests. And the same applied to the old Okinawan masters. That means that the exploration of the *bu* and the logic of Zen correspond to each other. But the *bu* does not come from Zen. The maxim "karate is Zen in motion" is metaphorically explaining the idea that the masters of karate can reach the sphere of Zen even without Zen. Because of the hard physical and technical education one can even reach higher spheres of enlightenment than in Zen. This was proven by many reports of adepts about miraculous techniques of great masters who could "strike without making the slightest sound".

A Sword with Blunt Blade

The sword that kills can become the sword that saves lives. This total transformation can only be achieved after years and years of devoted practice. If one "hardens" the soul only with Zen exercises one can never reach the spheres of "mutual retreat" (*ainuke*) and will never achieve the ability to handle the "life saving sword".

There is a book called *The Art of the Tengu* which is known as a once secret records of the methods and rules of the warrior. It tells the story of an old master of the martial arts who went to a remote mountain site to meet a Tengu[173] in order to get taught by him, as Ushiwaka-maru[174] once had done. Indeed the Tengu appeared and answered the master's questions:

[173] Tengu: Mythical beings of ancient Japan who dwelled in the solitude of the mountains. According to popular legends they were famous for their knowledge in martial arts. Sometimes, they passed on their skills to human beings. Numerous warriors and samurai who founded own martial arts schools (*ryū*), in particular in the field of *kenjutsu*, asserted that they had been unexpectedly inspired by a Tengu. Sometimes this purportedly happened in a dream they dreamt during a stay in the mountains where they had retired deliberately in

The master asked: "Can a Zen priest, who has surpassed the sphere of life and death, become a good sword fighter?" The Tengu answered: "A Zen priest and a sword fighter practice for different aims. The Zen priest intends to escape from the cycle of life, death and reincarnation. He strives for transcending the question for life and death by negating his own existence and accepting things as they happen. In doing so he wants to find eternal and immovable peace in his mind. If he is surrounded by enemies he surely will keep his peace of mind because he is already considering himself as being dead. That means that he has an immovable spirit. But his practice of Zen cannot help him to protect the physical life. It only helps not to fear death."

The Tengu continued: "It is often said that a samurai has got enlightened because he met this or that Zen priest. But this is only half the truth. Those who practice sword fighting and finally got enlightened with the help of Zen priests, thus reaching the highest spheres of budō *have gone through many years of educating their minds and refining their techniques to build a solid fundament. One cannot reach this all at once. This is why someone who is still not mature in the martial arts cannot reach enlightenment even with the help of the most famous Zen priest."*

Harigaya Sekiun, too, experienced a period of "animal spirit" before he managed to abandon it. That means that he strived for life-and-death struggles with his opponents.[175] Later he used to wear a long sword with blunted blade (*habiki*) that was no longer appropriate for killing. When his disciples asked for the reason he answered: "If you hit a man with your

---

order to find their "way" (*dō*) by asceticism (*musha shugyō*). No lesser man than Minamoto no Yoshitsune, one of the greatest warriors in Japan's history, has purportedly become a master of sword fighting in this way. The word Tengu is the Japanese reading of the Chinese character "Tien-kou" ("heaven's dog") The legend of these supernatural beings came to Japan in the 6th and 7th century. Often it is described as a being with a human body and a bird's head. The so-called "little Tengu" (*ko Tengu*) is a winged being, and the *konsha Tengu* has a human face with a very long nose. The supreme master of these mountain spirits is called Sojobo. He is represented with a long red nose and long white hair, and his power is symbolized by a fan consisting of seven feathers. Often the Tengu and the Yamabushi (fear-inspiring mountain monks) were thought to be the same. – Habersetzer, R. and G.: Encyclopédie des Arts Martiaux. Paris: Amphora 2004.

[174] Ushiwaka-maru: Boy's name of Minamoto no Yoshitsune (1159-1189). See also p. 25 et seq. – Publisher's comment.

[175] Harigaya Sekiun (1592-1662) has purportedly fought 50 duels in his lifetime, which he won without exception. – Habersetzer, R. and G.: Encyclopédie des Arts Martiaux. Paris: Amphora 2004.

sword, a little piece of the blade will break off so that one cannot use the sword anymore. But there is more than one enemy. Anyway, one could only kill the first one, so why not making the blade blunt. In doing so, one also avoids killing the first one."

Yamaoka Tesshū did not kill a single person in his whole life. But by endless and incredibly hard practice he killed his own self, his ego. This should not be forgotten. By giving up or sacrificing *bu* from the beginning, i.e. the spirit and the practice of fighting, one will not find peace. Peace is emerging in the moment the highest spheres of *bu* are reached and *bu* confronted with *bu* are "mutually retreating". Of course, in the real world, there are opponents and fights. But it is the value of the martial arts (*budō*) to realize the "mutual retreat" (*ainuke*) in this world as an act of humanity.

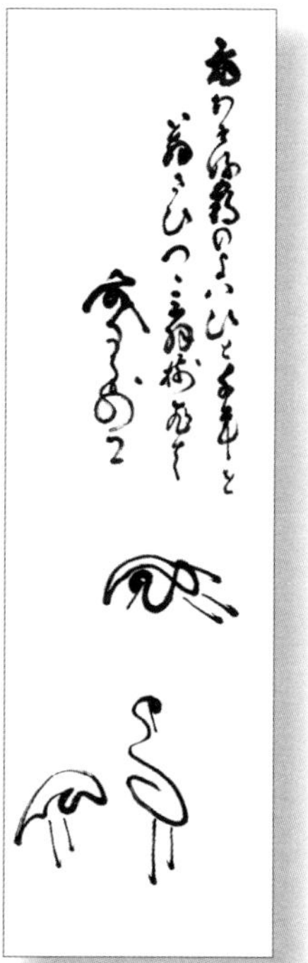

Like Miyamoto Musashi, Yamaoka Tesshū was a swordsman who also studied Zen, poetry, painting and calligraphy. He left some true masterpieces. This calligraphy means: "If people, too, lived for a thousand years, trying to dance playfully like cranes, eventually they would rust from old age, and the three birds of good fortune would fly away."

3 Karate as "Zen in Motion"

3.1 The Sphere of Emptiness (Kū) in Karate

Karate as the "Fist of the Nobles"

Karate was already called "Zen in motion" when my father was still alive. By practicing Zen, one reaches the spheres of inner purification or negation of the self (*muga*) by mere sitting meditation (*zazen*). By practicing karate, one reaches this sphere by moving. The term "Zen in motion" is often associated with the *Shōrinji kempō*, a martial art created by master Sō Dōshin[176] after World War II. The basic principle of master Sō was: "Fist and Zen are one" (*ken Zen ichi*). This idea is surely based upon Yagyū Munenori's and Miyamoto Musashi's maxim "sword and Zen are one" (*ken Zen ichi*).[177] Master Funakoshi Gichin had used the expression "Fist and Zen are one" before the war. In this spirit, the Japanese *Shōrinji kempō* can surely be considered as authentic Japanese *budō*, too.

Master Itosu once said, "karate is the fist of the nobles" (*kunshi no ken*). In his writings one can find sentences like: "Never use your fists and legs without sufficient reason and by no means for fighting in the streets" or "One does not harden the body for private quarrel". My father was absolutely bound to these ideas of his master and imparted them to his own disciples.

The Japanese word *kunshi*, designating noble, educated, wise, high-in-rank men, or lords, is a term of the Confucian philosophy. "Zen" on the

[176] Sō Dōshin (1911-1980), (birth name Nakano Michiomi), founded the style of *Shōrinji kempō* (also called *Shaolin-zu-kempō*) in 1947 on the basis of the Chinese quanfa (*kempō*) and Japanese martial arts (karate, *aikidō*). This style is strongly steeped in Zen Buddhism. In 1928 Nakano Michiomi had been sent on a secret mission to China (Manchuria) were he came under the influence of Taoist teachings and also came in touch with the Shaolin *kempō*. In 1932, in Peking, he became a disciple of Sifu Wen Lao-shi. In 1936 the latter appointed him officially to the 21st master of the Shaolin tradition and gave him his new name, Sō Dōshin. – Habersetzer, R. and G.: Encyclopédie des Arts Martiaux. Paris: Amphora 2004.

[177] The Japanese words for "sword" and "fist" are both pronounced as "ken" but written with different *kanji* (拳 – fist, 剣 – sword). – Publisher's remark.

Photo 96: The author and Mizuguchi Hirofumi, holding the *Ten Lessons* by Itosu Ankō.

other hand is a Buddhist term. But this does not mean that the concepts "Zen in motion" and "karate as the fist of the nobles" express either Buddhist or Confucian ideas. They are only expressions using concepts of Buddhism and Confucianism in order to express phenomena of Japanese thinking and spirituality. I want to repeat what had been written in *Itosu's Ten Lessons*: "Karate neither comes from Confucianism nor from Buddhism, Taoism or Shintō."

In the past, when someone was called *bushi* on Okinawa, one did not mean a member of the Japanese samurai class but a master of fist fighting. These masters were considered as people of high social and moral rank thus being like the *kunshi* according to the standards of Confucianism (such as Bushi Matsumura). People who merely had strong fists were not called *bushi* but "little fist" (*teguwa*).

Expressions like "Zen in motion" or "fist of the nobles" do not exist in Chinese *kempō*. They were created under the influence of Japanese sword fighting. Since, unlike karate, sword fighting in mainland Japan was under the protection of the Shōgun and other feudal lords, the rules of physical and mental techniques and the rules of killing were systematically developed, based on the ideas of Confucianism and Buddhism.

By the way: It is not difficult to understand what the expression "Zen in motion" means by simply watching performances of authentic karate *kata*.

The Sūpārinpai Kata and the Worldly Desires that Cause Suffering

The *Sūpārinpai kata* is the most superior *kata* of the *Naha-te*. It is written with the Chinese characters for the numerals 1, 100, 0 and 8, what is read as 108. Especially among the *kata* from *Naha* there are a lot which refer to numbers. *Sansērū* means 36, *Sēpai* means 18. Another one of the basic *kata* of the *Naha-te* is the *Sanchin*. In this case the number 3 (*san*) is included, which in Chinese also means "infinite". All these numbers are divisors of 108. The most superior *kata* in *Shuri-te* is called "54 Steps" (*Gojūshiho*), i.e. it refers to the half of 108. It is well-known that in Buddhism this number is very important. It is the number of worldly desires that cause suffering. On New Year's Eve the bells ring 108 times. The Buddhist prayer beads consist of 108 pearls. Some other numbers important for Buddhism like the 1080, the 54 and the 27 are related to the 108. Either they are divisors of it or multiples. Very often, the stairs leading to the temples have 108 steps. Whether one rings the bell on New Year's Eve or prays some prayer beads or climbs every step to the temple, it is always a religious exercise to free oneself form desires that cause suffering.

Of course, there are some *kata* which got their names from numbers not related to 108. For example, *Sēsan* means 13. The number 8 is also referred to rather often, probably because the respective character opens like a fan and therefore is considered in Japan as auspicious. The name of the *Kururunfa kata* means 17. The number 17 is the holy number of Taoism. According to this doctrine, everything consists of darkness and brightness. The highest number of darkness is the 8 (*gūsū*). The highest number of brightness is the 9 (*kisū*). Adding both results in 17. The constitution of Shōtoku Taishi (574-622) had 17 articles. So, under the strong influence of Taoism, the number

Photo 97: Mabuni Kenwa in a posture of the *kata Sūpārinpai.*

17 became even crucial for the Japanese lawmaking. And probably a certain influence of the Taoist thinking still exists.

But there are some people who claim that numerals in the names of the *kata* have nothing to do with the religious or philosophical meaning of certain numbers. These numerals would only express the number of techniques the *kata* consist of. In case of the *Sūpārinpai kata* this would be 108 and for the *Sansēru kata* 36 techniques. But to me this explanation does not seem to be plausible, because *kata* include a lot of invisible techniques and the techniques in general can be modified without limits.

For the *Shitō ryū* my father has created the *Jūroku kata* meaning "16". He named it "16" because he invented it in 1941, i.e. in the year Shōwa 16. In this case there was no other idea behind.

Karate – the Hand Reaching into the Spheres of Emptiness

I tend to think that many names of *kata* contain a Buddhist meaning, such as the *kata Sūpārinpai.* From the psychological point of view, the opponent visualized in the *kata* could be regarded to represent one's own "108 sufferings". Step by step, by destroying these sufferings with thrusts and kicks, one reaches the spheres of the "negation of the self" (*muga no kyō*) and of "emptiness" (*kū*).

In this respect there is a connection between karate and the concept of "emptiness" (*kū*). The modification of the written form of the term *karate* was initiated by master Funakoshi Gichin, who was the first to replace the *kanji*[178] that is pronounced *kara* and means "Tang" (China) by another one with the same reading but the different meaning "empty".[179] This character can also be read as *kū.*

Master Funakoshi wrote the word *karate* in the new way for the first time in 1929 after he had discussed the problem thoroughly with the Zen master Furukawa Gyōdō from the Enkaku-ji temple in Kamakura – with whom my father was also on close terms –, and with some of his karate students at the *Keiō* university. The character with the meaning "empty" symbolizes the spirit of karate – a way of fighting with bare hands and empty fists to defend oneself against an attacking enemy. The symbolic use of this character is based on a philosophical idea that has been laid down in the *Hannya Shingyō Sutra*[180]: "The color is like emptiness, and emptiness is like the color".[181] This means that finally the entire reality of things is nothing but emptiness. In this spirit the term karate can be interpreted as "the hand that reaches into the sphere of emptiness (*kū*)". The word "color" (*shiki*) represents everything that is material. The world of the "color" is the real world we can see with our eyes. But this does not mean at all that "emptiness" (*kū*) is a state of non-existence. "Emptiness" is the essence of the universe which transcends existence and non-existence. That is why the universe could also be called "the incarnation of life". All the things in the universe, the great universe itself are overflowing with life. This is the abundance of "emptiness". "Emptiness" becomes manifest only as "color". This is the meaning of the sentence "The color is like emptiness", because "emptiness" becomes "color". If one wants to see the life of the immense universe one must turn to the world because the real world is the realization of "emptiness".

In respect to karate, the *kata* correspond to the "color" one can see with the eyes. But at the same time they are "emptiness" that cannot be seen. In other words, a *kata* lacking vitality is also lacking "emptiness". There is no life inside.

---

[178] *Kanji*: Chinese characters as they are used in the Japanese script. Parallel to these in Japan the syllabaries Hiragana and Katakana are used. – Publisher's comment.

[179] That means that "Chinese hand" (唐手) was transformed into the "empty hand" (空手). – Publisher's comment.

[180] *Maka Hannya Haramita Shingyō*: Jpn. The Heart of Perfect Wisdom Sutra, also known as Heart Sutra. – Publisher's comment.

[181] *Shiki soku ze kū / kū soku se shiki.*

The Enlightenment of the Novelist

The author Akutagawa Ryūnosuke (1892-1927) wrote the story *The Samadhi of the Novelist*. This historical story is based on the diary of the writer Takizawa Bakin (1767-1848) who lived in the late Tokugawa period. It contains an episode that alludes to the terms "color" and "emptiness".

Bakin was already in his later years, more than 60 years of age, when he suddenly got stuck in the middle of writing his serialized novel "Satomi and the Eight Dogs"[182] and therefore endured a terrible time. One day his grandson Tarō came to him after having visited the Asakusa Kannon temple with his mother. Suddenly he said: "Grandpa, you must go on working. You must not lose your temper. Be patient and you will become even much more important as a writer." Bakin asked his grandson with surprise: "Who told you this?" And Tarō answered: "The Kannon from the Asakusa temple said it to me."

Akutagawa continued:

> *For a short moment, something like a solemn grandeur shone in his heart. A happy smile appeared on his lips. At the same time his eyes filled with tears. He did not mind whether it was perhaps just a joke Tarō had thought of or whether his mother had insinuated it to him. For him it was simply a miracle to have heard such words coming from his grandson's mouth. "Did the Kannon really say this? – Continue! Don't lose your temper! Go on, work harder!" The old writer laughed with tears in his eyes nodding with his head like a child.*

Bakin thought that the Kannon had used his grandson to encourage him and relieve him of his pain. With new forces he returned to his work and continued his stories about the eight dogs. There is no doubt that in this episode the Kannon was the "emptiness" and grandson Tarō was the "color".

Also Yukawa Hideki (1907-1981), the first Japanese Nobel laureate in physics, is said to have remembered in his late years the Kannon Bodhisattva to appear to him as an incarnation of the science in order to guide him on his way to the truth.

---

[182] *Nanso Satomi Hakkenden.*

The Goddess Kannon. 12th century ink painting on silk.

Seeing things with the eyes of *budō* is the same as seeing them with the eyes of the Kannon. Then one will see that the blossoms and the butterflies, the birds and the water, air, earth and human beings all belong to the same life, all are individual parts of an entity. Since ancient times several methods have been taught to reach this state of perception. One method among them is the sitting meditation (*zazen*). In Nichiren Buddhism, the *daimoku mantra* is repeated again and again.[183] In Jōdo Buddhism of the "School of the Pure Land", the believers invoke the Amidha Buddha (also Amitabha).[184] In some sects of esoteric Buddhism like Tendai or Shingon[185], one tries to become Buddha-like by a combination of rituals, physical meditation, prayers and spiritual exercise, that is by interaction of "body, words and mind" (*shin-ku-i no san mitsu*). Yoga meditation is used for similar purposes.

Karate, being "Zen in motion", and in particular *kata* practice can also be considered to be a method to reach the sphere of "emptiness" and the "negation of the self". Moreover, this is not only valid for karate. This is the case in any kind of *budō* practice.

The Buddha Nature in the Depths of the Heart

In the *Mumonkan*, the famous collection of *kōan* edited by the Chinese Zen priest Mumon Ekai (Chinese: Wumen Hui Kai, 1183-1260) there is a *kōan* made by Zen priest Hōen saying: "Who of both is the Qing Nü without soul? Find the answer and you will find the ultimate truth."[186] This *kōan* is about the unity of body and soul and is based on the following story:

> *In Tang*[187] *China, there was a man called Zhang Jian, who had a daughter with the name Qing Nü. She and her cousin Wang Zhou understood each other perfectly from childhood on. Zhang often said: "You get on so well. You are suited to each other like wife and husband. You should marry when you*

[183] The *daimoku* (Jpn.) is the central mantra and the basic practice in Nichiren Buddhism. It is pronounced "*Namu myōhō renge kyō*". "*Myōhō renge kyō*" is the Japanese reading of the title of the Lotus Sutra, and "*namu*" is a Buddhist term meaning at the same time doxology and confirmation of a belief; it is part of many Buddhist formulas and can be compared with the Jewish-Christian "Amen". Translated liberally the *daimoku* could be interpreted as "Blessed be the marvelous Lotus Sutra!". – Translator's comment.

[184] Such an invocation of a Buddha is called *nembutsu* ("envisioning Buddha"). – Publisher's comment.

[185] Cf. footnote 172 on p. 190.

[186] *Seijo* (Qing Nü) *rikon – nako ka kore shintei.*

[187] Tang era: 618-907.

are grown up." Naturally it was meant to be a joke, but both thought about it again and again. When they were grown up, the girl's father started to negotiate about marriage with an official and he would have given his daughter to this man even against her will. When Wang Zhou heard of this, he was shocked and decided to leave his family and lead a hermit's life in the mountains. He was leaving with a boat up the great Yangtze river[188]*, when he suddenly noticed somebody who desperately ran along the riverside. This was no one else but Qing Nü. She said: "When I heard that you had left home, I also ran away. Let me go with you." He answered: "It is so good you came. Let's go to another country and live together in happiness." After they had left home they soon had a child, and they lived in harmony for many years.*

But one day the memory of their parents became so strong that they decided to return. Now they traveled down the river in a boat and when they arrived in their hometown, Wang had his wife and child wait in the harbor and went alone to the house of Zhang Jian. When he met him he apologized saying: "I come to ask you to forgive us for running away from home and staying away without a message for such a long time. Meanwhile we have a child, and your daughter Qing Nü and me are living together in happiness. But now we have started to feel that we miss our parents' homes and decided to come back. So I ask you to forgive us for not showing enough respect towards our parents." Zhang Jian looked very surprised and answered: "Why are you talking such nonsense? Since you have left, she has been sleeping like dead all the time in her room." Wang Zhou replied: "No, you are wrong! She is living with me and just waiting at the boat in the harbor." – "No, she's sleeping in the back of the house." – "No, she's at the boat!"

This went on for a while until Wang Zhou decided to fetch his wife and child from the harbor. When he again stood in the entrance to Zhang Jian's house together with his wife and child, he had the strange vision of that Qing Nü appearing, who was said to have spent all the time sleeping in the back of the house. Then his eyes crossed with the eyes of the Qing Nü who had been with him all the time. And in this very moment both Qing Nüs seemed to merge into one human being.

So who was the real Qing Nü? The one who had been sleeping here in the house or the one who had fled with Wang Zhou? This incident is the subject of Zen priest Hōen's *kōan*.

---

[188] Yangtze, also Chang Jiang ("long river"), China's longest river (6,380 km, or 3,964 miles). – Publisher's comment.

In the Dhammapada (Jpn. *Hokku Kyō Sutra*), a collection of Buddha sayings that is said to come closest to the original voice of Buddha, one can read:

Self is the lord of self,
who else could be the lord?
With self well subdued,
a man finds a lord such as few can find.[189]

There is no doubt that the self living in the physical reality actually is the self. But this is not the true form, not the eternal self. The real self dwells in the depths of the soul. It is emptiness without form or shape or color. This is the Buddha nature (a quality all living creatures are born with enabling them to become Buddha themselves). Real human life is only possible when the Buddha nature has totally merged with the living body. Naturally it is not the body that reigns. The Buddha nature reigns and uses the body. The expression "Self is the lord of the self" of the Dhammapada means that the Buddha nature becomes the master of the physical body. I think that this is the sense of master Hōen's *kōan* "Who of both is the Qing Nü without soul?"

To my mind the mission of the human being is to strive for truth and improve the self, to raise the self while respecting the own imperfectness. This is to be done with the body one received from father and mother, nourished by the experience of pleasure and suffering. This should also be the utmost aim of people who go the way of karate.

[189] Verse 160. Translated by F. Max Müller. In Burlinghame, E.W.: Buddhist Parables. 1869. Reprinted 2008 by Red and Black Publishers, St Petersburg, Florida. – Publisher's comment.

3.2 "Zen in motion", and the Rules of Breathing

"Zen in motion" – the Unity of Body, Soul and Technique

To reach the unity of body, soul and technique expresses the idea that a technique emerges by the movement of the body which is infused with the soul that is united with the world and with the universe. The maxim "there is no first attack in karate" can only be understood when one has reached this sphere of unity. In the end it means "winning without fighting".

This expresses a state of mind which Miyagi Chōjun, who founded the *Gōjū* style and was a lifelong friend of my father, once put into the words: "Not being hit and not hitting – make a rule of avoiding harm."

The karate of the post-war era is dominated by competitive sports. And obviously there is a strong tendency to neglect the mental and spiritual elements and to reduce karate to body and technique. For this reason it is high time to reflect again on my father's maxim that "karate is Zen in motion" and master Funakoshi's idea that "there is no first attack in karate".

In the *Bubishi* the unity of soul, body and technique (*shin-gi-tai*) is explained. It is known that master Miyagi chose the name for his karate style, the *Gōjū ryū* from the "Eight Principles of Kempō" laid down in the *Bubishi*. These principles are the following:

1. The soul of men is one with the universe.
Jinshin dō tenshi.
The universe fills the soul of men.

2. The blood vessels are like the light of the sun and the moon.
Ketsumyaku motte jitsugetsu.
The human blood vessels keep the body going like sun and moon do with the world. This means that each human being is a little universe himself.

3. Hard and soft, breathing in and out make the rule.
Hō gōjū donto.
This sentence emphasizes the importance of breathing. The rule is the rhythm of the universe which is like a huge living being determined by the rhythm of hard and soft, inhaling and exhaling.
In order to receive the techniques from the unity of the soul and the world, breathing must be adapted to the world.

4. The body adapts to the circumstances.
Shin zuiji ōhen.
The body moves flexibly and spontaneously, adapting to the current circumstances. Soul (*shin*) and body (*tai*) become one.

5. The hand follows the rules of emptiness.
Shu hōkū sokunyū.
All actions are developed from the mental state of emptiness (*kū*). Soul (*shin*) and technique (*gi*) become one.

6. The legs are trained according to the model of the horse.
Ba shintai rihō.
This sentence emphasizes the importance of footwork that should be natural, flexible and sensitive like the prancing movements of a horse.
The soul which is one with the universe is also in the legs. When one walks, actually the soul walks.

7. The eyes look in four directions at the same time.
Gan yōshi shihō.
One always looks in all directions. But actually it is not the eye that looks. If the soul is in the eyes, seeing the things of the world, one sees like the Kannon.

8. The ears reach everywhere.
Ji nōchō hattatsu.
One must listen carefully in all directions. But it is not the ear that listens. The soul is in the ears and listens.

The first three of these eight principles of *kempō* refer to the soul, the rest of them to physical techniques. Because the latter are naturally dominated by the soul, these principles also deal with the "unity of soul, body and technique". If one understands the idea that karate is "Zen in motion", the deep meaning of these principles condensed to a few Chinese characters will appear in a fresh and vivid manner.

Up to this point emphasis was put on the mental and spiritual aspects. But karate practice reasonably concentrates on the development of physical strength and technical abilities. Because it is an art of fighting, first of all one must harden the body. Naturally one must exercise thrust by thrust and study blocking thoroughly until one is finally able to kill with one strike. But the development of body and techniques should be based on the practice of the *kata* handed down by our forefathers. If the body movements are learned in the appropriate way, the physical and technical development will also promote that of the soul. Unfortunately the traditional methodology of teaching originating from Okinawa is slowly getting lost more and more.

Arranging the Soul

The sentence "karate is Zen in motion" describes the ideal of reaching the spheres of the "negation of the self" (*muga*), while moving and executing *kata*. In this respect, as my father said, karate *kata* are unwritten or "body sutras".

Karate must be "Zen in motion", because one can, for example, only experience the "state of a falling dewdrop"[190] if one reaches the spheres of the negation of the self by moving. In particular for people who only occasionally practice *zazen*, the Zen Buddhist sitting meditation, it is rather difficult to reach these spheres by pure meditation. I guess this is something everyone who has tried it will admit. Deep thinking about the meditation riddles called *kōan* is a typical point of the Rinzai school of Zen Buddhism while the Sōtō school of Zen Buddhism favors "mere sitting" (*shikan taza*). But in Rinzai Zen, too, often only "mere sitting" is exercised, in particular when practicing at home. One sits until an incense stick is burnt down. This takes about 40 minutes. But what is to be done if disturbing thoughts keep surfacing?

Instead of sitting for a long time, it is easier for normal people to arrange or regulate their minds while moving. The three elements of arranging (*san chō hō*) – arranging the body (*chōshin hō*), arranging breathing (*chōsoku hō*) and arranging the soul (*chōshin hō*)[191] are organically related. In order to regulate the soul, first body and breathing have to be regulated. Because for *budō* intense, energetic movements are typical, one cannot avoid becoming conscious of the breathing. This makes the soul easier to be ar-

[190] See p. 142 et seq.

[191] In the identical words *chōshin hō*, *shin* one time means "body" and the other time it means "heart" or "soul". – Translator's comment.

ranged. So, first of all karate is an outstanding method to regulate one's breathing. In karate, breathing is systemized by the so-called "5 types and 10 forms" (*goshu jūkei*).[192] There is no other kind of *budō* with a similarly clear system of breathing. The breathing technique of the *Naha-te* can be said to be unrivaled worldwide.

Regulating Body and Breathing

Breathing is known to be particularly important in *aikidō*. Ueshiba Morihei who founded *aikidō* used words like "heavenly breath" or "breath of the earth". He is said to have had the mystical experience of his body being flooded with golden light coming from heaven, while golden vapor gushed out of the earth. This made him understand the breath of the universe and opened his mind for the way of *aiki* – the *aikidō*.

With regard to the regulation of the body I already mentioned that karate contains extremely sophisticated techniques that allow to mobilize the energy of the earth to become one's own power. In contrast to *zazen* or other kinds of meditation, in karate the fusion of energies is not only experienced in the mind, but by moving the body one actually becomes one with the energies of the earth. This energy or power of the earth is nothing else but gravitation. In religious or symbolic terms it is also called "energy of the Great Land" (*taichi no ki*) or "golden energy" (*kinki*) as master Ueshiba had perceived it.

In nearly all myths, popular religions and traditions, the god of the earth is depicted as dragon. Master Ueshiba declared himself of being literally "possessed" by the dragon god, whom he called "the dragon king of the nine fierce spirits of the cold plain of the billowing clouds of heaven"[193]. His son and successor as head of the school (*dōshu*), master Ueshiba Kisshōmaru (1921-1999), suggested this god to be probably the "god of

[192] See p. 209 et seq.

[193] *Ame no Murakumo Kuki Samnuhara Ryūō*. – According to Ueshiba Morihei this designates a "divine agency capable of eradicating all evil and pacifying the world", a symbol of the world's highest virtue. – See Ueshiba, M., Stevens, J. (ed.): The Essence of Aikidō. Tōkyō: Kodansha International 1999. – Publisher's comment.

Susanō slaying the Yamata no Orochi. Multicolored wood-block print by Toyohara Chikanobu (detail); around 1870.

the warriors" (*bushin*) embodied in the "sword of the billowing clouds of heaven"[194] which was drawn out of the tail of the mythical giant snake Yamata no Orochi by Susanō no Mikoto after he had killed the snake. This religious aspect emphasized by master Ueshiba is rather avoided in present *aikidō*, or treated with respectful distance. It had temporary influence only because it was his individual religious belief. Nevertheless, I feel that master Ueshiba's mystical ideas of the power of the earth have a very deep meaning. It is worth to have a closer look at Susanō no Mikoto. This mythical figure has been described in the *Kojiki*[195] as the god of storm and son of the creator deities Izanagi no Mikoto and Izanami no Mikoto, who have divided the land from the sea.

There is a symbolic picture showing master Ueshiba with the three holy

[194] *Ame no Murakumo Tsurugi.*

[195] See footnote 16 on p. 23.

treasures of Japan (*sanshu no jingi*) – mirror, jewels and sword.[196] The mirror is hanging from his neck in front of the breast. His stomach is decorated with lots of jewels, and he is carrying the sword on his back. According to tradition this sword is no other than the one Susanō has found in the tail of the giant snake and given to his sister, the sun goddess Amaterasu who is considered the divine ancestor of the Japanese emperors. Ueshiba's ideas contain something universal, which to my mind is worth becoming the subject of deeper analysis by religious studies. People practicing other kinds of *budō* or even many a student of *aikidō* may think that master Ueshiba with his heavenly inspiration and religiousness was just a little particular. But this should not be put aside so easily. Even by such religiousness important things can be found about *budō*.

Anyway, karate offers a very concrete physical method to become one with the earth. In order to become one with it, mentally one has to follow the threefold way of self arrangement (*sanchō hō*) of body, breath and soul. After all it becomes clear why the soul is easier to be regulated using karate than even by means of *zazen*.

Types and Forms of Breathing

The five methods of breathing (*kiiki no tondo*) are the following:

1. Inhaling slowly, exhaling slowly – *chōton chōto*
2. Inhaling slowly, exhaling quickly – *chōton tanto*
3. Inhaling quickly, exhaling quickly – *tanton tanto*
4. Inhaling quickly, exhaling slowly – *tanton chōto*
5. Inhaling and exhaling in waves – *keitondo*

In case of breathing in waves (*keitondo*) the first four methods are combined to further six forms of breathing: 1+2, 1+3, 1+4, 2+3, 2+4, 3+4. All in all there are five types of breathing, of which the 5th is subdivided into six forms. Thus, one obtains altogether ten forms. Hence the expression "five types and ten forms".

[196] In Japan these regalia symbolize the imperial power. – Publisher's comment.

When practicing karate *kata*, breathing always adopts one of these ten forms according to the respective movement. Because a karate *kata* consists of many different movements, one can learn in a natural way to combine each single movement with the most appropriate form of breathing. If somebody is gasping for air after having performed a *kata*, it is for sure that he does not master the breathing technique or that he has used wrong breathing techniques for certain techniques. Besides this, there is an individual aspect to be taken into account. Forms of breathing which are easy for one person may be difficult for others. So, it is important to progress in *kata* practice by paying special attention to the mutual relationship between techniques and breathing.

Yin and Yang in Breathing

There is Yin and Yang in breathing.[197] Everything in the world consists of Yin and Yang. The heaven is Yang, and the earth is Yin. The bright day is Yang, and the dark night is Yin. For human beings, men represent Yang and women Yin. Left is Yang, and right is Yin. Even in electricity this bipolarity can be found – as positive pole and negative pole.

[197] Yin and Yang (Jpn. *on* and *yō*): The principle "negative-positive" in Chinese philosophy. Dao, Yin and Yang form the original threeness in Chinese thinking. This was already enunciated in ancient times (Tao Te Ching by Laozi, written around the 6th century BC). "One Yin and one Yang, this is the Dao" is the mysterious aphorism summarizing Chinese Taoist metaphysics. Yin and Yang are two energetic poles by which the whole universe can be explained, from the macrocosm to the human being and finally to the microcosm. These two fundamental energies are contrary to each other, but one cannot be thought without the other. They govern all changes that can be observed in Nature. The primitive meanings of the terms are "shadow" (Yin) and "light" (Yang). Yin is a symbol for everything that is female, dark, earthly, receding, cold, docile, and Yang represents everything that is male, shining, heavenly, aggressive, hot and dominating. All aspects of life, all beings and all things are assigned to either of these categories. It is believed that the reciprocal effect of Yin and Yang is part of everything, and that balance between them is necessary. However, this balance is always unstable. This law of bipolarity has a strong influence on the Chinese martial arts. With the spread of the Chinese martial arts, the ideas of Yin and Yang have spread through the whole East Asian region. – Habersetzer, R. and G.: Encyclopédie des Arts Martiaux. Paris: Amphora 2004.

But nothing exists that is totally Yang or totally Yin. For example, noon is the climax of the bright day, Yang. But this moment is also the beginning of the dark half of the day, the night, Yin. Yin driven to the climax will change into Yang. Yang driven to the climax becomes Yin. The harmony of both arises from the contrast between them, but this harmony is also conflict. So, all the things in the world are in steady change and rebirth.

Inhaling is Yin, emptiness or non-physicalness (*kyō*). The breast is opened widely and the air is drawn in through the nose down to the bottom of the stomach. Exhaling is Yang, substance or physicalness (*mi*). The whole air contained in the body is pressed out from the bottom of the stomach through the mouth with a perceivable sound. Breathing is perfect when the breathing technique acquired consciously through *kata* practice functions in everyday life unconsciously by not remembering and not forgetting about it. To control breathing means to control life.

Having acquired correct breathing increases the ability to beginning something new, and it also helps to cope with unexpected defeats. By harmonizing Yin and Yang, emptiness and substance within oneself, all bodily functions can be developed in an optimal way. In doing so one also strengthens "the lower cinnabar field"[198] situated under the navel. Thus one can at any place and at any time control oneself and keep a clear and keen mind. So, the flame of life will powerfully burn in the heart, and one can live a life full of energy.

3.3 Preventing Disorder

Methods to Prevent Disorder

In the oldest treatise of Traditional Chinese Medicine, *The Yellow Emperor's Classic of Internal Medicine*,[199] one can find the expression "cure disorder before its outbreak" (*miran o osamu*). It is well-known that Traditional Chinese Medicine has the aim to prevent diseases, to regulate the organism

[198] Cf. footnote 71 on p. 89.

[199] Su Wen, Jpn.: *Kōtei daikei somon reisū.*

in a way that no symptoms appear so that it remains in the state of "not being ill". From the point of view of the Western Medicine, the Traditional Chinese Medicine is preventive because it keeps the human being in the state of "not being ill".

The wise man does not wait for the disease to appear, he cures it in advance. Giving medicine after the disease has already broken out means arranging things after they have already fallen into disorder. This is the same as starting to dig for a well only after when one has become thirsty, or to forge swords when the battle has already begun. This might already be too late. The wise man always tries to prevent any state of disorder. He aspires to "cure" each conflict completely, and before its outbreak. To my mind, this is the highest level of the ability to fight (*bu*), and it has been adequately expressed by the maxim "there is no first attack in karate".

There is an interesting episode about Yagyū Munenori. Once he was watching cherry blossoms in his garden. A young disciple stood close to him. Suddenly a thought occurred to him: "If I attacked master Yagyū with my sword right now, not even a man like him could escape." Just in the same moment Munenori looked around for a second and then quickly went back into the house. Later the disciple asked Munenori why he had suddenly shown distrust. The master answered: "Through many years of practice I have learned to sense any kind of turmoil arising in my environment. While watching the cherry blossoms, I was struck by the feeling that somebody was just intending to kill me. I looked around but there was no one else but you. So, I was rather confused, because I could not believe that one of my followers could intend to kill me." When the disciple heard his master's words, he confessed what kind of thought had crept into his mind and master Munenori clapped on his knees and said with a sigh of relief: "Ah, I understand. So that's that with my distrust."

There are many similar stories. One is about Tomita Shigemasa. Once, while being shaved by a servant, who just in the moment he had placed the knife under Shigemasa's chin, started to think: "If I tried to cut his throat now he could not escape; no one could, not even the greatest under the sky." Shigemasa looked up for a second and said: "What the hell are you just thinking? You make me shiver. Stop it!"

In February 2001, a joint seminar of *Shōtōkan ryū* and *Shitō ryū* was held in Venezuela. More than 600 karateka attended the event, mainly from South America. I was also invited and I met master Kanazawa Hirokazu[200], who is also very active in the international karate scene. After the seminar we both were awarded the Coronel-José-Jaoquín-Veroes medal by the parliament of the Federal State of Yaracuy. Master Kanazawa told me that once as a student he had to pick up master Funakoshi Gichin with a car to bring him to a karate lesson at his university. The master was already very old and he was sitting silently in the back of the car. Master Kanazawa glanced at him thinking: "I wonder whether master Funakoshi is still able to truly move." Abruptly master Funakoshi said: "Kanazawa, what on earth are you thinking?!" Of course master Kanazawa was very surprised. Evidently master Funakoshi had just "read his soul". I think, "reading the soul" (*ki o yomu*) is another expression for *sen no sen* and *sensen no sen* meaning to anticipate the attack, or even better to anticipate a series of actions and to react accordingly thus preventing the attack. In *kumite* situations I always know in advance what will come next. Will my opponent kick or thrust, move to the right or to the left? I just always know it for sure. When one masters *sensen no sen*, one reaches the sphere of winning without fighting. This is the realization of the essence of karate that is expressed by such expressions like "there is no first attack in karate" and "cure disorder before its outbreak".

The Story of the Marvelous Techniques of the Old Cat

The book *The Country Taoist*, which is part of the secret writings of the *Ittō ryū* and said to be the favorite book of Yamaoka Tesshū, includes a story titled *Marvelous Techniques of the Old Cat* (*neko no myōjutsu*).[201] Tesshū

[200] Kanazawa Hirokazu, born in 1931. After several years as chief instructor of the JKA (Japanese Karate Association) he founded his own association, the SKI (Shōtōkan Karate International). He argues for a *Shōtōkan* karate that is more conscious of its tradition but also open to sports competition. – Habersetzer, R. and G.: Encyclopédie des Arts Martiaux. Paris: Amphora 2004.

[201] *Inaka Sōshi* (The Country Taoist) by Chozanshi Issai, published in 1727. English version in Stevens, J. (ed.): Budo Secrets. Boston: Shambhala 2002.

usually made the secret documents available to his disciples but he did not show them this book. The story is about a cat that slept all the time so that it looked as if it was carved from wood. So, Tesshū was probably afraid this story might be misunderstood by his students and misused to justify their laziness. The message could have been interpreted by them in a way that for cats the highest state was the state of sleeping.

In the Edo era[202] *there once was a swordsman named Shoken. His home was plagued by a huge rat who roamed around freely, even during the day. Shoken's house cat was no match for the rat and fled in terror after being severely bitten. Shoken acquired several tough local polecats to combat the rat in a group. They were released in the house, and went for the rat, who crouched in a corner of a room waiting for them to come. The rat lashed out ferociously at one cat after the other and drove them all off. Angered by the abject failure of all the cats, the master decided to dispatch the rat with his sword. Despite his skill as a swordsman, he could not strike the rat – the animal leaped great distances through the air, moved like lightning, and boldly leapt right over the top of the swordsman's head. Shoken gave up in exasperation and decided to seek the aid of the amazing old cat from a nearby village.*

When the owner brought the old cat over to Shoken's house, Shoken was surprised at how ordinary and aged the cat appeared. However, he said, "Let's give it a try", and released the cat into the room where the rat was ensconced. As soon as it saw the cat approach, the rat froze. The cat nonchalantly walked over, seized the rat by the neck, carried it out of the room, and turned it over to Shoken.

That night, the other cats gathered and gave the old cat the seat of honor. They said to him, "We are all well known for our skill in rat catching, able to handle even weasels and otters, and our nails are razor sharp. However, there was nothing we could do against that rat. How is it that you were able to overcome that giant rat? Please impart to us the secrets of your art."

The old cat laughed and said: „Well, you are all still young and although you have experience in fighting with rats you still have a lot to learn. Before I begin, though, tell me about your training."

A black cat came forward and said: "I was raised in a family that specialized in training cats. I was taught how to leap over a seven foot screen, how to squeeze into tiny holes, and all kinds of acrobatic tricks. I was an expert at feigning sleep and then striking out as soon as a rat came near. Rats could not

[202] Edo era: 1603-1868.

escape me. I could catch them even as they fled across ceiling beams. I was never defeated until I met that old rat."

The old cat said: „Your training has centered exclusively on technique. All you think about is catching the rat. The old masters taught the kata *to enable us to develop good technique. And even the simplest techniques contain profound principles. You focus on external technique too much. This causes you to doubt the traditions of the masters and to devise new tricks. However, if you rely on technique too much, sooner or later you will come to an impasse because physical technique has a limit. Ponder this well."*

Next the tiger cat stepped forward and said: "I think that the development of ki *(life force) is most important. I have polished my* ki *for many years, and my spirit is very strong, filling heaven and earth. I could face down my opponents with overwhelming* ki *and defeat them from the start. I could immediately respond to any stimulus, any movement. I did not need to think; techniques naturally arose. I could freeze a rat running across a beam and make it drop to the floor. That old rat, though, came without a form and left not a trace. I was stymied."*

The old cat replied: „The ki *power you use is still a function of your own mind, and thus too self-centered. It is based entirely on your own level of self-confidence. As long as you remain conscious of your* ki *power and use it mentally to suppress an opponent, you will create resistance. And you will be sure to meet an opponent whose* ki *power is even stronger than yours. You may think that your* ki *power fills the universe in the same manner as the* kōzen no ki *(universal energy) employed by the Chinese sage Mencius, but it does not. In the case of Mencius,* ki *is bright and vigorous. His use of* ki *power is like a great river; your use of* ki *power is like a flash flood. We all know the proverb 'A biting cat gets bitten by the rat.' When a rat is cornered it forgets life, forgets desires, forgets winning and losing, forgets body and mind. That force is as strong as steel, and cannot be vanquished merely by* ki *power."*

There are two kinds of energy in the soul. One is called *kakki*. This is *ki* coming and going like a guest. The other one was named *seiki*, meaning "right or morale *ki*" by the ancient Chinese philosopher Mencius (Meng Zi, 372-289 BC). *Kakki* is like the energy of the water in the very moment the river overflows its banks. After the flood is over no more water is coming. The energy is exhausted. By contrast, *seiki* is inexhaustible. It is also called *kōzen no ki,* "overflowing energy" or "universal energy". The *ki* of the tiger cat was *kakki*; and it was unaware of the existence of the inexhaustible *seiki*.

Next, an older grey cat advanced quietly and said: "As you have stated, that type of ki *power can be very strong but still retains a form, however slight, that can be used against you. As for me, for many years now I have been polishing my heart. I do not rely on* ki *power; I never harbor thoughts of fighting with an opponent, and always try to harmonize myself to any attack. When an opponent is strong, I blend and follow his movements. My technique is like that of a curtain capturing and dropping to the floor a stone thrown against it. Until now, even the strongest rat could find no place to attack me. That rat, though, was amazing –* ki *power and harmonizing power had no effect on it."*

The old cat answered: "Your harmonizing power is not the harmonizing power of nature. It is a projection of your own mind and thus limited. Any trace of conscious thought destroys your equilibrium, and a sharp opponent will seize on that opening in an instant. Thought obstructs nature and hinders function. Do not think, do not act; follow the movements of nature, and self will disappear. Without a self, there will be no one to oppose you in heaven and earth.

"It is not my intent to dismiss all of your hard training as worthless. 'The Way has many vessels.' Techniques contain universal principles. Ki *power makes the body function and vivifies the cosmos. Harmonizing power enables one to blend naturally with any attacking force, even rocks, without being broken. As soon as there is the slightest conscious thought, however, contrivance and willfulness appear, and that separates you from the natural Way. You see yourself and others as separate entities, as opponents. If you asked me what technique I employ, the answer is* mushin *(no mind).* Mushin *is to act in accordance with nature, nothing else. The Way has no limits; so do not think of this talk of mine as the ultimate secret.*

"Long ago, there was a cat in my neighborhood that seemed to do nothing but nap all day. That cat looked spiritless, almost like a cat made out of wood. No one ever saw it catch a rat, yet wherever it was and wherever it went, no rat dared to appear. I once visited the cat and asked it to explain the reason. I asked four times for an answer but it remained silent. It was not that the cat did not want to answer but rather that it did not know how to answer. As the old saying goes, 'Those who know, do not speak; those who speak, do not know.' That cat forgot about itself, forgot about objects, and dwelled in a state of purposelessness. That cat actualized the divine martial virtue of 'non-killing'. I am still no match for that cat."

This "wooden cat" expressed the essence of *budō* by curing the "disorder" before its outbreak. Becoming free from intentions (*mushin*), means to become one with nature. If there is no self there is no enemy either. The proper way is probably to get rid of one's intentions and, without moving oneself, to make the opponent surrender or at least refraining from fighting. This is the sphere described by the expression "there is no first attack in karate". Only from this sphere one is able to "cure disorder before its outbreak". Miyamoto Musashi called this state "rock body" (*iwa no mi*) and considered it to be the crucial point of the *Nitō ryū* ("school of the two swords") he had founded.

At the end of his life, Musashi had retreated for Zen practice to the Reigandō grotto[203] on the mountain Iwato located on the island of Kyūshū in the western part of the present Kumamoto prefecture. One day he was exercising *zazen* together with a Zen priest called Dairen, both sitting on a rock. All of a sudden a snake came along. It crawled onto the priest's knees but then around Musashi, anxious not to touch him. This caused Musashi to regard himself to be still spiritually immature and he said: "This shows that I have not yet become truly one with nature." If Musashi had more practiced *zazen*, the snake might have crawled over his body.

The living human being is not made of wood or stone. His soul should not be fixed to a certain part of the body. If the soul is caught somewhere the human being cannot move freely. This should not happen. The soul must be immovable while in steady circulation. That is what it is about when talking about the unity of soul and universe.

Theory and Experience

I already mentioned above that I can always anticipate the opponent's actions because my body knows in advance what is coming. In order to do this one must be able to "read" something from a very complex picture. This comprises to correctly judge the own body position and the position of the opponent, the distance, the breathing, the center of gravitation and the whole preceding process of fighting. By the way: The same applies to

[203] In the vicinity of the Reigandō grotto the temple Ungan-ji was situated. Miyamoto Musashi (1584-1645) had retreated into the cave, in which he wrote his famous *Book of Five Rings*. He completed this work some weeks before his death. – Habersetzer, R. and G.: Encyclopédie des Arts Martiaux. Paris: Amphora 2004.

the masters of chess or *go*. But the assessment of the situation is not based upon theory but upon experience. The power of judgment arises from the whole body and not only from the head. It comes from the five senses, and beyond this from a complex intuition transcending the five senses. Of course it is correct to say that "there is no limit to the techniques". But the techniques that can be developed from a certain body position are limited. If, for example, I am standing with my back turned to the opponent, I cannot carry out a straight thrust against him. The required experience is acquired in a natural way by repeating many thousand times *kata* and analytic practice (*bunkai*) which are based on a correct and realistic understanding of karate. Thus, one cannot only analyze the situation to foresee the next actions of the opponent, one can also move the own body accordingly and use the right techniques. Reaching higher stages of practice, one can even obstruct the opponent's techniques before he has begun to develop them. This is really possible.

Trying to explain all this with words might finally lead to nothing. If one tries to explain karate in a complicated way, it is easy to do so. Personally, I prefer simple explanations. But it is not that simple to explain it in a comprehensive way. One of the secret poems of *budō* that is part of the oral tradition teaches: "The essence is as close as my eyelashes but I cannot see it." If one reveals the essence of a technique, which in the old *budō* was strictly kept secret to everyone, one can often hear: "Oh, I should have known this earlier!" But to my mind it is better to understand it by practicing. Finally a technique can never be fully explained with words.

The Spirit of Death Defiance

The five cats appearing in the story about the marvelous techniques of the old cat represent the five stages of skills: The first one, the young, black, quick and sharp-minded cat relied on its technical skills. The second one, the tiger-striped cat, paralyzed its opponents with energetic shock. The third one, the elderly cat, mastered the distance to the opponents (*maai*) and tried to come into harmony with them. The fourth one, the old cat, always acted without any intention. Finally the fifth one, the sleeping "wooden" cat, "acted" by having turned into a "rock". In fact, the secret of the marvelous techniques of the Old Cat is already revealed in the words addressed to the young black cat: "The old masters taught the *kata* to enable us to develop good technique. And even the simplest techniques contain profound principles. You focus on external technique too much..." The old cat admonished the young one to study the old techniques thoroughly as a means to enhance the mental energy and to develop the soul. The whole process of development up to the spheres of the "wooden" cat is contained in the *kata*. So, everybody practicing karate should keep the teachings of the old cat in mind.

But are these teachings respected in the current world of karate? Is it not governed by the spirit of the young black cat, focused on external technique and technical competition? Or has karate rather become something like the art of the tiger cat that like a demon overwhelms the opponent with destructive mental energy and the bloodthirsty will to kill?

A lot has been written about karate in this book. There is one more thing I would like to add. All techniques in karate are receiving or blocking techniques. But if the blocking hand is at the same time the striking hand this is called "simultaneous mutual strike" (*ai uchi*)[204]. *Ai uchi* is a potentially deadly method. One should be well prepared for it. To acquire the determination needed for *ai uchi* one must practice *kumite*. But in present competitive *kumite*, with sophisticated rules about how to get points and to win, the courage needed for *ai uchi* cannot be learned, because the real enemy is the self, the ego. The self is what has to be fought against. If one is led by the idea "I must achieve a victory over my opponent!" one cannot realize *sen no sen*, i.e. one cannot anticipate the opponent's attack, and of course one can even much less anticipate his response to one's response (*sensen no sen*). If one is possessed by the thought: "I want to win! I want to survive!" one will become totally rigid and inflexible.

One must expose the body to the sphere of death. One must dare everything, whatever it takes. No step backward is allowed. In this spirit one must practice the *kata* that are based on the true logic of karate thousand and even ten thousand times and analyze the performance again and again.

---

[204] See footnote 133 on p. 157.

Preventing Disorder

The Japanese word *shiai,* meaning match, competition, is written with two characters, the first meaning "to try, to check" and the other "to connect, to meet". So, the meaning of the word is "to meet, or to face trial". In the past the same word *shiai* was written with one different character, meaning "to die, death". When in ancient times swordsmen met for these trials, they "met with, or faced death". Today one would enter a *shiai* with a bamboo sword, the body safely protected. But in the past, real swords were used and the person who lost the match usually lost his life. If in such a "meeting with death" the state of the immovable soul (*fudōshin*) is disturbed, this is called *tatare mai*, i.e. "one does not want to be struck". Then one clings to the small self and fears surprise. Since ancient times there have been the so-called "four warnings" in *kendō* against fear (*kyō*), shock (*kyō*), doubt (*gi*) and confusion (*waku*).

The *Ittō ryū* technique called "downward cut" (*kiri otoshi*)[205] is a sacrifice technique (*sutemi*) to free the soul from these tendencies. But also the *Yagyū ryū*, favoring the counterstrike technique, which from the point of view of technical logic is the opposite pole to the *Ittō ryū*, is based upon the belief "in the god-like power of the sword arising from the spontaneous attack with no regard for the self". And just because *sutemi* is a sacrifice technique, it is life saving and life creating for the own self as well as for the opponent. The "attack in harmony with the other" (*gasshi uchi*)[206] of the *Yagyū ryū*, respecting the whole personality of the opponent, represents the "life saving sword". But before one is able to master the *gasshi uchi* one must have killed or "negated" the self, the ego. So, the essence of the two technically contrary styles is the same.

Often one can hear: "He was strong when he was young. His technique was marvelous." But this sentence indirectly also expresses that strength and technical abilities have disappeared over the years. That means that his techniques were no *sutemi* techniques but merely build upon power and speed. To master *sutemi* techniques, one must become free of intentions

---

[205] See footnote 68 on p. 87.

[206] See footnote 67 on p. 86.

(*mushin*) and one with nature. The soul must become one with the world, i.e. also one with the opponent. If one further develops this mental and spiritual state one will be able to "cure disorder before its outbreak" without doing anything, just by existing. If one approaches the opponent in such a state of unity with the world, this is *sen no sen*, "anticipating and going ahead of the attack" and finally one reaches the ability of *sensen no sen*, "further anticipating the response to one's response". If one confronts the opponent in this state of unity, this is the "soundless *kamae*". The mental and spiritual energy that emerges from this unity is the "real energy" (*seiki*) or the "overflowing energy" (*kōzen no ki*).

The techniques, the energetic adaptation and influence (*kiai*) or the distance (*maai*) are only correct when they are based upon this unity. This spirit should be embodied in all aspects of everyday life. In every moment of life a "calm mind" (*heijōshin*) should be governed by an "immovable soul" (*fudōshin*) inside. This is the marvelous art the old cat has taught us. And karate cannot be called true and real until this stage is reached. But if one comes to this point, one will be in the same sphere as an enlightened Zen priest. Only the path will have been different.

In karate one aspires to reach the godlike fighting spirit of non-killing and the mental state of the unity with the world. From this the "holy fist" arises that is able to "cure the disorder before its outbreak". This is "Zen in motion". The soul, having become one with the world, is filling eyes, ears, mouth, hands and feet, and contributes to the creation of a peaceful society.

The karate *kata* teach the techniques through physical unity with the world, and the psychological regulation by mental unity with the world. Their teachings are without words but extremely efficient. Practicing the *kata* taught in their correct old forms again and again helps to learn and to refine the essential techniques, strengthens the soul and builds the character – finally the whole human being is shaped by them.

Bu – Never Accomplished

In the early 1960s I was invited to Panama to attend the first south American *kumite* meeting. At that time there were no rules and nothing was used to protect face or hands. Many fighters were injured, had their noses broken etc. So, my skills as a "*jūdō* chiropractor" were urgently needed. Besides this, the referees were not up to their job at all and so the mood of the audience was rather tense. Hence the spectators made their feelings clear in a noisy way. And in this situation I was asked to do a *kata* performance. At that time, at *jūdō* events the masters used to do performances of their art during the intermissions. At these occasions they wore *hakama* trousers adorned with their family crest. So, I also wore my *hakama* with the Mabuni family crest and performed the *Gojūshiho*, the *kata* of the "54 steps". This is an old *kata* taught by the masters of the *Shuri-te* as the very last *kata* in the training of a disciple. Today even children practice it on karate events. But in the past, this *kata* was only allowed to be practiced by people over 40 years of age. 70 percent of the techniques included in this *kata* are receiving or blocking techniques. Therefore this *kata* represents the essence of the way of karate – "there is no first attack in karate". My father liked to perform this *kata* whenever he was asked to.

In the middle of all this noise I was regulating my breathing, positioning the opponent in my imagination and starting slowly to execute the first blocks. Step by step the movements of my fists were filled with the soul and I felt that I was becoming one with the *kata*. After the last blocking technique I stayed in the state of *zanshin*, breathing slowly. Suddenly I realized that the audience were all sitting on their heels in the formal *seiza* position and watching me in total silence. Then a storm of applause broke out. But at that time I did not feel particularly happy about this as one might imagine. In fact I did not even really realize it. It was as if everything around had disappeared and I had performed the *kata* alone in the world. The people who had been watching my performance were no one else but me. All the souls had become an entity and the bloodthirsty atmosphere that had governed before had totally changed. I had "stopped the spear". *Bu*, the martial power, was transformed into harmony.

Becoming one with heaven and earth means to get rid of the "small self", to realize the "great self" and to become one with the "great life". This is called "unity of God and human beings" (*shinjin gōitsu*). This expression could well be associated with Ueshiba Morihei, the founder of *aikidō*. But my father, too, used this term in his book *Introduction into Attack and Defense Techniques in Karate Kempō*: "The *kiai* creates unity of God and human beings, and in an intense fire the self is destroyed." This sphere of unity cannot only be reached while executing *kata*. It can be maintained in everyday life, too. If one succeeds in this way one will be able to "cure disorder before its outbreak" just by being present, similar to the "wooden cat" with her "marvelous technique". But having reached this state does not mean that one will remain in it automatically.

In order to stay there one must practice all life long. The time one is living in is always "now", this very moment. But is it really possible to live in "this very moment" in mental and spiritual unity? One is dying and reborn in "this very moment". The individual moments one is living in this unity will accumulate gradually to one day, one year, and finally a whole life.

I have placed a poem written by my father at the beginning of this book, expressing his idea of practicing karate: "I enjoy my mind getting empty while rowing to the island of *bu*." We who have devoted our lives to the way of karate are striving for this "island of *bu*". We go on with our practice as long as we live. But the "island of *bu*" my father was striving for was not a place in another world far from reality. His "island of *bu*" was the here and now.

The place one is going, standing, sitting, lying, every place where the body just is, must be the *dōjō*. "Karate is life. Life is karate." This maxim is leading us on our way.

Sometimes I even do exercises in my dreams. Then often my father appears and joins me in my practice. I have spent my life in a way that I actually cannot think of anything else but karate. But I enjoy every single day. As long as there is life inside me I continue on the way of karate with all my energy. This is a way that never ends. Now, in my old age, I think I am beginning to understand my father's words which I would like to paraphrase a little to adapt it to my present feelings: "I enjoy my mind getting empty going the way of karate."

Afterword by the Editor of the Japanese Edition

I compiled and edited this book in January and February 2001 according to the verbal explanations made by master Mabuni. Actually, the essence of *budō* cannot be explained by using words. One could even say that the essence of *budō* is just the part which there are no words for. Nevertheless we tried to find appropriate words. Master Mabuni spoke about the various subjects with sincerity and deep understanding and I feel very grateful and lucky that I got the chance to contribute to this memorable project and to spend some time together with this holy man of the fist whose name will be engraved in the history of karate forever.

I started to practice karate 25 years ago when I was a 6th grade pupil. There were times when I thought I could make a career based on karate and tried very hard in this direction. But then I met a karate master who became very important for my orientation. This was Mabuni Kenei, who is the last *budō* master on mainland Japan to represent the traditional Okinawan karate.

After I had met him, I started to think that I should study directly under his guidance. In May 1999 I decided to try to get into contact with master Mabuni. At that time I had to go to Ōsaka every week and so I asked him whether I could get lessons in his *dōjō* once a week. But for professional reasons time planning was difficult for me. I was surprised to hear master Mabuni saying: "Well, you may come when you have the time to."

At the age of 34 Master Mabuni was appointed as head of the *Shitō ryū*. Since this time he has become highly respected as one of the greatest experts, and now he is one of the eldest in the world of *karatedō*. And such a great man was still going to the *dōjō* every day to supervise his students' practice giving all his physical and mental energy for their education.

Although I came only once a week for an extra lesson, master Mabuni always offered himself as a partner for the exercises. Once we practiced joint-locking techniques by means of the *bunkai* of the *Seipai kata*. As always, he offered his own hand to try a joint-locking technique. I was reluctant to do it with full force. But he said: "More, more!" Even for a beginner like me he gave everything. Once he came with a taped thumb. When I asked for the reason of this injury he answered: "Just sprained it while practicing with a youngster." This sentence tells a lot about his attitude towards teaching.

As explained in this book, since ancient times *kata* are the center of karate practice. But in present competitive karate, *kata* are rather despised since they are considered as being out of touch with reality. In master Mabuni's lessons I understood for the first time, that as part of a *kata*, even the slightest movements can have a very deep meaning. Master Mabuni himself is regarded to be the "personification of the *kata*". His karate reminds us of the old masters. He practiced with young people like me, with tough guys bearing the 5th or 6th *dan* or tall and heavy foreigners. But with his ability to read the *ki* and anticipate the opponent's actions, he can control any attack, and his techniques are always *kata* applications. *Kata* are not at all out of touch with reality. They are a wealth of living techniques and the crystallized wisdom of all masters of the past.

During his lessons, during pauses or at other occasions he talks a lot about karate and human life. His thinking, based upon more than 70 years of experience in *budō*, is always deep and full of truth. His ideas are pointing to the chance to go beyond the limits of our present world. It is only a natural result that I wanted to help spreading his teachings.

Since the book is based upon the verbal explanations of master Mabuni the editor has to assume the whole responsibility for the written version. So, I pray that I was able to correctly express the outstandingly rich technical knowledge accumulated in so many years of practice and his great and all-embracing personality and do not damage his reputation in any way.

I am very grateful for master Mabuni Kenei having entrusted me with compiling and editing his book. Although after planning the book it took nearly two years to realize it, he never urged me. This, too, shows his attitude to give things the time they need.

Finally I want to thank the publisher of the publishing house *Sankosha*, mister Takahashi Teruo, for his great help in editing the book and for publishing it.

Yokoyama Masahiko, 25 October 2001

Table of Contents